THE

CRITTENDEN COMMERCIAL ARITHMETIC

AND

Business Manual.

DESIGNED FOR THE USE OF

MERCHANTS, BUSINESS MEN,

ACADEMIES, AND COMMERCIAL COLLEGES.

BY

JOHN GROESBECK,

CONSULTING ACCOUNTANT,

PRINCIPAL OF CRITTENDEN'S PHILADELPHIA COMMERCIAL COLLEGE.

Fifth Edition, Revised and Enlarged.

PHILADELPHIA:

E. C. & J. BIDDLE, 508 MINOR STREET.

NEW YORK: J. W. SCHERMERHORN & CO.

BOSTON: WOODMAN & HAMMETT. *CINCINNATI:* R. W. CARROLL & CO.

CHICAGO: E. SPEAKMAN & CO.

1868.

"Knowledge is the guide of practice."

"If a man's wits be wandering, let him study arithmetic."—BACON.

"Washington studied the intricate forms of business. He copied out bills of exchange, notes of hand, bills of sale, receipts, and all the varieties of the class, with a precision and elegance that were remarkable."

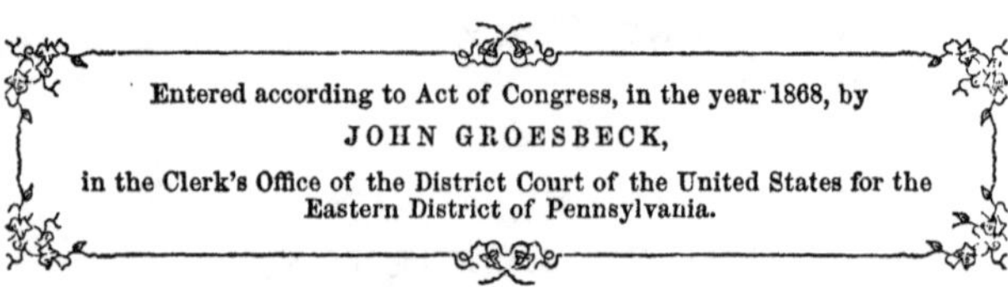

STEREOTYPED BY MACKELLAR, SMITHS & JORDAN,
PHILADELPHIA.
PRINTED BY J. B. RODGERS.

PREFACE

TO THE FOURTH EDITION.

THE object of this book is to impart that practical knowledge which is daily required in business life.

Business is based upon comprehensible principles and facts, a knowledge of which will promote efficiency in actual transactions. Practice only can impart skill in application; but practice enlightened by knowledge sooner acquires proficiency, and is saved from many errors and much useless labor.

Among the qualifications necessary in mercantile pursuits, none are more essential than a thorough acquaintance with the methods of calculation employed, and a familiarity with the various forms of business papers.

The limits of the text-books on Arithmetic in common use prevent that extended explanation of commercial customs and regulations, and the presentation of the requisite details, necessary for a clear understanding of the manner in which the calculations are to be applied; and, while the principles of numbers are fully elucidated, the short, practical, and labor-saving methods actually used by business men are omitted. The pupil frequently finds, when he enters into active life, that he is poorly prepared, and that he must learn more expeditious and varied methods of calculation than those he has been taught at school.

Success and advancement in any pursuit depend in a great measure upon the qualifications possessed when entering upon it, as the exactions of active life leave little opportunity to remedy deficiencies of preparation. He who would succeed must not wait until surrounded by the bustle, demands, and complications of actual business, any more than the captain should defer obtaining a knowledge of navigation until his vessel is at sea, or the physician put off the study of medicine until called upon to prescribe. He should go prepared into the busy walks of life, ready to surmount every difficulty and to excel in every thing he undertakes.

The calculations presented in the following pages have been selected as the best and most important in actual use in business circles, and which are daily becoming more and more necessary to be well understood by those who wish to make an efficient preparation for the employments of the counting-house. Several of them, it is believed, are now published for the first time. Not only the principles, but the mechanical processes, should be completely mastered, in order to acquire that readiness, rapidity, and accuracy of application which are essential to secure an eminent position as an accountant, or to become a competent business man.

The forms of papers are those with which every person should be familiar, and include a greater variety than has yet appeared in any one collection. They are accompanied by explanations of their nature and use, and the obligations and relations of the parties to them, and will impart such accurate ideas of business practices as will be of great service to those of limited experience.

Many subjects have been introduced which, though rarely taught in schools, are of great importance in the counting-room and in actual life. The student of book-keeping especially will find much to aid him in his attempts to acquire a knowledge of that science.

The author has been connected for the last eleven years with Crittenden's Philadelphia Commercial College, for which this manual was primarily prepared, and, in addition to his knowledge of the wants of the student, has been frequently consulted by merchants and others upon difficult questions that have occurred in their practice. These difficulties have been carefully noted, and many of their intricacies are here solved and explained.

He takes this opportunity to acknowledge his indebtedness to numerous friends for their valuable assistance in the preparation of the work, and to render them his sincere thanks. He would also express his obligations to the officers of numerous banks and mercantile houses, of the Mint, the Custom-House, and of various public and private establishments, for the opportunities afforded him of obtaining reliable information on many subjects of interest and value.

Three large editions of the work having been exhausted within a few months, it has been carefully revised and considerably enlarged, and no effort has been spared to render it worthy of its very favorable reception. To those who have kindly favored him with their communications,—as invited in the first edition,—the author tenders his thanks, and would here repeat that he will deem it a special favor if business men, teachers, and others, will communicate any suggestion, new or improved method of calculation, or useful information on business topics, that may add to its accuracy and completeness.

CONTENTS.

COMMERCIAL ARITHMETIC.

BUSINESS FORMS AND INFORMATION.

CHARACTERS AND ABBREVIATIONS

USED IN BUSINESS.

@ At.

℅ Account.

¢ Cents.

% Per cent.

℀ Number.

1^{1} One and one-quarter.

1^{2} One and one-half.

1^{3} One and three-quarters.

15 doz. $\frac{5}{\$12}$, $\frac{5}{\$15}$, $\frac{5}{\$18}$. Fifteen doz., 5 of which are \$12 per doz., 5 doz. @ \$15, and 5 doz. at \$18 per doz.

1 hhd. Sugar.
1100
155 | 945lbs., 1100 pounds gross weight, 155 lbs. tare, or weight of hhd., 945 lbs. net weight.

4 ps. 42, 36, 28, 32 } 138 yds. The numbers in the bracket are the number of yds. in each piece respectively.

10 doz. $\frac{4}{5}$ @ 2/– $\frac{6}{8}$ @ 3/6. 4 doz. No. 5 @ 2 shillings per doz.; 6 doz. No. 8 @ 3*s*. 6*d*. per doz.

7 × 9, or 7 by 9 in. 7 in. wide, 9 in. long.

(A) W.W., and similar characters and letters, are placed on packages to designate a particular lot or shipment.

(Goods are numbered and marked, that they may be distinguished without minute description.)

Acc't.	Account.
Adv.	Adventure.
Am't.	Amount.
Ass'd.	Assorted.
Bal.	Balance.
Bbl.	Barrel.
Blk.	Black.
Bo't.	Bought.
B. L., or B. of L.	Bill of Lading.
Co.	Company.
Cr.	Creditor.
Com.	Commission.

Cons't.	Consignment.
Dft.	Draft.
Disc't.	Discount.
Do. or ditto.	The same.
Doz.	Dozen.
Dr.	Debtor.
Ea.	Each.
E.E.	Errors excepted.
E. & O.E.	Errors and omissions excepted.
Exch.	Exchange.
Exps.	Expenses.
Fig'd.	Figured.
Fol.	Folio.
Forw'd, or fwd.	Forward.
fr.	From.
Fr.	French.
Fr't.	Freight.
Guar.	Guarantee.
Gal.	Gallon.
Hhds.	Hogsheads.
Ins.	Insurance.
Insol.	Insolvency.
Inst. (instant)	This month.
Invt.	Inventory.
Int.	Interest.
Mdse.	Merchandise.
Mo.	Month.
Net.	Without deduction.
No.	Number.
Pay't.	Payment.
Pd.	Paid.
Pk'gs.	Packages.
Per, or pr.	By.
Per cent.	By the hundred.
Prem.	Premium.
Prox. (proximo)	The next month.
Ps.	Pieces.
Rec'd.	Received.
Ship't.	Shipment.
S. S.	Steamship.
Sunds.	Sundries.
Ult. (ultimo)	The last month.
Yds.	Yards.
Yr.	Year.

COMMERCIAL ARITHMETIC.

METHODS OF ADDITION.

1. Addition constitutes the greater part of all the calculations of business and common life; and the ability to add with rapidity and accuracy is of more practical utility than all the other arithmetical operations combined. This ability, however, can be readily acquired by the exercise of memory and the right kind of practice. A regular method should be pursued; encumbering the mind with amounts to be carried from one operation to another should be avoided; and a practical familiarity with the sums of combinations of numbers should be cultivated as much as possible. Any thing which lessens the number of operations to be performed promotes rapidity. By closely adhering to the following methods, a short time only will be required for acquiring considerable proficiency.

2. In writing numbers, care should be taken to make the figures clear and plain, so that a 3 will not be mistaken for a 5, or a 7 for a 9; and also that the figures in one line do not run into those in the line below, and that all the figures of a column be placed directly under each other.

3. Commence at the foot of the column and add upward, and, if the column is long, always set down the carrying figure. This relieves the mind from apprehension of loss of time, from being compelled, by interruptions which often occur in business, to leave the work when nearly through the addition of several columns of figures; and then, if necessary, any column may be re-added without the trouble of adding the preceding.

Always add the carrying figure to the next column *on commencing.*

2

4. The following methods of retaining the carrying figure are adopted by most accountants :—

FIRST METHOD.

```
$13213.30
 25342.13
 12468.31
  1143.13
 35321.34
 13476.21
  2113.13
---------
103077.55
  2222.11
```

SECOND METHOD.

```
      15
     15
    ---
    27
   27
  20
 23
10
---------
103077.55
```

In the first method, the figure to be carried is written *small* immediately under the figure to which it belongs.

In the second method, the whole result of each column is set down by itself, the sum of each column being written one place to the left under the sum of the column preceding it; then, when all the results are written, the right-hand figures, including all the footing of the last column, will give the total result.

5. *If the figures are not set down in regular order under each other*, instead of trying to follow the column upward, take the figure which is the same number of places from the right hand as the figure with which you started, not regarding whether it is below tens or hundreds, or very near the right-hand figure, or at some distance from it. For instance, if you wish to add a column of hundreds which have been set down irregularly, instead of looking for the next figure above, look for the next figure which is three places from the right. This method will save time, and avoid perplexity and uncertainty.

6. To secure accuracy, the addition should be performed twice,—in different directions: this gives new combinations, and, if there has been a mistake, is a preventive of its repetition, which is likely to occur, especially when the mind has been too long engaged.

7. If the columns of figures are long, it is generally better to place the footings on a separate piece of paper and test their correctness, before placing them in ink on the book; as mistakes can then be corrected without defacing the page by erasures.

8. Familiarity with the totals of combinations should be the object of all practice. Counting is not adding. It is quite as easy, and considerably quicker, to say at once, 8 and 7 are 15, than to count 8, 9, 10, 11, 12, &c., up to the result 15; and also to say, 3, 6, 10, 15, than to say, 3 and 3 are 6, 6 and 4 are 10 10 and 5 are 15.

COUNTING-HOUSE DRILL TABLES.

Drill Table No. 1.

20	20	20	20	20	20	20	20	20	20
19	19	19	19	19	19	19	19	19	19
18	18	18	18	18	18	18	18	18	18
17	17	17	17	17	17	17	17	17	17
16	16	16	16	16	16	16	16	16	16
15	15	15	15	15	15	15	15	15	15
14	14	14	14	14	14	14	14	14	14
13	13	13	13	13	13	13	13	13	13
12	12	12	12	12	12	12	12	12	12
11	11	11	11	11	11	11	11	11	11
10	10	10	10	10	10	10	10	10	10
9	9	9	9	9	9	9	9	9	9
8	8	8	8	8	8	8	8	8	8
7	7	7	7	7	7	7	7	7	7
6	6	6	6	6	6	6	6	6	6
5	5	5	5	5	5	5	5	5	5
4	4	4	4	4	4	4	4	4	4
3	3	3	3	3	3	3	3	3	3
2	2	2	2	2	2	2	2	2	2
1	1	1	1	1	1	1	1	1	1
2	3	4	5	6	7	8	9	10	11

Drill Table No. 2.

20	21	22	23	24	25	26	27	28	29	30
19	20	21	22	23	24	25	26	27	28	29
18	19	20	21	22	23	24	25	26	27	28
17	18	19	20	21	22	23	24	25	26	27
16	17	18	19	20	21	22	23	24	25	26
15	16	17	18	19	20	21	22	23	24	25
14	15	16	17	18	19	20	21	22	23	24
13	14	15	16	17	18	19	20	21	22	23
12	13	14	15	16	17	18	19	20	21	22
11	12	13	14	15	16	17	18	19	20	21
10	11	12	13	14	15	16	17	18	19	20
9	10	11	12	13	14	15	16	17	18	19
8	9	10	11	12	13	14	15	16	17	18
7	8	9	10	11	12	13	14	15	16	17
6	7	8	9	10	11	12	13	14	15	16
5	6	7	8	9	10	11	12	13	14	15
4	5	6	7	8	9	10	11	12	13	14
3	4	5	6	7	8	9	10	11	12	13
2	3	4	5	6	7	8	9	10	11	12
1	2	3	4	5	6	7	8	9	10	11

The above columns should be added until the addition can be easily performed and without hesitation.

9. In the following columns, add all the figures enclosed in each bracket as *one number*, and name only results in the same manner as when the figures are taken separately. Thus, in adding column No. 4, say 7, 11, 16, &c.

10. When a figure is repeated several times, count the number of times it occurs, and multiply by the figure. Thus, if the figure 8 occurs seven times in a column, multiply 7 by 8 for the result, instead of adding seven 8's together.

11. When three figures occur in regular order,—as 4, 5, 6, or 6, 7, 8,—three times the middle figure will be their sum; when five figures occur, take five times the middle figure. When there are four figures in regular order, take twice the sum of the extremes; when there are six, take three times the sum of the extremes.

(1.)	(2.)	(3.)	(4.)
324	678	3 3 4	1 1 2
235	789	3 4 5	1 2 3
143	976	4 6 3	2 6 4
421	899	3 7 7	4 1 1
312	989	7 8 4	2 5 5
234	988	4 6 6	3 1 2
343	878	2 8 1	5 3 3
423	673	8 3 7	3 2 4
225	789	2 9 3	2 6 5
123	968	3 0 5	2 8 1
334	887	4 5 5	0 4 4
212	987	5 5 1	1 2 2
324	798	2 3 9	0 4 1
123	976	3 7 5	1 2 1
431	687	7 6 5	2 0 4
212	997	3 4 2	4 1 3
4419	13959	72 1 2	

ADDITION OF SEVERAL COLUMNS AT ONE OPERATION.

12. To add two or more columns at one operation.

To the lower number add first the units of the next number above, then the tens, then the hundreds; and so continue.

OPERATION.

23	
31	$22 + 5 = 27,\ 27 + 10 = 37$
24	$37 + 4 = 41,\ 41 + 20 = 61$
15	$61 + 1 = 62,\ 62 + 30 = 92$
22	$92 + 3 = 95,\ 95 + 20 = 115$ Ans.
115	

OPERATION.

234	
112	$322 + 3 = 325 + 20 = 345 + 400 = 745$
423	$745 + 2 = 747 + 10 = 757 + 100 = 857$
322	$857 + 4 = 861 + 30 = 891 + 200 = 1091$ Ans.
1091	

Practice will enable a person to add amounts of two or more figures at one operation: thus, 22 + 15 = 37, 37 + 24 = 61, 61 + 31 = 92, 92 + 23 = 115 Ans. As soon as the combinations become familiar, addition by this method can be performed without difficulty; but, for ordinary purposes, one column at a time is sufficient. In Ledger accounts, when the last two or three columns are not all filled, they may be added at one operation with advantage.

13. Very long columns of figures are sometimes added in the following manner :—

FIRST METHOD.	SECOND METHOD.	
247	247	
362	362	
228	228	
436	436	1273
1273	128	
128	326	
326	121	575
121	121	
1848	316	
121	405	842
316		Ans.
405		
2690 Ans.		

ADDING HORIZONTALLY.

14. In some branches of business the ability to add numbers which are written horizontally instead of being placed under each other, is often required. Thus,—

824 + 325 + 652 = 1801

All the units are first added, then the tens, and then the hundreds. A little practice will soon overcome any difficulty which may be experienced at first.

Add 434, 216, 4217, 3217.

Add 216, 1231, 432, 1800, 2167.

Add the following numbers as they stand :—

325	116	365	
431	275	218	Ans. 1730.

BALANCING ACCOUNTS.

15. It is frequently of advantage to the accountant to find the difference between two sums by addition, instead of by subtraction. For example, if he wishes to find the difference between 2427 and 1235, instead of taking the trouble of placing the smaller number under the larger, he will add, mentally, to 1235 a sum that will make the whole equal to 2427, writing the figures as he proceeds under 1235.

2427 1235
1192—balance.

When both sides of an account contain several amounts, first add the larger side in the usual manner; *then commence at the top of the columns, on the smaller side of the account, and add downwards, inserting the necessary figures to make the required balance.* Thus, to find the balance of the following account:

Dr. **V. I. Andrews.** **Cr.**

1867.			1867.		
Jan. 3.	To Mdse.	$84.00	Jan. 10.	By Cash,	$45.00
" 10.	" "	72.00	" 17.	" "	67.00
" 24.	" "	43.00		*Balance,*	*87.00*
		$199.00			

First, add the larger side; then say, $5+7=12$, and 7, *the figure required to make the balance,* $=19$. Set down 7 and carry 1. $1+4+6=11$, and the remaining figure of the balance $=19$. To test the accuracy of the work, add the whole of the smaller side, and include the balance.

EXAMPLE II.

Dr. **George L. Burtis.** **Cr.**

1867.			1867.		
Feb. 9.	To Mdse.	$187.37	Feb. 15.	By Cash,	$150.00
" 26.	" "	37.42	Mar. 10.	" "	437.75
Mar. 4.	" "	260.38			
Apr. 9.	" "	720.16			
May 6.	" "	132.50			
" 9.	" "	350.00			

CANCELLATION.

16. Cancellation is the process of shortening operations in multiplication and division by rejecting equal factors.

17. Cancelling, or rejecting a factor of any number divides the number by that factor.

18. Cancelling a number is the same as dividing that number by itself, and, consequently, the quotient is 1.

19. Dividing the multiplicand or multiplier will give the same result as dividing the product.

$$360 \times 24 = 8640, \quad 8640 \div 6 = 1440.$$
$$360 \div 6 = 60, \quad 60 \times 24 = 1440.$$
$$24 \div 6 = 4, \quad 4 \times 360 = 1440.$$

20. If the dividend and divisor be both multiplied or both divided by the same number, the quotient will not be changed.

$$32 \div 8 = 4$$

$$32 \times 5 = 160,$$
$$8 \times 5 = 40, \quad 160 \div 40 = 4.$$

$$32 \div 4 = 8,$$
$$8 \div 4 = 2, \quad 8 \div 2 = 4.$$

$$8)\tfrac{32}{8} = \tfrac{4}{1} = 4.$$

21. Dividing the divisor will give the same result as multiplying the quotient.

$$14)126(9, \quad 9 \times 2 = 18.$$
$$14 \div 2 = 7, \quad 126 \div 7 = 18.$$

22. Dividing the dividend will give the same result as dividing the quotient

$$14)126(9, \quad 9 \div 3 = 3.$$
$$126 \div 3 = 42, \quad 42 \div 14 = 3.$$

1. Divide the product of 6, 8, and 9 by 4 times 3.
2. A merchant bought 27 yards of cloth at $2.25 per yard, and paid for it in tea at 75 cts. per lb. How many pounds were required? Ans. 81 lbs.
3. What will 28 pieces of cloth cost, each piece containing 27 yards, at 25 cts. per yard?

FRACTIONS.

RULES FREQUENTLY USED.

23. To multiply whole numbers by fractions.

RULE.—*Multiply by the numerator, and divide the product by the denominator.*

EXAMPLES.

1. Multiply 464 by $\frac{3}{4}$.

$464 \times 3 = 1392$; $1392 \div 4 = 348$ Ans.

2. Multiply 12672 by $18\frac{3}{4}$.

```
      12672
        18¾
   4)38016—product by 3.
      9504—product by ¾.
    101376    "    "  8.
    12672     "    "  1.
    237600—product by 18¾.
```

24. To multiply a fraction by a fraction.

RULE.—*Multiply the numerators together for a new numerator, and the denominators together for a new denominator.*

1. Multiply $\frac{2}{5}$ by $\frac{4}{7}$.

$2 \times 4 = 8$
$5 \times 7 = 35$ Ans. $\frac{8}{35}$.

2. Multiply $\frac{4}{5}$ by $\frac{6}{11}$.
3. " $\frac{18}{29}$ " $\frac{3}{4}$.
4. " $\frac{7}{17}$ " $\frac{12}{31}$.

25. To divide by a fraction.

RULE.—*Invert the divisor, and multiply as in the previous rules.*

1. Divide $\frac{5}{9}$ by $\frac{3}{4}$.

$\frac{3}{4}$ inverted $= \frac{4}{3}$
$5 \times 4 = 20$
$9 \times 3 = 27$ Ans. $\frac{20}{27}$.

2. Divide $\frac{4}{7}$ by $\frac{2}{3}$.
3. " $\frac{8}{11}$ by $\frac{5}{6}$.
4. " $3\frac{1}{2}$ " $\frac{2}{3}$.
5. " 9 " $\frac{3}{5}$.
6. Divide $\frac{8}{15}$ by $\frac{2}{3}$.
7. " $\frac{1}{4}$ " $\frac{1}{2}$.
8. " $\frac{1}{2}$ " $\frac{1}{4}$.
9. " $\frac{6}{7}$ of 21 by $\frac{5}{11}$.
10. " $\frac{1}{2}$ of $\frac{6}{7}$ by $\frac{9}{10}$.
11. " $\frac{1}{4}$ of $\frac{6}{7}$ by $\frac{9}{10}$.
12. " $\frac{8}{35}$ by $\frac{4}{7}$.

27. To divide by a mixed number.

Rule.—*Multiply the whole number in the divisor by the denominator of the fraction, and to the product add the numerator. Multiply the dividend by the denominator of the fraction; then divide as usual. The remainder, if any, must be divided by the denominator of the fraction to obtain the true remainder.*

1. Divide 480 by $5\frac{1}{2}$.

$$\begin{array}{rr} 5\frac{1}{2} & 480 \\ 2 & 2 \\ \hline 11) & 960 \\ \hline \end{array}$$

$87\frac{3}{11}$; or 87, $1\frac{1}{2}$ Rem.

2. Divide 2675 by $18\frac{3}{4}$.
3. " 18992 by $133\frac{1}{3}$.
4. " 425 by $31\frac{1}{4}$.
5. " 341 by $7\frac{1}{3}$.
6. " 1227 by $97\frac{4}{5}$.

28. To reduce a decimal to a common fraction.

Rule.—*Write the decimal as it stands, omitting the decimal point, for the numerator. For the denominator, write 1 with as many ciphers annexed as there are decimal places in the numerator.*

EXAMPLES.

1. Reduce .25 to an equivalent common fraction.
   Ans. $\frac{25}{100}$, which reduced to its lowest terms $= \frac{1}{4}$.
2. Reduce .375 to a common fraction.
   Ans. $\frac{375}{1000} = \frac{3}{8}$.
3. Reduce .1875 to a common fraction. Ans. $\frac{3}{16}$.
4. Reduce .625 to a common fraction. Ans. $\frac{5}{8}$.

29. To reduce common fractions to decimals.

Rule.—*Annex ciphers to the numerator, and divide by the denominator, prefixing a point to the quotient. There must be as many places in the quotient as there have been ciphers annexed; if not enough, prefix ciphers.*

Note.—For practical purposes, it will be sufficiently accurate if the division be carried to four or five places.

EXAMPLES.

1. Reduce $\frac{3}{4}$ to a decimal.

$$4)3.00$$
$$.75 = \frac{75}{100} \text{ Ans.}$$

2. Reduce $\frac{3}{8}$ to a decimal. Ans. .375.
3. " $\frac{6}{7}$ " " Ans. .8571+.
4. " $\frac{1}{4}$ " "
5. " $\frac{2}{3}$ " "

30. MULTIPLICATION OF DECIMALS.

RULE.—*Multiply as in whole numbers, and from the right of the product point off as many figures for decimals as there are decimal places in both* MULTIPLICAND *and* MULTIPLIER.

If there are not figures enough in the product, prefix ciphers.

EXAMPLES.

1. Multiply 4.25 by 6.5.

```
   4.25
    6.5
  -----
   2125
  2550
  -----
 27.625 Ans.
```

2. Multiply 84.5 by 4.

```
  84.5
     4
  -----
 338.0 Ans.
```

3. Multiply 6.425 by 4.25.
4. " 18.5 " 6.75.
5. " 12.575 " 9.375.
6. " .25 " 6.0025.
7. " .275 " 3.0025.
8. " 18.625 " 5.25.
9. What is the cost of $12\frac{3}{4}$ lbs. @ $6\frac{1}{4}$ cts. per lb.?
10. What is the cost of $7\frac{2}{5}$ yds. at $18\frac{3}{4}$ cts. per yd.?

NOTE.—It is sometimes more convenient to change common fractions to decimals before multiplying. $18\frac{3}{4} \times 12\frac{1}{2} = 18.75 \times 12.5$.

31. DIVISION OF DECIMALS.

RULE I.—When the decimal places in the dividend and divisor are equal, *divide as in whole numbers; the quotient will be in whole numbers.*

RULE II.—When the decimal places in the dividend exceed those in the divisor.

Divide as in whole numbers, and from the right hand of the quotient point off as many decimals as the decimal places in the dividend exceed those in the divisor. Should there be a deficiency of figures in the quotient, it must be supplied by prefixing ciphers. If there be a remainder, annex ciphers, and continue the division as far as desired, each cipher annexed being equivalent to one more decimal in the dividend.

RULE III.—When the decimal places in the divisor exceed those in the dividend.

Annex ciphers to the dividend, and proceed as before.

EXAMPLES.

1. Divide 156.25 by 6.25. Ans. 25.
2. " 234.70525. by 64.25. Ans. 3.653.
3. " .8727587 by .162.
4. " 6.25 by .1875.
5. " 327$\frac{3}{8}$ by 4.

PRINCIPLES OF FRACTIONS.

32. Numbers written in the form of a fraction denote division, the numerator being the dividend, and the denominator the divisor.

33. Multiplying or dividing both the numerator and denominator of a fraction by the same number does not change the value of the fraction.

34. Multiplying the numerator, or dividing the denominator, of a fraction multiplies the fraction.

35. Dividing the numerator, or multiplying the denominator, divides the fraction.

DENOMINATE NUMBERS.

36. A **Denominate Number** is composed of simple numbers of different denominations.

37. Reduction is the process of changing numbers from one form, or denomination, to another, without altering their values. (For Tables, see WEIGHTS AND MEASURES.)

REDUCTION DESCENDING.

38. To reduce numbers from a higher denomination to a lower.

RULE.—1. *Multiply the number of the highest denomination by the number which one of this denomination makes of the next lower.*

2. *Add to the product the number in the next lower denomination, if any.*

3. *Proceed in the same manner through the lower denominations to the one required.*

EXAMPLES.

1. Reduce £10 7*s.* 10*d.* to pence.

```
       10
       20 shillings in a pound.
      ---
      200
        7
      ---
      207 shillings.
       12 pence in a shilling.
     ----
     2484
       10
     ----
Ans. 2494 pence.
```

2. How many pints in 22 bushels, 6 qts. 1 pint?
3. How many inches in 6 rods, 2 yds. 8 ft. 6 inches?
4. How many minutes in one day?
5. How many pounds in 1 ton, 3 cwt. 3 qrs. 10 lbs.?
6. Reduce 75 bushels to pints.

REDUCTION ASCENDING.

39. To reduce a number from a lower denomination to a higher.

RULE.—*Divide the given number by the number required to make one of the next higher denomination.*

Divide the quotient thus obtained as before, and so proceed to the denomination required.

NOTE.—The remainders, if any, are of the same denomination as the numbers divided.

EXAMPLES.

1. In 1275 pence, how many pounds?

```
12)1275
   ——————
20) 106s. 3d.
   ——————
    £5  6s.      Ans. £5 6s. 3d.
```

2. Reduce 15485 lbs. to tons.
3. Reduce 632687 feet to miles.
4. In 7846 grains of gold, how many lbs.?

40. To find the value of one denomination in numbers of another denomination having different relations.

RULE.—*Reduce the given numbers to a denomination which is common to both, then reduce the result to the denomination required.*

EXAMPLES.

1. How many Ells English in 600 Ells French?

REMARK.—Both denominations can be reduced to quarters.

600 Ells French = 3600 qrs.
3600 qrs. reduced to Ells English = 720, Ans.

2. Estimating a gallon wine measure to contain 231 cubic inches, and a gallon beer measure to contain 282 cubic inches, how many gallons beer measure are there in 640 gallons wine measure?

3. If a dollar is worth in Canton 4*s.* 4*d.*, how many dollars are equal in value to £1500?

FRACTIONS OF DENOMINATE NUMBERS.

41. To reduce a fraction of one denomination to whole numbers, or to an equivalent fraction, of another denomination.

RULE.—*Multiply or divide the fraction by the same numbers that would be employed in the reduction of whole numbers.*

EXAMPLES.

1. What is the value of $\frac{3}{16}$ of £1?

   $\frac{3}{16} \times 20 = \frac{60}{16} = 3\frac{12}{16}s.$

   $\frac{12}{16} \times 12 = \frac{144}{16} = 9d.$ Ans. 3*s.* 9*d.*
2. What part of £1 is $\frac{1}{4}$ of a penny?

   $\frac{1}{4} \div 12 = \frac{1}{48}.$

   $\frac{1}{48} \div 20 = \frac{1}{960}.$ Ans. $\frac{1}{960}.$
3. What part of a bushel is $\frac{3}{4}$ of a quart?
4. Reduce $\frac{6}{7}$ of a day to lower denominations.
5. Add $\frac{3}{4}$ of a pound to $\frac{5}{6}$ of a shilling. Ans. 15*s.* 10*d.*
6. Reduce $\frac{7}{8}$ of a lb. to the fraction of a cwt.
7. What part of an acre is $\frac{3}{4}$ of a rod?

42. To reduce a denominate number to a fraction of another denomination.

RULE.—*Reduce the given numbers to the lowest denomination mentioned, for the numerator, and a unit of the denomination of the required fraction to the same denomination, for the denominator.*

EXAMPLES.

1. Reduce 7*s.* 4*d.* 1*far.* to the fraction of a pound.

   7*s.* 4*d.* 1*far.* = 577*far.*

   £1 = 960 " Ans. $\frac{577}{960}.$
2. Reduce 1 pint to the fraction of a gallon.
3. What part of a bushel are 3 qts.?
4. What part of a week are 3 hours?
5. What part of a mile are 5 feet?

DECIMALS OF DENOMINATE NUMBERS.

43. To reduce a denominate number to a decimal of a higher denomination.

RULE.—*Annex ciphers to the lowest denomination, and divide by that number which will reduce it to the next higher denomination, and annex the quotient as a decimal to that higher. Then divide that higher denomination as before, and so continue dividing until the whole is reduced to the denomination required.* Or,

Reduce the given number to a common fraction of the denomination required, and reduce this fraction to a decimal.

EXAMPLES.

1. Reduce £7 15*s.* 6*d.* 3*far.* to the decimal of a pound.

4	3.00	
12	6.75000	3*far.* = .75 of a penny.
20	15.5625	6.75*d.* = .5625 of a shilling.
	£7.778125	15.56250*s.* = .778125 of a £.

Ans. £7.778125.

2. Reduce £617 1*s.* 1*d.* to the decimal of a pound.

12	1.0000
20	1.0833
	£617.05416. Ans.

NOTE.—For a shorter practical method for sterling money, see page 43.

3. Reduce 3 bus. 1 pk. 3 qts. to the decimal of a bushel.
4. Reduce 3 qrs. 12 lb. 8 oz. to the decimal of a ton.
5. Reduce 2 gals. 1 qt. 1 pt. to the decimal of a gallon.

44. To reduce a denominate decimal to whole numbers.

RULE.—*Multiply the given decimal as in reduction of whole numbers, and point off in the product as in multiplication of decimals.*

The numbers on the left of the decimal point will be the whole numbers required.

NOTE.—Only the decimal part of each number should be multiplied.

EXAMPLES.

1. What is the value of .625 of a pound?

$$\begin{array}{r} .625 \\ 20 \\ \hline 12.500 \\ 12 \\ \hline 6.000. \end{array}$$

Ans. 12*s*. 6*d*.

2. What is the value of .875 of a ton?
3. What is the value of 1.875 of a bushel?
4. What is the value of .425 of a pound troy?
5. What is the value of 2.19375 of a year?

MISCELLANEOUS EXAMPLES.

1. How much money is required to pay for the following goods?

$32\frac{1}{2}$ yards muslin, at $16\frac{2}{3}$ cts. per yard.		
$18\frac{3}{4}$ lbs. tea, @ \$1.15 per lb.		
$17\frac{1}{2}$ lbs. coffee, at $22\frac{1}{2}$ cts. per lb.		
$15\frac{1}{2}$ lbs. lard, at $16\frac{1}{4}$ cts. per lb.		
$23\frac{3}{4}$ lbs. chrome yellow, at $37\frac{1}{2}$ cts. per lb.		
$19\frac{7}{12}$ feet brass, at $23\frac{1}{2}$ cts. per foot.		
Ans.		

2. If a piece of land is worth \$317.50, what is $\frac{5}{8}$ of it worth? What is $\frac{3}{7}$? What is $\frac{3}{8}$?

3. A man sold $4\frac{3}{5}$ acres of land for \$320. How much did he receive per acre?

4. A United States, or Winchester, bushel contains 2150.42 cubic inches: how many cubic inches in $13\frac{4}{5}$ bushels?

5. What is $\frac{2}{3}$ of $\frac{5}{19}$ of \$117? of \$585?

6. Bought $15\frac{4}{5}$ tons Russian hemp for \$4325.50: what was the price per ton?

7. What is the cost of 3 metres gold chain, at \$3.25 per inch, each metre containing 39.371 inches?

8. What is the value of 15 gals. 1 qt. 1 pt. of wine, at \$3.75 per gallon?

PRACTICE.

45. Practice is a brief method of ascertaining the total value of a quantity by combining the values of convenient aliquot parts.

46. An **Aliquot Part** is some fraction of a quantity whose numerator is 1.

EXAMPLES.

1. What is the value of 336 yds. cloth, at 18¾cts. per yd.?

12½¢ = ⅛ of a dollar.
6¼ = ½ of 12½¢.

8)$336	value at	$1	per yd.
2)42	" "	12½¢	" "
21	" "	6¼¢	" "
Ans. $63	" "	18¾¢	" "

2. How much will 1232 bushels wheat cost, at $1.31¼ per bushel?

1232
1.31¼

4)1232	cost at	$1.00	per bu.
4) 308	"	25¢	" "
77	"	6¼¢	" "
Ans. $1617	"	$1.31¼	" "

3. What will 28 bus. 3 pks. 4 qts. clover-seed cost, at $3.50 per bus.?

	$98.00	= cost of	28 bus.
½ of 3.50 =	1.75	= " "	2 pks.
½ " 1.75 =	.87½	= " "	1 "
½ " .87½ =	.43¾	= " "	4 qts.
Ans.	$101.06¼	= " "	28 bus. 3 pks. 4 qts.

4. What will 270 yds. silk cost, at £1 5*s.* 6*d.* per yard?
Ans. £351 18*s.*

5. What will 326 bbls. flour cost, at $7.87½ per bbl.?

6. Required the cost of 12 gals. 3 qts. 1 pt. of molasses, at 62½cts. per gallon.

CONTRACTIONS

IN

MULTIPLICATION AND DIVISION.

The following contractions are useful for imparting readiness and dexterity in the mechanical processes of multiplication and division. If thoroughly mastered, they will be found to be of great service, and will amply repay the time and labor expended in acquiring them. They include, in a condensed form, nearly all of practical value that has yet been published; together with some methods which, it is believed, now appear in print for the first time.

The labor of making out bills and invoices, entering sales, taking account of stock, and many similar operations, may be much lessened by their use; as extensions can be made without writing out the operations, while the liability to mistakes is diminished, because there is less labor, and fewer figures are employed.

CONTRACTIONS IN MULTIPLICATION.

47. To multiply two numbers of two places each when the units or tens are alike.

RULE.—*Multiply units by units; then,* IF THE UNITS ARE ALIKE, *multiply the sum of the tens by the units, and the tens by tens.* IF THE TENS ARE ALIKE, *multiply the sum of the units by the tens, and the tens by tens; in all cases carrying as usual.*

EXAMPLES.

1. Multiply 34 by 54.

34	$4 \times 4 = 16$
54	$5 + 3 = 8 \times 4 = 32 + 1$ (carried) $= 33$
1836	$3 \times 5 = 15 + 3$ (carried) $= 18$

2. Multiply 45 by 43.

45	$5 \times 3 = 15$
43	$5 + 3 = 8 \times 4 = 32 + 1$ (carried) $= 33$
1935	$4 \times 4 = 16 + 3$ (carried) $= 19$

3. Multiply 44 by 64.
4. " 32 " 72.
5. " 28 " 18.
6. " 45 " 35.
7. " 123 " 33.
8. " 65 " 55.
9. " 124 " 34.
10. Multiply 36 by 34.
11. " 64 " 64.
12. " 35 " 34.
13. " 72 " 73.
14. " 37 " 35.
15. " 45 " 45.
16. " 66 " 66.

$45 \times 45 = 5 \times 4$ with the square of 5 annexed.
$75 \times 75 = 8 \times 7$ " " 5 "

48. This rule includes the multiplication of two numbers whose units or tens are ones, the squaring of numbers, multiplying when the units are alike and the sum of the tens is ten, &c.

As it is capable of several hundred applications, its value is obvious. A little practice will give the ability to write the products without setting down the figures to be multiplied. It is believed that this is the first time the above rule has appeared in print.

49. To multiply by numbers, the half, third, or fourth of which is a convenient multiplier.

RULE.—*Multiply the half of one number by twice the other, or one-third of one number by three times the other, &c.*

EXAMPLES.

1. Multiply 28 by 16.

$28 \times 2 = 56$
$16 \div 2 = 8$ $\qquad 56 \times 8 = 448.$

2. Multiply 35 by 27.

$27 \div 3 = 9$
$35 \times 3 = 105$ $\qquad 105 \times 9 = 945.$

50. This rule is well adapted for mental operations, and is especially applicable to numbers which can easily be changed to tens, hundreds, &c.

3. Multiply 42 by 15.

$42 \div 2 = 21$
$15 \times 2 = 30$ $\qquad 21 \times 30 = 630.$

4. Multiply 76 by 15.	9. Multiply 48 by $13\frac{1}{3} = 16$ by 40.
5. " 134 " 35.	10. " 36 " $22\frac{1}{2}$.
6. " 43 " 24.	11. " 24 " $23\frac{1}{3}$.
7. " 182 " 18.	12. " 136 " 45.
8. " 56 " 28.	13. " 28 " $17\frac{1}{7}$.

$56 \times 4 = 224$, $28 \div 4 = 7$, $224 \times 7 = 1568$.

51. To multiply when one part of the multiplier is a factor or multiple of the other.

RULE.—*Multiply by the smaller part of the multiplier; then multiply the product so obtained by the number which shows how many times this smaller part is contained in the other, placing the right-hand figure of the second product under the right-hand figure of that part of the multiplier to which it belongs*

EXAMPLES.

1. Multiply 285 by 164.

```
16 ÷ 4 = 4          285
                    164
                  -----
                   1140  product by 4.
                   4560  4 times the product
                  -----
                  46740    by 4 = 285 × 16.
```

2. Multiply 654 by 436.

```
   654
   436
  ----
  2616    product by 4.
 23544  9 times the prod.
------
285144    by 4 = 654 × 36.
```

3. Multiply 364 by 126.
4. " 387 " 279.
5. Multiply 4267 by 142.
6. " 276 " 357.
7. " 812 " 426.
8. " 373 " 369.
9. " 235 " 424.
10. " 644 " 321.
11. " 342 " 535.
12. " 822 " 642.
13. " 545 " 927.

14. The custom-house value of a franc is 18.6 cents: what is an invoice amounting to 32165 francs worth in United States currency?

15. What is an invoice of cassimeres, valued at £3225, worth, the custom-house value of a pound sterling being $4.84?

52. To multiply by any number ending with 9.

RULE.—*Multiply by the next higher number, and subtract the multiplicand.*

EXAMPLES.

1. Multiply 42 by 39.

   39 + 1 = 40
   42 × 40 = 1680
   1680 — 42 = 1638 Ans.

2. Multiply 45 by 99.
3. Multiply 432 by 59.
4. " 125 " 699.
5. " 175 " 290.
6. " 325 " 909.
7. " 424 " $9\frac{1}{2}$.
8. " 36 " $68\frac{3}{4}$.

53. To multiply by two figures at once.

RULE I.—*Multiply both figures in the multiplier by each figure in the multiplicand separately.* Or,

RULE II.—*Multiply units by units; then to the product of each succeeding figure in the multiplicand by the units of the multiplier, add the product of the figure preceding it by the tens, and carry as usual. Multiply the last figure of the multiplicand by the tens of the multiplier.*

NOTE.—When large numbers are to be multiplied, for the purpose of remembering which figure has been used, place a dot over each figure of the multiplicand as soon as multiplied.

EXAMPLE UNDER RULE I.

Multiply 3265 by 24.

3265	$24 \times 5 = 120$, $24 \times 6 = 144 + 12$ (carried)
24	$= 156$.
78360	$24 \times 2 = 48 + 15$ (carried) $= 63$, $24 \times 3 +$ 6 (carried) $= 78$.

EXAMPLES UNDER RULE II.

1. Multiply 34 by 43.

43	$3 \times 4 = 12$, write 2.
34	$4 \times 4 = 16 + 1$ (carried) $= 17$ to carry.
1462	$3 \times 3 = 9 + 17$ " $= 26$, write 6.
	$4 \times 3 = 12 + 2$ " $= 14$.

2. Multiply 212121 by 23.

212121		2	1	2	1	2	1
23							23
4878783		2×3	1×3	2×3	1×3	2×3	1×3
	2×2	1×2	2×2	1×2	2×2	1×2	
	Ans. 4	8	7	8	7	8	3

With a little practice, the products may be written without the trouble of writing the numbers under each other, which often, as in making out invoices, entering sales, &c., effects a considerable saving of time. When thoroughly understood, the liability to mistakes is less than by the ordinary method, because there are fewer operations.

3. Multiply 42 by 14.	5. Multiply 63 by 31.
4. " 36 " 16.	6. " 26 " 51.

Find the answers to the following by multiplying the numbers as they stand:—

24 yards calico	@ 14c. per yd.	Ans. \$3.36.
52 lbs. sugar	@ 17c. per lb.	"
36 bus. oats	@ 51c. per bus.	"
48 bus. corn	@ 63c. per bus.	"
362 yds. carpeting	@ 77c. per yd.	"
28 lbs. tea	@ 74c. per lb.	"
72 yds. muslin	@ 42c. per yd.	"
34 gross pens	@ 85c. per gross.	"

54. To multiply when the multiplier is a convenient or aliquot part of 10, 100, 1000, &c.

RULE.—*Annex as many ciphers to the multiplicand as there are in the number of which the multiplier is an aliquot part; then*

Take such part of the multiplicand so increased, as the multiplier is of the number of which it is an aliquot part.

EXAMPLES.

1. Multiply 424 by 25.

$25 = \frac{1}{4}$ of 100. $42400 \div 4 = 10600$.

2. Multiply 4936 by $12\frac{1}{2}$.

$12\frac{1}{2} = \frac{1}{8}$ of 100. $493600 \div 8 = 61700$.

ALIQUOT PARTS OF 10.	ALIQUOT PARTS OF 100.		ALIQUOT PARTS OF 1000.
$2\frac{1}{2} = \frac{1}{4}$	$6\frac{1}{4} = \frac{1}{16}$	$18\frac{3}{4} = \frac{3}{16}$	$83\frac{1}{3} = \frac{1}{12}$
$3\frac{1}{3} = \frac{1}{3}$	or $\frac{1}{4}$ of $\frac{1}{4}$	or $\frac{1}{8} + \frac{1}{2}$ of $\frac{1}{8}$	$125 = \frac{1}{8}$
$1\frac{2}{3} = \frac{1}{6}$	$8\frac{1}{3} = \frac{1}{12}$	$31\frac{1}{4} = \frac{5}{16}$	$166\frac{2}{3} = \frac{1}{6}$
$1\frac{3}{7} = \frac{1}{7}$	or $\frac{1}{3}$ of $\frac{1}{4}$	$37\frac{1}{2} = \frac{3}{8}$	$250 = \frac{1}{4}$
$1\frac{1}{4} = \frac{1}{8}$	$12\frac{1}{2} = \frac{1}{8}$	$62\frac{1}{2} = \frac{5}{8}$	$333\frac{1}{3} = \frac{1}{3}$
$1\frac{1}{9} = \frac{1}{9}$	$14\frac{2}{7} = \frac{1}{7}$	$66\frac{2}{3} = \frac{2}{3}$	$375 = \frac{3}{8}$
	$16\frac{2}{3} = \frac{1}{6}$	$75 = \frac{3}{4}$	$625 = \frac{5}{8}$
	$25 = \frac{1}{4}$	$83\frac{1}{3} = \frac{5}{6}$	$833\frac{1}{3} = \frac{5}{6}$
	$33\frac{1}{3} = \frac{1}{3}$	$87\frac{1}{2} = \frac{7}{8}$	$875 = \frac{7}{8}$

55. *This table can also be used to show the value of an aliquot part. For example,* $\frac{5}{8}$ *of* 1000 *equal* 625; $\frac{5}{6}$ *of* $100 = 83\frac{1}{3}$.

3. Multiply 48 by $2\frac{1}{2}$.
4. " 18 " $3\frac{1}{3}$.
5. " 384 " $12\frac{1}{2}$.
6. " 486 " $16\frac{2}{3}$.
7. " 165 " $33\frac{1}{3}$.
8. " 96 " $1\frac{2}{3}$.
9. Multiply 320 by $6\frac{1}{4}$.
10. " 840 " $8\frac{1}{3}$.
11. " 225 " $14\frac{2}{7}$.
12. " 648 " 125.
13. " 726 " $166\frac{2}{3}$.
14. " 2456 " $37\frac{1}{2}$.

15. What is the cost of $12\frac{1}{2}$ yds. cloth @ $18\frac{3}{4}$c. per yd.?
$12\frac{1}{2} = \frac{1}{8}$; changing $18\frac{3}{4}$ to a decimal, $18.75 \div 8 = \$2.34\frac{3}{8}$.

56. Aliquot parts may be conveniently used when the multiplier is but little more or less than an aliquot part.

EXAMPLES.

1. Multiply 24 by $17\frac{2}{3}$.

$17\frac{2}{3} = 16\frac{2}{3} + 1$; $16\frac{2}{3} = \frac{1}{6}$.

$$\begin{aligned} 24 \times 16\tfrac{2}{3} &= 400 \\ 24 \times 1 &= 24 \\ \hline & 424 \text{ Ans.} \end{aligned}$$

2. Multiply 36 by $18\frac{2}{3}$.
3. " 48 " $13\frac{1}{2}$.
4. " 33 " 35.
5. " 36 " $34\frac{1}{3}$.

57. To multiply mixed numbers in which the fractions are alike.

RULE.—*To the product of the whole numbers add that part of their sum which is expressed by the fraction, and the product of the fraction multiplied by itself.*

NOTE.—Perform the operation mentally whenever it can be done.

EXAMPLES.

1. Multiply $6\frac{1}{2}$ by $4\frac{1}{2}$.

$$\begin{aligned} 6 \times 4 &= 24 \\ \tfrac{1}{2} \text{ of } (6+4) &= 5 \\ \tfrac{1}{2} \times \tfrac{1}{2} &= \tfrac{1}{4} \quad 29\tfrac{1}{4} \text{ Ans.} \end{aligned}$$

2. Multiply $8\frac{1}{4}$ by $4\frac{1}{4}$.
3. " $6\frac{1}{3}$ " $9\frac{1}{3}$.
4. " $8\frac{1}{3}$ " $4\frac{1}{3}$.
5. " $7\frac{1}{5}$ " $8\frac{1}{5}$.
6. " $4\frac{1}{2}$ " $4\frac{1}{2}$.
7. " $6\frac{3}{4}$ " $6\frac{3}{4}$.
8. Multiply $12\frac{1}{4}$ by $3\frac{1}{4}$.

$\frac{1}{4}$ of $15 = 3\frac{3}{4}$

$\frac{3}{4} + \frac{1}{16} = \frac{13}{16}$. Ans. $39\frac{13}{16}$.

9. Multiply $16\frac{2}{3}$ by $9\frac{2}{3}$.
10. " $8\frac{1}{3}$ " $6\frac{1}{3}$.

58. When the whole numbers are alike, and the fraction is one-half, the half of the sum of the whole numbers equals one of the numbers, and the operation can be shortened by multiplying the whole number by itself plus 1, and annexing $\frac{1}{4}$:—

$$4\tfrac{1}{2} \times 4\tfrac{1}{2} = 5 \times 4 + \tfrac{1}{4} = 20\tfrac{1}{4}.$$

59. This rule will apply to whole numbers, by taking the units as so many parts of ten, and the tens as so many parts of one hundred. Thus, to multiply 45 by 45: 40 equals 4 tens, 5 equals one-half of ten, and one-fourth of one hundred equals 25; then, $5 \times 4 = 20$, to which annex $\frac{1}{4}$ of 100, that is, 25, and we have 2025.

11. Multiply 65 by 65.
12. " 35 " 35.
12. Multiply 650 by 650.
13. " 450 " 450.

60. To multiply mixed numbers when the whole numbers are alike.

Rule.—*To the product of the whole numbers add that part of one of them which is expressed by the sum of the fractions, and the product of the fractions.*

EXAMPLES.

1. Multiply $12\frac{1}{4}$ by $12\frac{1}{2}$.

$$12 \times 12 = 144$$
$$\tfrac{1}{4} + \tfrac{1}{2} = \tfrac{3}{4}$$
$$\tfrac{3}{4} \text{ of } 12 = 9$$
$$\tfrac{1}{4} \times \tfrac{1}{2} = \tfrac{1}{8}$$
$$144 + 9 + \tfrac{1}{8} = 153\tfrac{1}{8} \text{ Ans.}$$

2. Multiply $8\frac{1}{3}$ by $8\frac{1}{6}$.
3. " $9\frac{1}{4}$ " $9\frac{1}{12}$.
4. " $8\frac{1}{5}$ " $8\frac{1}{20}$.
5. " $6\frac{1}{2}$ " $6\frac{3}{4}$.
6. " $12\frac{1}{3}$ " $12\frac{1}{6}$.
7. " $7\frac{1}{7}$ " $7\frac{3}{7}$.
8. " $8\frac{1}{4}$ " $8\frac{3}{4}$.

Note.—*When the sum of the fractions equals one, and the whole numbers are alike, that part of one of them which is expressed by the sum of the fractions is equal to itself, and the operation can be shortened by multiplying the whole number by itself plus 1, and annexing the product of the fractions.*

Thus, to multiply $8\frac{1}{4}$ by $8\frac{3}{4}$:—

$$\tfrac{3}{4} + \tfrac{1}{4} = \tfrac{4}{4}, \text{ or } 1; \qquad \tfrac{4}{4} \text{ of } 8 = 8$$
$$9 \times 8 = 72 \qquad \tfrac{1}{4} \times \tfrac{3}{4} = \tfrac{3}{16} \qquad 72\tfrac{3}{16} \text{ Ans.}$$

10. Multiply $4\frac{2}{3}$ by $4\frac{1}{3}$.
11. " $12\frac{1}{6}$ " $12\frac{5}{6}$
12. " $7\frac{1}{5}$ " $7\frac{4}{5}$.
13. " $6\frac{1}{4}$ " $6\frac{3}{4}$.
14. " $8\frac{1}{3}$ " $8\frac{2}{3}$.

15. Multiply 4.25 by 4.75.

$$4.25 = 4\tfrac{1}{4} \qquad 4.75 = 4\tfrac{3}{4}$$
$$5 \times 4 = 20 \qquad \tfrac{1}{4} \times \tfrac{3}{4} = \tfrac{3}{16}$$
$$\tfrac{3}{16} = .1875$$
$$20.1875 \text{ Ans.}$$

61. To multiply any mixed numbers.

Rule.—*Multiply by the fraction of the multiplier, then by the whole number;*—or, *Reduce both multiplier and multiplicand to improper fractions, and then proceed as in multiplication of fractions.*

EXAMPLE.

Multiply $6\frac{1}{3}$ by $9\frac{1}{2}$.

$6\frac{1}{3}$
$9\frac{1}{2}$
$3\frac{1}{6}$ prod. by $\frac{1}{2}$.
3 " of $\frac{1}{3}$ by 9.
54 " " 6 " 9.

Ans. $60\frac{1}{6}$.

Or, $6\frac{1}{3} = \frac{19}{3}$ $9\frac{1}{2} = \frac{19}{2}$

$\frac{19}{3} \times \frac{19}{2} = \frac{361}{6} = 60\frac{1}{6}$.

62. To multiply by numbers which are from 1 to 12 less than 100, 1000, &c.

RULE.—*Multiply the multiplicand by the difference between the multiplier and 100, 1000, &c., and subtract the product from the product of the multiplicand by 100, 1000, &c.*

EXAMPLES.

1. Multiply 35 by 98.

$98 = 100 - 2$
$35 \times 2 = 70$
$35 \times 100 = 3500$
$3500 - 70 = 3430$ Ans.

2. Multiply 125 by 198.
3. " 205 " 96.
4. " 375 " 89.

5. Multiply 215 by 98.

NOTE.—When from 1 to 12 more than 100, add the product of the multiplicand by the unit figure, after annexing the required number of ciphers.

$325 \times 102 = 32500 + 650 = 33150$ Ans.

6. Multiply 475 by 101, 103, 106.

63. To multiply two numbers which are equidistant from any number which may be squared mentally.

RULE.—*From the square of the mean number subtract the square of the difference between the mean number and one of the given numbers.*

EXAMPLES.

1. Multiply 98 by 102.

100, the mean number between 98 and 102;
Square of $100 = 10000$; $4 =$ the square of the difference;
$10000 - 4 = 9996$ Ans.

2. Multiply 32 by 28.

Square of 30 = 900;
900 — 4 = 896.

3. Multiply 41 by 39.

4. Multiply 88 by 92.
5. " 37 " 43.
6. " 46 " 34.
7. " 73 " 87.
8. " 41 " 59.

When the sum of the units equals ten, and one of the tens is an odd number and the other is an even number, the numbers are equidistant from some number of tens, which is obtained by taking half of the sum of the tens plus 1.

9. Multiply 45 by 95.

10. Multiply 35 by 65.

64. This rule includes multiplying by numbers of two places each, *when the sum of the units is 10 and the difference of the tens is 1;* by numbers *the sum of whose units equals 10, and whose tens are alike;* mixed numbers, in which *the sum of the fractions equals 1, and the difference of the whole numbers is 1.*

11. Multiply $12\frac{1}{2}$ by $11\frac{1}{2}$. Ans. $143\frac{3}{4}$.
12. Multiply $7\frac{1}{3}$ by $6\frac{2}{3}$.

13. Multiply $4\frac{1}{4}$ by $3\frac{3}{4}$.
14. " 61 " 59.
15. " 126 " 114.

65. To square any number of 9's instantaneously.

RULE.—*Beginning at the left, write 9 as many times less 1 as there are 9's in the given number, an 8, as many ciphers as 9's, and 1.*

The square of 999 = 998001; square of 9999 = 99980001. The square of any number of 3's equals $\frac{1}{9}$ the square of the same number of 9's.

CONTRACTIONS IN DIVISION.

66. Multiplying or dividing both the dividend and divisor by the same number does not alter the quotient.

67. To divide by any number ending in 5, or an aliquot part of 10, or any number of tens.

RULE.—*Multiply both the dividend and divisor by any number that will make the divisor equal some number of tens or hundreds; then divide as usual.*

NOTE.—*If there is a remainder, it must be divided by the number by which the dividend was multiplied, to obtain the true remainder.*

EXAMPLES.

1. Divide 4480 by 35.
   $35 \times 2 = 70$
   $4480 \times 2 = 8960$
   $8960 \div 70 = 128$ Ans.
2. Divide 3644900 by 175.
   $175 \times 4 = 700$
   $3644900 \times 4 = 14579600$
   $14579600 \div 700 = 20828$ Ans.
3. Divide 6785 by 45.
4. " 3725 " 75.
5. " 628750 by 55.
6. " 2628000 " 225, by $22\frac{1}{2}$, $17\frac{1}{2}$, $23\frac{1}{3}$, $17\frac{1}{7}$, $18\frac{1}{3}$, or $18\frac{2}{5}$.

68. To divide by an aliquot part of 100, 1000, &c.

RULE.—*Multiply the dividend by the number which expresses how many times the given divisor is contained in 100, 1000, &c., and point off as many places as there are ciphers in the number divided by the given divisor.*

EXAMPLES.

1. Divide 485 by 25.
   $100 \div 25 = 4$
   $485 \times 4 = 19.40$ Ans.
2. Divide 8480 by $12\frac{1}{2}$.
   $100 \div 12\frac{1}{2} = 8$
   $8480 \times 8 = 678.40$ Ans.
3. Divide 69600 by $16\frac{2}{3}$.
4. Divide 4762000 by $33\frac{1}{3}$.
5. " 2875 " $62\frac{1}{2}$.

$62\frac{1}{2} = \frac{5}{8}$ of 100

```
   2875
      8
  ─────
5)23000
  ─────
  46.00 Ans.
```

$62\frac{1}{2} = \frac{5}{8}$ or $\frac{10}{16}$: therefore, if the number is multiplied by 4 and the product by 4, and *three* places be pointed off, the same result will be obtained.

69. To divide by numbers greater or less than 10 or 100 by an aliquot part

RULE.—*Find what part of the given divisor the difference between it and 10 or 100 equals;* then

Increase the dividend by this aliquot part of itself, if the divisor is less, but diminish it if the divisor is more than 10 or 100, and point off as many decimals as there are ciphers in the number of tens taken.

EXAMPLES.

1. Divide 3165 by $7\frac{1}{2}$.

$10 - 7\frac{1}{2} = 2\frac{1}{2}$

$2\frac{1}{2} = \frac{1}{3}$ of $7\frac{1}{2}$

To 3165

Add 1055 $= \frac{1}{3}$ of 3165

422.0 Ans. 422.

2. Divide 6345 by 15.

$15 = 10 + 5$

$5 = \frac{1}{3}$ of 15

From 6345

Subtract 2115 $= \frac{1}{3}$ of 6345

423.0 Ans. 423.

3. Divide 18764 by $66\frac{2}{3}$.
4. " 2465 " 75.
5. " 42736 " $83\frac{1}{3}$.
6. " 37254 " $88\frac{8}{9}$.
7. Divide 18992 by $133\frac{1}{3}$.
8. " 7462 " $166\frac{2}{3}$.
9. " 4265 " $116\frac{2}{3}$.
10. " 3256 " $87\frac{1}{2}$.

70. To divide by any number but little less than 100, 1000, &c.

RULE.—*Cut off from the right of the dividend as many figures as the divisor contains.*

Multiply the figures on the left of the point by the difference between the divisor and 100, 1000, &c. Point off as many figures as there are in the divisor, and write the product under the dividend.

Multiply the part of this product on the left of the point, if any, by the same multiplier, cut off, and set down as before.

Continue so until the number of figures in the product do not exceed those in the divisor; then add the several results, and to the sum add the product of the number of units carried to the left of the point, if any, by the number used as a multiplier.

The part on the left of the point will be the quotient; that on the right, the remainder.

If the remainder exceeds the divisor, carry one to the quotient, and take the difference between the divisor and remainder for the true remainder.

EXAMPLES.

1. Divide 5532 by 98.

```
98)55|32
    1|10
     | 2
   ------
   56|44
```

$100 - 98 = 2$

$55 \times 2 = 110$

$1 \times 2 = 2$

$56\frac{44}{98}$ Ans.

2. Divide 485 by 95.

```
95)4|85
    |20
   -|--
   5|05
    | 5, the product of 1 (the number carried
   -|--    across the point) by 5.
   5|10
```

3. Divide 11201 by 98.
4. " 3267 " 97. Ans. 33$\frac{66}{97}$.
5. Divide 4268 by 93.
6. " 4264 " 88.
7. " 2487 " 91.

CALCULATIONS USED IN PARTICULAR BRANCHES OF BUSINESS.

71. To find the value of tons and hundred-weight without the use of fractions.

RULE.—*Multiply the number of hundred-weight by 5, and annex the product to the tons, as so many hundredths of tons; then multiply by the given price per ton, and point off two decimals.*

EXAMPLES.

1. What is the cost of 18 tons, 17 cwt. coal @ $4 per ton?
   $17 \times 5 = 85$ $18.85 \times 4 = 75.40$. Ans. $75.40.
2. What is the cost of 35 tons, 15 cwt. hay at $12 per ton?
3. What is the cost of 48 tons, 17 cwt. coal, at $6.50 per ton?

72. To find the value of shillings and pence in the decimals of a pound sterling.

RULE.—*Multiply the shillings by 5, and call the product hundredths.*

Multiply the pence by 4⅙, and call the product thousandths.

The sum of these two values will be the decimal required.

EXAMPLES.

1. Reduce 12*s.* 6*d.* to the decimal of a pound.

$$12 \times 5 \ = .60$$
$$6 \times 4\tfrac{1}{6} = .025$$
$$.625$$

2. Reduce £187 13*s.* 3*d.* to the decimal of a pound.

$$13 \times 5 \ = .65$$
$$3 \times 4\tfrac{1}{6} = .0125$$
$$.6625 \qquad \text{Ans. £187.6625.}$$

73. To change aunes to yards.

NOTE.—An aune is a French measure, equal to $1\frac{1}{4}$ yards.

RULE.—*Annex a cipher, and divide by 8.*

EXAMPLES.

1. In 484 aunes, how many yards?

$$4840 \div 8 = 605 \text{ Ans.}$$

2. In 3848 aunes, how many yards? In 1265? In 1847?

NOTE.—$1\frac{1}{4} = \frac{5}{4}$, or $\frac{10}{8}$. This rule can easily be applied to numerous other calculations. The contents of boards $1\frac{1}{4}$ inches thick, &c., may be computed in this manner; the selling price of goods in order to gain 25% on the cost; and others.

3. What is the selling price of goods, which cost 64 cents per yard, to gain 25%?

$$640 \div 8 = 80$$

$$64$$
$$16 = 25\% \text{ of } 64$$
$$80$$

74. To find how many gallons of linseed oil in a given number of pounds, at $7\frac{1}{2}$ lbs. per gallon.

RULE.—*Add one-third of the number of pounds to itself, and point off one decimal.*

EXAMPLES.

1. How many gallons in 675 lbs.?

$$675$$
$$225 = \tfrac{1}{3} \text{ of } 675$$
$$90.0 \qquad \text{Ans 90 gals.}$$

2. In 1846 lbs. how many gallons? in 675, in 339 lbs.?

PROPORTION.

75. Ratio is the relative magnitude of two numbers of the same kind, and is found by dividing one by the other: thus, the ratio of 3 to 12 is 4.

76. A ratio is denoted by two dots similar to a colon: thus, 5 : 15 expresses the ratio of 5 to 15, and is read, As 5 is to 15.

77. It may also be written in the form of a fraction: thus, $\frac{16}{4}$ expresses the relation of 4 to 16.

78. The two numbers compared are called the terms of the ratio, the first being the divisor, and the other the dividend.

79. The first term is called the *antecedent*, and the last the *consequent.*

80. The terms of a ratio must be of the same kind, or such as may be reduced to the same denomination. We cannot compare 3 yds. with 6 dollars, but we can compare 3 yds. with 5 feet, because we can reduce yards to feet, and say, As 15 feet are to 5 feet.

81. Multiplying the consequent, or dividing the antecedent, multiplies the ratio.

82. Dividing the consequent, or multiplying the antecedent, divides the ratio.

83. Multiplying or dividing both antecedent and consequent does not alter the ratio. (See CANCELLATION, Art. 20.)

84. Proportion is an equality of ratios.

Thus, 2 : 4 : : 10 : 20 expresses that the ratio between 2 and 4 is the same as between 10 and 20, and is read, As 2 is to 4, so is 10 to 20.

The first and fourth terms are called the *extremes;* the second and third, the *means.*

85. *In every proportion the product of the means equals the product of the extremes.*

From this principle, having three terms of a proportion, we are enabled to find the fourth.

SIMPLE PROPORTION, OR, RULE OF THREE.

86. A Simple Proportion is expressed by an equality of two ratios, and consists of four terms. When three of the members of a proportion are given, two of them must be of the same kind, and the other must be of the same kind as the fourth term, or answer.

87. For finding the fourth term, we have the following

Rule.—*Place the given number which is of the same kind as the required answer, as the third term.*

Then, if from the nature of the question the number sought should be larger than the third term, place the greater of the two remaining terms for the second term, and the less for the first; but if the number sought should be less than the third term, place the less of the two remaining numbers for the second, and the greater for the first.

Reduce, if necessary, the first and second terms to the same denomination, and if the third term is a compound number, reduce it to the lowest term mentioned in it.

Then multiply the second and third terms together, and divide the product by the first term: the quotient will be the fourth term, or answer.

EXAMPLES.

1. If 25 barrels of flour cost $165, what will 35 barrels cost?

$$25 : 35 :: 165$$

$$\begin{array}{r} 165 \\ 35 \\ \hline 25)\overline{5775} \\ \hline 231 \end{array}$$

Ans. $231.

Since dollars are of the same kind as the answer sought, we place $165 as the third term. Then, as 35 barrels will cost more than 25 barrels, we place 35, the larger number, for the second term, and 25, the smaller, for the first.

By Analysis.—If 25 barrels cost $165, one barrel will cost $6.60, and 35 barrels will cost 35 times $6.60 = $231.

2. If 7 yards of broadcloth cost $24.50, how much will 12 yards cost at the same rate?

3. If 18 bushels of wheat cost $27, what will 50 bushels cost?

4. What will 27 yards of cloth cost, if 48 yards cost $36?

5. What will 100 shares of railroad stock cost, if 175 shares can be bought for $125?

6. If 12 men build 16 rods of a wall in a day, how many rods will 9 men build?

7. How much will 14 yds. 3 qrs. of cloth cost, at the rate of 10 yds. 1 qr. for $20?

8. What will 22 gals. 2 qts. of wine cost, at the rate of $15.50 for 6 gals. 1 qt. 1 pt.?

9. If $\frac{5}{6}$ of an acre cost $320.25, what will $\frac{3}{4}$ of an acre cost, at the same rate?

COMPOUND PROPORTION.

88. A **Compound Proportion** is one which involves two or more simple ones.

89. Every example in Compound Proportion can be solved by two or more simple proportions.

90. All the terms of a compound proportion appear in couplets, except one, which is always of the same kind as the answer sought.

RULE.—1. *Write the number which is of the same kind as the answer sought, for the third term.*

2. *Arrange the two terms of each ratio separately, as in simple proportion.*

3. *Multiply the continued product of the second terms by the third term, and divide the result by the continued product of the first terms.*

NOTE.—The work may frequently be much abridged by cancellation.

EXAMPLES.

1. If 12 men in 30 days earn $270, how many dollars will 18 men earn in 36 days?

12 : 18 : : 270
30 : 36

360 : 648 : : 270
648

360)174960($486 Ans.
1440

3096
2880

2160
2160

$270 is the same kind as the required term. 18 men will earn more than 12 men, and more can be earned in 36 days than in 30. 12 × 30 = 360. 18 × 36 = 648.

Or, by cancellation, 12 : 18 : : 270. (9 over 270)
30 : 30 (3 under)

3 × 9 × 18 = 486, Ans.

By Analysis.—If 12 men earn $270 in 30 days, 1 man will earn $\frac{1}{12}$ of $270 = $22.50 in 30 days, and $\frac{1}{30}$ of $22.50 = 75¢ in 1 day. If 1 man earn 75¢ in 1 day, 18 men will earn 18 times 75¢, or $13.50, in 1 day, and 36 times $13.50 = $486 in 36 days.

By Simple Proportion.—12 : 18 : : 270 : 405. (men. men.)
30 : 36 : : 405 : 486. (days. days.) Ans. $486.

DISTRIBUTIVE PROPORTION.

91. Distributive Proportion is the method of dividing a number, or quantity, into parts which are proportional to given numbers.

NOTE.—*This rule is also called Fellowship, or Partnership, the Rule of Proportional Division, and Partitive Proportion. For Partnership, see page* 174.

92. The principle of this rule can be easily applied to the solution of numerous questions of a practical nature, such as determining the profits and losses of partners in trade, apportioning the shares of participators in prize-money, finding the relative proportion of ingredients requisite to form a given quantity of a compound, apportioning taxes, school-rates, averaging, &c.

RULE.—*Multiply the whole quantity to be divided by each proportional number, and divide each product by the sum of the proportional numbers.* Or, use the following formula:—

Sum of the proportional numbers : *Quantity or number to be divided* :: *Each proportional number.*

EXAMPLES.

1. Divide 300 into two parts which shall be to each other as 3 to 9.

3 + 9 = 12
12 : 300 : : 3 : 75 the less number.
12 : 300 : : 9 : 225 the greater number.

300 proof.

2. Divide $600 proportionately among 4 men whose shares are to each other as 3, 4, 5, 6.

3 + 4 + 5 + 6 = 18
18 : 600 : : 3 : 100 first man's share.
18 : 600 : : 4 : 133⅓ second " "
18 : 600 : : 5 : 166⅔ third " "
18 : 600 : : 6 : 200 fourth " "

3. Divide 450 shares of railroad stock among 3 persons in proportion to the number of shares already held by them. A. owns 400, B. 200, C. 300. What number will each receive?

4. A., B., C., and D. invest $50,000 in a shipment to Cuba. A. invests $15,000, B. invests $20,000, C. invests $10,000, and D. invests $5000. They gain $30,000. What is each partner's share of the profits?

5. A., B., and C. do a piece of work for $140. A. does $\frac{1}{5}$, B. $\frac{1}{10}$, and C. $\frac{7}{10}$. How much ought each to receive?

6. Gunpowder is composed of 76 parts of nitrate of potass, 14 of carbon, and 10 of sulphur. How much of each ingredient will be required to make 12 cwt. gunpowder?

Ans. 9 cwt. 13$\frac{11}{25}$ lbs. nitrate of potass.
1 cwt. 2 qrs. 20$\frac{4}{25}$ lbs. carbon.
1 cwt. 22$\frac{10}{25}$ lbs. sulphur.

7. A., B., and C. engaged in trade, and agreed to share the gains and losses in proportion to the amount each invested, A. invested $5000, B. $8000, C. $7000. They gained $6600. What was each man's share?

5

COMPOUND DISTRIBUTIVE PROPORTION, OR, DOUBLE FELLOWSHIP.

93. In Compound Distributive Proportion, each share is affected by different periods of time, or by different quantities or rates.

RULE.—*Multiply each share by the time, or quantity, or rate, by which it is affected, and the products will be the proportional numbers. Then proceed as in Simple Distributive Proportion.*

EXAMPLES.

1. A. and B. entered into partnership. A. invested $100 for 2 months, B. invested $200 for 3 months. They agreed to divide the gains and losses in proportion to the capital of each and the time for which it was invested. Their gains were $280. How much was the share of each?

$100 × 2 mos. = 200 for 1 month.
$200 × 3 " = 600 " 1 "

800 : 280 : : 200 : 70, A.'s share.
800 : 280 : : 600 : 210, B.'s share.

2. If an iron enameller manufactures a mixture worth $100, which he applies with equal thickness to the following lots, what does the mixture on each of the plates cost?

14 plates, 8 in. wide, 10 in. long. 8 × 10 = 80 sq. in. each.
10 " 10 " " 20 " " 10 × 20 = 200 " " "
20 " 15 " " 20 " " 15 × 20 = 300 " " "

14 plates each 80 sq. in. = 1120 sq. in.	9120 : 100 : : 1120 : 12.27+
10 " " 200 " " = 2000 " "	9120 : 100 : : 2000 : 21.92+
20 " " 300 " " = 6000 " "	9120 : 100 : : 6000 : 65.78+
9120	

$12.27, the cost of 14 plates. 1 plate costs 88 cts. nearly.
1 sq. inch costs $\frac{88}{80}$ or $1\frac{1}{10}$ cts. nearly.

3. A., B., and C. hired a pasture for $45. A. had 15 cows pastured 2 months, B. had 8 cows pastured 3 months, and C. had 9 cows pastured 4 months. How much should each pay?

4. If 4 oz. gold 22 carats fine be mixed with 8 oz. gold 18 carats fine, how much fine gold will there be in 6 oz. of the mixture?

NOTE.—*The fineness of gold is usually expressed by saying that gold is so many carats fine; that is, that so many parts out of 24 are pure gold.*

$$4 \text{ oz.} \times \tfrac{22}{24} = \tfrac{88}{24} \text{ oz. fine gold.}$$
$$8 \text{ oz.} \times \tfrac{18}{24} = \tfrac{144}{24} \text{ " " "}$$

$\frac{88}{24} + \frac{144}{24} = \frac{232}{24} = \frac{29}{3}$, the quantity of fine gold in 12 oz.
$8 + 4 = 12$; then, 12 oz. : $\frac{29}{3}$ oz. : : 6 : $4\frac{5}{6}$. **Ans.** $4\frac{5}{6}$ oz.

Or, *By Analysis*.—If there are $\frac{29}{3}$ oz. pure gold in 12 oz. of the mixture, there is $\frac{1}{12}$ of $\frac{29}{3}$ or $\frac{29}{36}$ oz. in 1 oz. of the mixture; and in 6 oz. there are 6 times $\frac{29}{36} = \frac{29}{6}$ or $4\frac{5}{6}$ oz.

MEDIAL PROPORTION, OR ALLIGATION.

94. Alligation is the process of finding the value of a compound or mixture of articles of different values, or of forming a compound which shall have a given value, or one in which the articles shall be in a given proportion.

95. To find the average value of several articles when the quantity and rate are given.

RULE.—*Multiply each quantity by its rate, and divide the sum of the products by the sum of the quantities. The quotient will be the average value.*

EXAMPLES.

1. If 10 lbs. of tea worth 60¢ per lb. be mixed with 20 lbs. worth 40¢ and 30 lbs. worth 75¢, what is one pound of the mixture worth?

OPERATION.

25 lbs.	@ 60¢	=	15.00
25 "	" 36	=	9.00
40 "	" 75	=	30.00

90 lbs. are worth $54.00
1 lb. is worth $54.00 ÷ 90 = 60¢. **Ans.**

2. If I mix 100 lbs. sugar worth 10¢ per lb., 36 lbs. worth 15¢ per lb., 80 lbs. worth 12¢ per lb., and 40 lbs. worth 9¢ per lb., what will one pound of the mixture be worth?

96. To find what quantities of ingredients of different values will form a compound of a given value.

RULE.—*Find the gain or loss on one of each ingredient, then take as much of any ingredient as will make the gain and loss equal.* Or,

At the left of the column containing the rates, write the mean rate. Then connect each rate that is less than the mean rate with one that is greater, and write the difference opposite the rate with which it is connected.

If more than one difference stand opposite to any number, add the differences together.

The differences, or sums of difference, written opposite any rate will denote the quantity of the ingredient to be taken at that rate.

NOTE.—I. If any article is of the mean rate, it need not be linked, as it is of the average value, and will not affect the rate.

II. Every pair of numbers joined, forms of itself a compound of the right proportions, whether taken separately, or in connection with others. This operation only gives the ratios of the several ingredients. If all the quantities found, be multiplied or divided by the same number, they may be increased or diminished at pleasure, without affecting the proportion.

III. When part, or all, of the numbers contain fractions, they may be reduced to a common denominator, and their numerators used.

IV. A variety of answers may be obtained by linking differently, all of which will be correct.

EXAMPLES.

1. In what proportion must a grocer mix coffee worth 15¢, 18¢, 20¢, 22¢, and 24¢ per pound, that the mixture may be worth 21¢ per pound?

FIRST OPERATION.

By selling at 21¢
1 lb. worth 15¢ I gain 6¢
1 " " 18 " " 3
1 " " 20 " " 1
Total gain, 10

1 lb. worth 22¢ I lose 1¢
1 " " 24 " " 3
Total loss, 4

To make the gains and losses equal, instead of 1 lb. he can take 6 lbs. at 22¢, or 2 lbs. at 24¢.

Or 3 lbs. at 15¢ and gain 18¢
3 " " 18 " " 9
9 " " 24 " lose 27

SECOND OPERATION.

21	15	—3	3
	18	—3	3
	20	—1	1
	22	—1	1
	24	—6 + 3 =	9
			17.

PROOF.

3 lbs.	@ 15¢	=	45
3 "	" 18	=	54
1 "	" 20	=	20
1 "	" 22	=	22
9 "	" 24	=	2.16
17 "	" 21¢	=	$3.57

2. If a grocer wishes to mix tea worth 70¢, 80¢, $1, and $1.10 per pound, that the mixture shall be worth 90¢ per pound, how many pounds of each must he use?
Ans.

97. To find what quantity of each of the other ingredients must be used to make a compound of a given value, when the quantity of part, and the value of all, are given.

RULE.—*Find the proportional numbers as in the last case, and divide the given quantity by its proportional number.*

Multiply each remaining proportional quantity by the quotient so obtained, and the several products will be the required quantities.

EXAMPLES.

1. How many pounds of sugar, worth 8¢, 12¢, and 24¢ per pound, must be mixed with 40 pounds worth 20¢, that the mixture may be worth 22¢ per pound?

OPERATION.

22 { 8	2	Then 2 × 20 = 40 @ 8¢ =	3.20
12	2	2 × 20 = 40 " 12 =	4.80
20	2	2 × 20 = 40 " 20 =	8.00
24	14 + 10 + 2 = 26	26 × 20 = 520 " 24 =	124.80
	32	Ans. 640 " 22 =	$140.80

40, the limited quantity, divided by 2, the proportional quantity of sugar at 20 cts., = 20, the ratio.

2. How much wine worth $1.25, $1.30, and $1.40 per gallon must be mixed with 40 gallons worth $1 per gallon, 10 gallons at $1.20 per gallon, and 5 gallons at $1.70 per gallon, that the mixture may be worth $1.35 per gallon?

OPERATION.

40 gals. at $1.	= 40.00	1.35 { 1.10		5
10 " " 1.20	= 12.00	1.25		5
5 " " 1.70	= 8.50	1.30		5
55	60.50	1.40	25 + 10 + 5 =	40
Average price per gallon, $1.10.				55

55, the limited number of gallons, which average $1.10, divided by 5, the proportional quantity, gives 11 for the ratio. Then

5 × 11 = 55	at $1.10 =	$60.50
5 × 11 = 55	" 1.25 =	68.75
5 × 11 = 55	" 1.30 =	71.50
40 × 11 = 440	" 1.40 =	616.00
605	" $1.35 =	816.75

Ans. 605 gals.

98. To find the quantity required of each ingredient to make a compound of a given quantity, when the value of the ingredients is given.

RULE.—*Find the proportional parts as before, and divide the quantity of the mixture by the sum of the proportional parts.*

Multiply each quantity by the quotient thus obtained, and the several products will be the required quantities of each.

EXAMPLES.

1. A merchant received an order for 460 lbs. of sugar, at 15¢ per pound. He has in his store sugars worth 10¢, 12¢, 20¢, and 25¢ per pound. How much shall he take of each to fill the order?

OPERATION.

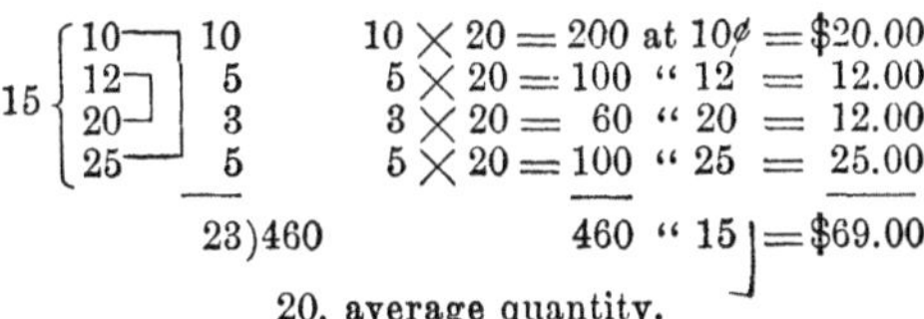

.Ans. 200 lbs. at 10¢, 100 lbs. at 12¢, 60 lbs. at 20¢, 100 lbs. at 25¢.

99. If a quantity is at the average rate, it may be disregarded until the other quantities are found, and then enough of that quantity taken to make the whole equal to the required compound.

100. As each combination is perfect in itself, if the result is in mixed numbers, when whole numbers are required, we may select some multiple of the pairs, and thus make up the quantity sought.

MISCELLANEOUS EXAMPLES.

1. What is the fineness of a composition consisting of 2 lb. 8 oz. gold 18 carats fine, 3 lb. 6 oz. 14 carats fine, 1 lb. 6 oz. 22 carats fine, and 1 lb. 6 oz. alloy?

2. A cask contains 30 gallons wine worth $3 per gallon. What quantity will the cask contain after pouring in water until the contents are worth but $2.50 per gallon?

3. A farmer wishes to mix rye at 70 cts. per bushel with corn at 90 cts. and oats at 50 cts. What quantity of each must he take to make the mixture worth 75 cts. per bushel?

4. A merchant wishes to fill a barrel which will hold 200 lbs. with sugar worth respectively 8 cts., 12 cts., and 14 cts. per lb., so that the mixture may be worth 13 cts. How much of each must he take?

5. A man bought 50 bbls. flour for $500,—some at $8 per bbl., some at $9 per bbl., and some at $12 per bbl. How many of each kind did he purchase?

PERCENTAGE.

101. Percentage is a method of computing by means of a fraction whose denominator is 100.

The term *per cent.* is an abbreviation of the Latin *per centum*, which signifies *by the hundred.*

102. The **Rate** per cent. is the number of hundredths. Thus, 8 per cent. is eight-hundredths, and may be expressed $\frac{8}{100}$, or .08, or 8%. $\frac{1}{8}\% = \frac{1}{8}$ of $\frac{1}{100} = \frac{1}{800} = .00125$.

Per cent. is simply the proportion of a hundred, and is not any of the denominations of Federal money: 10 per cent. is not 10 cents, nor 10 dollars, but $\frac{10}{100}$; 10 per cent. of \$50 = \$5; 10 per cent. of 85 bbls. = $8\frac{1}{2}$ bbls.

Percentage is used in most commercial calculations, such as Interest, Commission, Insurance, Profit and Loss, &c.

103. CASE I.—To find the percentage of any number or quantity, the rate per cent. being given.

RULE.—*Multiply the given number by the rate per cent., and divide by 100* (i.e. *point off two decimals*).

EXAMPLES.

1. What is 8% of \$640?

$640 \times 8 = 5120.$ Ans. \$51.20

8% of $640 = \frac{8}{100}$ of $640 = \frac{5120}{100} = 51.20.$

The percentage on sterling money and denominate numbers is found after reducing the numbers to the lowest denomination given, or to the decimal of the highest, and then proceeding as in simple numbers. (See Decimals of Denominate Numbers, p. 28.)

2. What is 6 per cent. of £15 9*s.* 6*d.*?

By Art. 43. 9*s.* 6*d.* = £.475

$$\begin{array}{r} 15.475 \times 6 = .92850 \\ 20 \\ \hline 18.57000 \\ 12 \\ \hline 6.84000 \end{array}$$

Ans. 18*s.* $6\frac{84}{100}$*d.*

£15 9*s.* 6*d.* = 3714*d.* 3714 × 6 = 22284

222.84*d.* = 18*s.* $6\frac{84}{100}$*d.*

104. CASE II.—To find what rate per cent. one number is of another.

RULE.—*Annex two ciphers to the percentage, and divide by the number on which the percentage is reckoned.*

EXAMPLE.—What per cent. of 40 is 8?

800 ÷ 40 = 20. $8 = \frac{8}{40}$ of 40; $\frac{8}{40}$ of 100 = 20.

2. A student at an examination in which 50 questions were asked answered 45 correctly. What per cent. did he answer?

105. CASE III.—To find a number when the value of a certain per cent. of it is known.

RULE.—*Annex two ciphers to the percentage, and divide by the rate per cent.*

EXAMPLE.—42 is 25% of what number?

4200 ÷ 25 = 168.

2. A man sold a house, and gained $2850, which was $12\frac{1}{2}$ per cent. of what he received. How much did he sell it for?

106. CASE IV.—To find what number is a certain per cent. *more* or *less* than a given number.

RULE.—When the given number is MORE than the required number, *annex two ciphers to the given number, and divide by 100* PLUS *the rate per cent.*

When the given number is LESS than the required number, *annex two ciphers to the given number, and divide by 100* LESS *the rate per cent.*

EXAMPLES.

1. What amount of gold, at a premium of 25 per cent., can I buy for $720 in currency?

100 + 25 = 125; 72000 ÷ 125 = 576. Ans. $576.

2. Purchased merchandise and sold it for $1680, thereby losing 20 per cent. What did the merchandise cost?

100 — 20 = 80; 168000 ÷ 80 = 2100. Ans. $2100.

EXAMPLES IN PERCENTAGE.

What is 6 % of $26.45 ?

26.45 × 6 = 158.70. Ans. 1.58\frac{7}{10}$.

NOTE.—The figures on the left, after pointing off, are of the lowest denomination in the number multiplied. If there are cents in the given number, two more places must be pointed off for cents.

1. If a merchant who buys goods on 6 months' credit is allowed a deduction of 5 % for paying his bill within 30 days, what can he save on a bill of $560? How much on $3650?

2. If a man fails to pay his water rent until he is charged 12% for delay, how much will he lose if his water rent is $18.75?

3. If 1 % per month, counting from the time of payment, is allowed on all taxes paid before July 1st, and 1 % per month charged on all taxes remaining unpaid thereafter, how much more does A. pay than B., if B. pays his taxes Feb. 1st, and A. pays his taxes Nov. 1st, their tax-bills being each $180?

4. A merchant owes $6500, and his property is worth only $5425. What per cent. of his debt can he pay?

5. A man shipped 3800 bbls. of flour to England, and during a storm 19 bbls. were thrown overboard. What per cent. was lost?

6. If a man pays an income-tax of $177.50, the rate being 5%, what is the amount of his income above the deduction allowed by the government?

7. If I have $374.50 in currency, how much gold can I buy when it sells at a premium of 7 %?

8. The population of a certain village increased in 5 years from 6000 to 7800. What was the average rate of increase per year?

9. What is the difference to a salesman between selling a bill of $1000, on which there is a profit of $100 of which he receives $\frac{1}{8}$, and selling the same amount for a commission of 1½ per cent.? What will be the difference to the firm if the goods are sold for $950 instead of $1000, and what the difference to the salesman?

10. A merchant sold a lot of cloth at $3 per yard, and thereby gained 20 per cent. What per cent. would he have gained if he had sold the cloth at $3.75 per yard?

COMMISSION, BROKERAGE, &c.

107. Commission is the charge made by Factors, or Commission Merchants, Brokers, and other agents, for buying and selling merchandise, stocks, &c., making collections, or transacting any other business for another. It is usually calculated at so much per cent. on the amount of money received or expended.

108. A **Broker** is one who makes a bargain for another, but who has not the goods in his possession.

109. Guarantee is the charge made for assuming the risk of loss from non-payment by the purchaser.

110. The *Consignment* is the quantity of goods sent to be sold; the person who sends them is called the *Consignor;* the commission merchant, or person to whom the goods are sent, is called the *Consignee.* (See Account Sales.)

111. The excess of the amount of sales or collections over the charges, is called the *Net Proceeds.*

112. Stocks are usually bought and sold at a certain per cent. on their *par value*, or at so much per share.

(See The Stock Exchange.)

113. Rates of Commission adopted by Philadelphia Merchants.

The charges for selling flour, grain, seeds, and other produce shall be 2½ per cent. on the gross amount of sales, and the incidental expenses, handling, cooperage, measuring, fire insurance, &c. shall be charged in addition.

That, in order to secure uniformity, these incidental expenses shall be as follows, viz.:—

On flour, not less than 3 cents per barrel for labor, 3 cents per barrel for inspection and cooperage, 3 cents per barrel for storage. (See Storage, page 64.)

On wheat, when received by rail, not less than 1 cent per bushel for measuring, storage, and labor.

All other grain, when received by rail, 1½ cents per bushel for measuring, storage, and labor.

On wheat and other grain, when received afloat, 1½ cents per bushel for measuring, and actual expenses incurred when stored, which shall not be less than the charge made by rail.

On seeds, dried fruit, butter, dressed hogs, feed and meal in bags, and other miscellaneous produce, 2½ per cent. commission, and 1 per cent. for storage, measuring, &c.

A charge of not less than ⅛ of 1 per cent. for fire insurance shall be added in all cases, except where sales are made afloat.

After the first month shall have expired, the charge for storage shall not be less than 3 cents per barrel per month on flour, and ½ cent per bushel on grain, with ⅛ of 1 per cent. per month fire insurance.

Rules.—In all cases where acceptances are made on produce, in anticipation of sales, the commission merchant shall be at liberty to sell, in order to meet the drafts at maturity.

Delivery will be accomplished on the part of the seller when he places at the door of his warehouse flour or meal in a position to be removed by the purchaser's porters or stevedores; and grain, when pointed out to the purchaser or his agent.

The expenses of towing and wharfage of boats and vessels shall be paid by the purchaser of the cargo, when moved for his accommodation.

RECEIVING COMMISSION.

	Cents.			Cents.	
Bacon	50	℔ ton.	Shingles	20	℔ 1000.
Bark	50	"	Shot	6¼	keg.
Beef	50	"	Soap, foreign	4	box.
Butter and Lard	50	"	Staves	20	1000.
Clay	50	"	Steel, in bars or bundles	20	ton.
Clover-seed	2	bushel.	Sugar	15	hhd.
Coal	10	"	do.	5	barrel.
Corn Meal	3	barrel.	do.	1½	bag.
do.	12	hhd.	Tallow	25	hhd.
Dye Woods	25	ton.	Tea	4	chest.
Flour	3	barrel.	Tin, block	15	ton.
Grain, all kinds	1	bushel.	Tobacco	25	hhd.
Hemp	6	bale.	do.	6	bale.
Hoop Poles	20	1000.	do. manufac.	2	box.
Indigo	8	chest.	Whisky	25	hhd.
do.	4	ceroon.	do.	6¼	barrel.
Iron	20	ton.	Whiting	25	hhd.
Leather	$1.00	ton.	Wine	25	pipe.
Lumber	20	1000 ft.	do.	6¼	cask.
Nails	20	ton.	Wood, dye	30	ton.
Plaster	10	ton.	Wool	12½	sack.
Seeds	1	bushel.			

COMMISSIONS FOR PURCHASING.

On produce generally, one-half the charges made for selling, and 2½ per cent. on all other goods.

COMMISSION FOR RECEIVING AND SHIPPING HENCE TO OTHER PORTS.

	Cents.			Cents.	
Flour and Meal......	6¼	℔ barrel.	Grain, all kinds......	1	℔ bushel.
Corn Meal............	25	hhd.	Peas and Beans......	1	"
Flour and Meal......	3⅛	hf. bbl.	Seeds, all kinds......	3	"

COMMISSION FOR LOADING MERCHANDISE IN CARS AND BOATS.

On store goods and merchandise generally, 75 cents per ton.

LEAKAGE AND BREAKAGE.

On spirits, 2 per cent.; ale, beer, and porter, in bottles, 10 per cent.; all other liquors, in bottles, 5 per cent.

EXAMPLES IN COMMISSION.

1. Received $245 for selling goods at a commission of 5%. How much did I sell?

$$245 \times 100 = 24500$$
$$24500 \div 5 = 4900. \quad \text{Ans. } \$49.00.$$

2. A broker purchased for me 50 shares of railroad stock, of the par value of $50 per share. His charge was ⅛%. How much did I pay him?

3. A country trader buys through a commission merchant an invoice of goods for $2550. The commission merchant charges 2^2% for buying. How much must the trader remit to pay for the goods and commission?

4. Thomas & Sons sold for me, at auction, a lot of goods to the amount of $14,500. Their charges are as follows:—Commission, 2^2%; guarantee, 2^2%; advertising, $22.50; drayage, labor, and storage, $32.50. How much is due me?

5. A house was sold for $2400, which was 80% of its cost. What was the cost?

6. Paid a broker $24 for investing money in bank stock for me, selling at par at a commission of ¼%. How much did he invest?

7. Paid a merchant 3% commission, and received $3880 as net proceeds. What was the amount of sales?

8. What number diminished by 3% of itself is equal to 796?

9. Received, as net proceeds of a consignment, $760, after paying 2^2% commission for selling. What was the amount of sales?

10. Received $224 dividend on 50 shares railroad stock, which cost $3200. What was the rate per cent.?

11. An agent sold property for $18,240, and received $121.60. What was the rate of commission?

12. If I pay a commission merchant $125 for commission and guarantee on a sale of $2500, what rate does he receive?

13. A commission merchant wishes to buy exchange with the net proceeds of a sale amounting to $714. The rate of exchange is 2%. How large a bill can he buy? Ans. $700

14. A Cuban merchant wishes to draw on New York for an amount which will leave him the sum of $6141.39, after paying a premium of 4^2% for negotiating and exchange. For how much must he draw? Ans. $6430.77.

15. A merchant received $525, with which to buy goods He is to receive a commission of 2^2% on the amount of purchase, for buying. How much is his commission, and what is the amount of purchases?

16. I have remitted $3600 to my agent in Montpelier, with which to buy wool, first deducting his commission of 3% for purchasing. How much will he expend for wool? How much will be his commission?

17. Invested in wheat the proceeds of a consignment of flour, less my commission on both at 3%, which amounted to $60. What did I sell the flour for, and what did I pay for the wheat? Ans. Flour, $1030, Wheat, $970.

$\frac{100}{100} - \frac{3}{100} = \frac{97}{100}$, net proceeds of the flour.

$\frac{100}{100}$ of wheat $+ \frac{3}{100}$ com. $= \frac{103}{100}$ of the wheat.

Then $\frac{97}{100}$ of the flour $= \frac{103}{100}$ of the wheat, and $\frac{97}{103}$ of the flour equalled the wheat, and $\frac{6}{103}$ of the flour equalled the commission, $60.

18. A commission merchant sold goods for $6262, and received $150, which included a charge for freight of $9.34. What rate of commission did he receive?

19. Sold lumber on commission at 5%. Invested net proceeds in dry goods at 2% commission. My whole commission was $70. What was the value of the lumber and the dry goods? Ans. Lumber, $1020, Dry goods, $950.

Suggestion.—Net proceeds of lumber equal $\frac{95}{100}$, or 95%. Commission on dry goods equals $\frac{2}{102}$ of 95% $= 1\frac{44}{51}\%$. $1\frac{44}{51} + 5 = 6\frac{44}{51}$. Then, if $6\frac{44}{51}\%$ equals $70, 5% equals $51, 2% equals $19.

20. J. B. Myers & Co. sell for me a quantity of dry goods on commission at 6%. How much must be sold that my agent can buy flour with the proceeds to the value of $5400, after retaining his commission, for buying, of $2^2\%$?

Ans.

21. Sold goods at $2^2\%$ commission, which I invested in sugars, and sold them at a profit of 15 per cent., realizing a gain of $240. How much commission did I receive, and how much did the goods sell for?

22. A merchant bought an invoice of grain, which, including $1\frac{1}{8}\%$ commission, cost $$5050.62\frac{1}{2}$, and paid $15.25 for freight. He sold the grain at a profit of 15% on its first cost, and invested the proceeds in sugar, which he sold at 5% profit, receiving a note due in 48 days, including grace. This note he had discounted at 6%, at bank. What was the cost of the grain, and how much were his profits?

Ans. Cost of grain, $4994.43; total profits, $916.66.

The following transaction occurred in a Philadelphia commission house:—

23. A commission merchant received an order to purchase merchandise worth $1000, on which he paid $50 for drayage. He was to effect insurance at the rate of 1% on 10% advance of total cost of merchandise, drayage, commission for buying, and cost of insurance, and was to receive 3% commission on total cost of merchandise, drayage, and insurance. What was the amount insured, and how much did he receive for commission, and how much for insurance?

Ans. $1203.28, Com. $31.86, Ins. $12.03.

Suggestion.—1% of 3% = .0003, which added to 1% = .0103, which increased by 10% of itself equals .01133, the rate of insurance on $1. $1050 increased by 3% of itself equals $1081.50, which increased 10% equals $1189.65. Then, to find the amount to be insured to cover $1189.65 and the insurance, or .01133 of itself, we divide $1189.65 by $1 less .01133, which gives us $1203.28.

STORAGE.

Storage is charged at a certain price per barrel, bale, box, etc., according to regulations adopted by the Chambers of Commerce or Boards of Trade of the different cities.

All goods stored are subject to one month's storage. In some places, if they remain any part of a month they are charged for a full month; in others, after the first month, if taken out within fifteen days, a half-month is charged; if after fifteen days, a whole month. The owners of the goods pay for putting the goods in store, stowing away, and the expenses of delivery.

When goods are received and delivered at the pleasure of the consignor, the dues for storage are usually determined by an average.

To compute storage.

Rule.—*Multiply the number of barrels, or other articles, first entered, by the number of days between the time of entrance and the time of the first delivery, or second entrance.* Then

Multiply each balance by the number of days it continues unchanged.

The sum of all the products will be the number of articles in store for one day. To find the number stored for one month, divide the sum of the products by 30.

Example.—What is the cost of storage, at 1¢ per bushel per month, of wheat received and delivered as per following account, closed Oct. 2d, 1866?

Account of Storage of Wheat received and delivered for account of A. Y. Rodgers & Co., St. Louis.

Date.		Received.	Delivered.	Balances.	Days.	Products.
1866.						
July	2	200		200	9	1800
"	11		150	50	5	250
"	16	350		400	5	2000
"	21		300	100	20	2000
August	10	400		500	5	2500
"	15		450	50	5	250
"	20		50	0	0	0000
Septemb'r	5	200		200	5	1000
"	10	100		300	5	1500
"	15		200	100	17	1700
		1250	1150			30)13000
Bal. on hand Oct. 2,			100			433⅓
		1250	1250			

$433\frac{1}{3} \times 1¢ = \$4.33$, Ans.

INSURANCE.

114. Insurance is a contract of indemnity by which one party engages, for a stipulated sum, to insure another against a loss or injury to which he may be exposed.

115. The **Insurer** is the person who takes the risk. He is sometimes called the Underwriter, from the custom of individual insurers writing their names, together with the amounts for which they will be responsible, *under* a description of the property insured.

116. The **Premium** is the sum paid for insurance, and is a percentage on the amount insured.

117. The **Policy** is the instrument containing the contract, and describes the property or person insured, and the terms on which the insurance is effected.

118. Insurance companies are generally incorporated bodies; but persons, such as commission merchants, shippers, and others, insure, at times, as well as companies.

119. Mutual Insurance Companies are those in which the persons insured become members of the company, and liable to a certain extent for its losses; they also share in the gains of the company, if any.

120. Policies are of two kinds,—*Open Policies*, and *Closed or Valued Policies.*

121. A *Valued or Closed Policy* is one in which the amount insured is definitely determined at the time the insurance is effected. Houses, furniture, and goods in store are insured in policies of this kind.

122. An *Open Policy* is one upon which amounts yet to be ascertained and insured may be entered at different times. (See page 69.) They are used by persons who insure goods which are to be conveyed from one place to another. The person taking an open policy gives a note, called a *Premium Note*, to the insurance company, as security for the premium on the amounts he anticipates insuring before the date on which the note matures. This note at maturity is returned to him on payment of the premiums on the amounts he has had insured. A nominal premium is mentioned in the policy when made out, but actual premiums are fixed at the time the risk is reported, and are regulated by a scale of prices arranged by the company.

When the insurance is on goods to be imported from a foreign country, the value of the currency of that country is also stated. As it is customary to insure for about 10% more than the cost of the invoice, this is included in the valuation of the foreign currency. English money is thus estimated at $5.25 per pound sterling.

When the insured ships goods, or receives information of goods shipped to him, he must notify the insurance company as soon as he is in receipt of bill of lading or other advice of shipment.

Some open policies which insure invoices shipped abroad, contain the clause that "no risk shall attach until the amount and description of the same shall be approved and indorsed thereon by the company, and to be valued at the sum so indorsed;" but open policies designed to cover goods to be received will cover all consignments if reported immediately on receipt of bill of lading or advice of shipment. In all open policies, to the description of the property are added the words "lost or not lost," so as to include all goods not known to be actually lost.

123. To guard against fraud, property is not usually insured for its full value, and no more can be recovered than the amount of actual loss. The party insured must also have an interest in the property insured, and, when goods or furniture are destroyed, must be able to give a full enumeration or description of the property.

Dwelling-houses, and permanent property about the value of which opinions differ, and which deteriorate in time, may generally be insured for from one-half to three-fourths their estimated value; goods at sea, or in transportation, from 5 per cent. to 25 per cent. more than their cost or invoice price, in order to cover the expenses of freight, insurance, and a share of the profits; goods in store, at their cash value; but the goods are not usually specified until a fire has occurred.

124. Insurance companies will not insure more on any one risk than a stated amount, which usually ranges from $3000 to $20,000, according to the capital of the company insuring, and the hazard of the risk. They will frequently, however, take a larger amount, and then reinsure themselves for part in another company.

125. The rate for insuring varies according to the degree of risk incurred, either from original liability, or from the difficulty of preservation or recovery when fires take place; and some property is so hazardous that insurance companies decline to insure it at any rate. On private dwellings the rates are about 2 per cent. for a perpetual policy, and ¼ of 1 per cent. annually; goods at sea, from ¼ per cent. to 3 per cent.

The following rates are taken from those adopted by the New York Board of Fire Underwriters:—

For insuring $100 in dry goods, groceries, boots and shoes, crockery, furs, leather, paper, wine and liquors, dry drugs, carpets, jewellers' stocks, from 55 to 95 cts. Retail stocks of tobacco and cigars, books and stationery, music and prints, organs, wood and hollow ware, hats and caps with manufacturing, cabinet ware, paints and oil, toys, vessels in port, from 90 cents to $1.20 per $100. Wholesale drugs, steam tugboats, steam and sail vessels, lumber-yards, from $1.25 to $1.65. Tar, naval stores, sugar-houses, from $1.50 to $2.50.

126. The advantages to commerce from insurance are immense. "Without the aid that it affords, comparatively few individuals would be found disposed to expose their property to the risk of long and hazardous voyages; but by its means insecurity is changed for security, and the capital of the merchant whose ships are dispersed over every sea, and exposed to all the perils of the ocean, is as secure as that of the agriculturist." The dangers from not being insured are so many and so great that none but millionaires can afford to remain uninsured; and it is considered by some a moral duty to insure in all cases where the interests of creditors or of one's family are in danger from the omission of it.

EXAMPLES IN INSURANCE.

1. What is the premium for insuring $4500 @ 1^2%?

$4500 \times 1^2 = 67.50$. Ans. $67.50.

2. What will it cost to insure a house for $2600 at a premium of 2%, the policy and survey costing $1.50?

3. Effected insurance on a cargo from Liverpool, worth £1872 11*s.* 5*d.*, at a premium of 1^2%. What is the premium, the pound sterling being valued at $5.25?

4. If the premium on a perpetual policy is 2%, which will be returned on payment of 5% of the premium for every year the policy is held, what is the difference in the cost of a perpetual policy insuring a house valued at $4000, and returned at the end of four years, and an annual policy taken at a premium of ¼ of 1% per year for the same time?

4000 @ 2% = 80. 5% of 80 = 4. $4 \times 4 = 16$.

4000 @ ¼% = 10. $10 \times 4 = 40$. $40 - 16 = 24$.

Ans. $24.

5. What is the cost of insuring furniture worth $3000, at a premium of 80 cts. per $100, the policy and survey costing $1.50?

6. A merchant insured his goods to the amount of $5000 in one company at a premium of 1^2%, and $2800 in another company at a premium of 1^1%. The policies cost $1 each. What did he pay in all?

7. If I take a risk of $10,000 at a premium of 1^1%, and reinsure it at 1^2%, what will be my gain?

8. If I take a policy covering goods in my store for 1 year, to the amount of $15,000, at a premium of 1^2%, and within that time I insure consignments to the amount of $23,000, at the same rate, how much do I gain?

9. At ⅛ of 1% per month, what will be the cost of insuring goods worth $2800 which remain in store 3 months?

JAMES, KENT, SANTEE & CO.'S OPEN POLICY WITH THE DELAWARE INSURANCE COMPANY.

Name of Vessel.	Place of Shipment.	Place of Destination.	Time of Sailing.	Amount of Invoice in Foreign Currency.	Value of Currency.	Valuation agreed upon in American Currency.	Rate.	Premium.	Date of Approval.	Signatures.
Oriola.........	Liverpool	Philada.	1868 Mar. 1	£10,000	$5.25 per £	$52,500.00	$\frac{3}{4}$%	$393.75	Mar. 15	R. G. Gray, *Secretary.*
Cutwater......	London..	New York	" 3	5,250	"	27,562.50	$1\frac{1}{2}$%	413.44	Apr. 5	R. G. Gray.
Julia Trundy	Liverpool	"	" 5	2,875	"	15,093.75	1%	150.94	" 30	R. G. Gray.
Blue Nose.....	"	Philada.	" 27	6,000	"	31,500.00	$1\frac{1}{4}$%	393.75	" 15	R. G. Gray.
City of Boston	"	"	Apr. 14	500	"	2,625.00	2%	52.50	May 2	R. G. Gray.
Lafayette......	"	"	" 19	340	"	1,785.00	$1\frac{1}{2}$%	26.77	" 10	R. G. Gray.
Aurora.........	Havre...	New York	" 25	fr. 32,450	30¢ per fr.	9,735.00	1%	97.35	" 15	R. G. Gray.
Kangaroo.....	"	Philada.	May 3	fr. 25,000	"	7,500.00	$1\frac{1}{2}$%	112.50	" 22	R. G. Gray.
Wm. S. Balch	Liverpool	"	" 10	£4,200	$5.25 per £	22,050.00	$1\frac{1}{4}$%	275.63	" 25	R. G. Gray.

The above illustrates the manner of entering amounts insured on open policy. The terms of the policy are omitted, for want of space. The calculations should all be performed by the student.

MARINE OR GENERAL AVERAGE.

127. General Average means a contribution made by all parties concerned towards a loss sustained by some of the parties in interest, for the benefit of all. In such cases, the loss arising from the contribution falls within the provisions of the insurance policy.

128. No general average takes place unless it can be shown that the *danger was imminent*, that the sacrifice was *voluntary* and *considered indispensable* for the safety of the rest, and that the portion which was saved *was saved by reason of the sacrifice.*

129. Particular Average is any partial loss, without being voluntarily encountered, and is borne wholly by the owner of the property damaged. In cases of particular average, the indemnity is to be adjusted upon a comparison of the gross proceeds of the sound and the damaged goods.

130. Jettison (from the French *jeter*, to throw) is the portion of goods thrown overboard.

131. Salvage is an allowance or remuneration made to those by whose exertions ships or goods are saved from the dangers of the seas, fire, or enemies.

132. The cargo, including the part sacrificed, is valued at the price it would have sold for in *cash* at the port of destination.

The ship, and freight, and every thing on board which pays freight, contribute to general average. The wages of seamen do not contribute, that they may have no interest in opposing a sacrifice necessary to the general safety.

From the freight $\frac{1}{3}$ is usually taken (in New York $\frac{1}{2}$) for seamen's wages, pilotage, &c., to find its contributory value.

In the valuation of repairs, masts, cables, &c., it is customary to deduct $\frac{1}{3}$,—thus estimating the old as worth $\frac{2}{3}$ the value of the new.

Statement of General Average of the "Fairweather," PERRAN J. COOKE, *Master, from New York to New Orleans, in consequence of losing part of her rigging by a violent gale, in getting aground on Stirrup Key, and by throwing part of her cargo overboard, as appears by protest, &c.*

AMOUNT OF LOSSES.					
Paid Geo. Burton and Wm. H. Taylor, of the sloops Emily and Shamrock, for assistance in getting vessel off, as per agreement,			$8000.00		
Protests, postages, stamps, &c.,			5.00		
Value of goods thrown overboard:					
Fosdick & Co.'s goods,		$1800.			
G. Porchs' "		3840.			
Gustav Piaggio's "		4000.	9640.00		
Freight of goods thrown overboard,			6000.00		
Adjustment of average, and certificate,			25.00		
		Total losses,	$23670.00	23670	00
CONTRIBUTORY INTERESTS.					
Ship Fairweather, valued at		$45000. pays		10651	50
Goods of Fosdick & Co.,	$12500.	"	2958.75		
" " G. Porchs,	17250.	"	4083.07		
" " Gustav Piaggio,	4000.	"	946.80		
" " J. Burnside & Co.,	5250.	"	1342.68		
Total cargo valued at, as per invoices,		$39000. "		9231	30
Freight, $24000, less 1/3, =		$16000. "		3787	20
		$100000. "		23670	00
Rate of contribution, 23.67 per cent.					
PARTICULAR AVERAGE ON THE SHIP.					
Repairs, new masts, yards, &c., as per bills,			4275.00		
Less 1/3 for new,			1425.00		
Ship's value, $45000, at 6 1/3 per cent. =			$2850.00		

The different parties, if fully insured, can recover from the insurance companies the amount contributed to the general loss.

133. The rules for adjusting averages—with all the incidents of general average, salvage, and the like—are different in different countries. In most commercial ports the calculations are made by Adjusters of Averages,—a class of men who have a knowledge of the customs of the place and an extended experience, both of which are necessary in order to have a full understanding of the subject. The proportions of general average are calculated as follows :—

134. To apportion general average.

RULE I.—*Divide the sum of the losses by the sum of the contributory interests, and multiply each contributory interest by the quotient thus found; the product will be the contribution of each interest to the general loss.*

Or, RULE II.—BY PROPORTION.

$$\left\{\begin{matrix}\text{Sum of the}\\ \text{contributory interest}\end{matrix}\right\} : \left\{\begin{matrix}\text{sum of the}\\ \text{losses}\end{matrix}\right\} :: \left\{\begin{matrix}\text{each contributory}\\ \text{interest}\end{matrix}\right\} : \left\{\begin{matrix}\text{sum to be}\\ \text{contributed.}\end{matrix}\right\}$$

MISCELLANEOUS EXAMPLES.

1. What sum must be insured, at a premium of $1^1\%$, to cover the total loss, insurance included, of a cargo valued at $2731,25, charges $10.25, policy $1?

2. What will it cost to insure goods worth $3500, at a premium of $\frac{3}{4}\%$, if the policy includes 10% advance on the value of the goods?

3 I paid $32 for an insurance on goods worth $4800, shipped from Boston to Philadelphia. What rate did I pay?
Ans.

4. A merchant shipped a cargo valued at $15,000 from New York to Cuba, which he insured at $2^1\%$. The additional charges were $425. For how much must he sell the cargo to gain 20% on the entire cost?

5. Insured a cargo worth fr. 97,500, shipped from Havre to New York per the Marie Pierre. What was the cost of insurance at $1^3\%$, if the franc was valued at 25 cents and the cost of policy was $1? Ans. $427.56.

6. Insured in the Girard F. & M. Insurance Company goods valued at $17,000, and paid $127.50. What was the rate?

TAXES.

135. **Taxes** are sums of money assessed on persons, property, incomes, or products, usually for some public purpose.

136. When assessed on persons without regard to property, they are called *Capitation or Poll Taxes;* and in some places the payment of a poll tax is required before the privilege of voting is granted.

137. **Property Tax** is assessed on real and personal estate, and is sometimes apportioned at a certain per cent., but usually as so many cents on $100, or so many mills on $1.

Real Estate includes immovable property, such as houses, lands, &c. All other property, such as money, notes, stocks, mortgages, furniture, tools, cattle, &c., is called *Personal Property.*

138. Taxes are also assessed by the United States Government on incomes, manufactures, sales, &c.

139. The persons who estimate the value of the property to be taxed, and apportion the taxes, are called the *Assessors.*

140. Before assessing taxes, it is necessary to ascertain the sum to be raised, including expenses for collection and the proportion which it is expected will be uncollectable.

141. To find what sum must be assessed to raise a given net amount.

RULE.—*Subtract the rate allowed for collection from $1, and divide the net amount to be raised by the remainder: the quotient will be the entire sum to be assessed.*

EXAMPLES.

1. What sum must be assessed to raise $950,000 net, allowing 5% for collection?

$1.00 — .05 = .95. $950000 ÷ .95 = $1000000, Ans.

PROOF.—5% of $1000000 = $50000. $1000000 — $50000 = $950000.

142. It is also necessary to find the number of persons liable to pay a poll tax, if any; to estimate the value of all property, both real and personal, to be taxed, and to make an inventory of it; to determine what portion of the tax is to be raised upon the polls, or articles of property upon which there is a specific tax (if any), and to divide it equally among them.

The amount to be raised by a specific tax must be deducted from the total amount of tax to be raised. Then,

143. To find how much must be paid on each dollar of taxable property to raise the remainder of the tax, we have the following

RULE.—*Divide the amount to be raised, by the amount of taxable property, less that part on which nothing can be collected: the quotient will be the answer.*

EXAMPLES.

1. The tax assessed by a certain town is $37,500; its property is valued at $2,500,000. What rate per cent. is the tax? and how much will be paid by a man whose property is assessed at $12,000?

37500 ÷ 2500000 = .015, or, 1½ cts. tax per dollar.
12000 × 1½% = $180, Ans.

PROOF.—When a tax list is made out, the amount of the taxes of all the individuals in it should equal the whole tax assessed.

TAX TABLE AT THREE MILLS PER DOLLAR.

$		$	$		$	$		$	$		$
1	pays	.003	10	pay	.03	100	pay	.30	1000	pay	3.00
2	pay	.006	20	"	.06	200	"	.60	2000	"	6.00
3	"	.009	30	"	.09	300	"	.90	3000	"	9.00
4	"	.012	40	"	.12	400	"	1.20	4000	"	12.00
5	"	.015	50	"	.15	500	"	1.50	5000	"	15.00
6	"	.018	60	"	.18	600	"	1.80	6000	"	18.00
7	"	.021	70	"	.21	700	"	2.10	7000	"	21.00
8	"	.024	80	"	.24	800	"	2.40	8000	"	24.00
9	"	.027	90	"	.27	900	"	2.70	9000	"	27 00
10	"	.030	100	"	.30	1000	"	3.00	10000	"	30.00

2. A tax of $5130 is to be raised by a certain town; the property to be taxed is assessed at $430,000. There are 240 polls, each taxed $1. What amount must be levied, allowing 5% commission for collecting? what will be the tax on $1? and what will be the tax of each of the following persons?

A., who pays a tax on $6000, and 1 poll.
B., " " " " " 5400, " 2 "
C., " " " " " 1550, " 4 "

OPERATION.

Tax to be levied on the town, $5130. Rate of collection, 5%. 100 — 5 = 95. 5130 ÷ .95 = 5400, the amount to be assessed.

5% of 5400 = 270, amount paid for collection.

240 polls at $1 = $240.

Total amount to be raised,	$5400
Less amount of poll tax,	240
Amount to be raised on property,	5160

5160 ÷ 430,000 = .012, or 12 mills on a dollar.

A.'s tax, $6000 @ .012 =	$72
1 poll,	1
Total,	$73

B.'s tax, $5400 @ .012 =	$60.80
2 polls,	2.00
Total,	$62.80

C.'s tax, $1550 @ .012 =	$18.60
4 polls,	4.00
Total,	$22.60

3. How much tax will a person pay whose property is assessed at $6400, if he pays $1\frac{3}{4}$% city tax, and $\frac{1}{2}$ of 1% State tax, besides paying 5% United States tax on an income of $1800?

4. What rate of tax is required to raise $27,500 on property assessed at $1,850,000?

5. What amount of taxes will a person pay whose income is $12,800 per year, from which a deduction of $1900 is allowed for expenses, 5% being charged on all incomes less than $10,000, and 10% on all over that sum; his city and State tax is 15 mills per dollar on property assessed at $75,000, besides paying a tax of $2 on his gold watch, a tax of $6 on his carriage, and a license tax of $10?

INTEREST.

144. Interest is compensation for the use of money or value. The sum for the use of which interest is paid is called the Principal; the sum of the Principal and Interest is called the Amount.

145. Legal Interest is the rate established by law. Usury is interest greater than the legal rate, and is prohibited by law. In some States, however, parties are allowed to give and receive higher than legal rates by special contract. All interest in ancient times was called usury.

146. When no rate is mentioned, the legal rate is always understood. Debts of all kinds draw interest from the time they become due, but not before, unless specified. Interest on interest remaining unpaid is considered illegal.

147. The legal rate in most of the States, and on debts due the United States, is 6% per annum. In New York, Michigan, South Carolina, Wisconsin, Georgia, and Minnesota, it is 7%; in Alabama and Texas, 8%; Louisiana, 5%; California and Kansas, 10%; and in Oregon, 12½%.

148. The legal rate in England and France is 5%; in Canada, Nova Scotia, and Ireland, 6%.

149. In Pennsylvania, commission merchants and agents of parties not residing in the State are authorized to enter into an agreement to pay a rate not exceeding 7% on balances of money remaining in their hands, and to receive a rate not exceeding that amount, for advances of money made by them on consignments from persons living and transacting business beyond the limits of the State.

150. In Arkansas, Illinois, Iowa, Michigan, Mississippi, Missouri, and Tennessee, interest as high as 10% can be taken by special contract; in Louisiana and Florida, as high as 8%; in Minnesota, Texas, and Wisconsin, as high as 12%; in California and in Massachusetts (since July 10, 1867), any per cent.

151. Most merchants settle their accounts semi-annually, or oftener, and the interest is calculated for days. The interest on Notes and Bonds which have some time to run, is generally calculated for months and days.

COMPUTING TIME.

152. To find the time between two dates, omit the day of the date and include the day of maturity.

For instance, if Tuesday is the tenth day of the month, to the next Tuesday, the seventeenth, is seven days; but if both Tuesdays are included, we have eight days, if both are omitted, only six days.

153. When months are mentioned, they are construed to mean calendar months, by which is meant the time from one day in one month to the same day in another month.

Notes or securities falling due on the 30th or 31st of any month which has only 28, 29, or 30 days in it, are considered to be nominally due on the last day of the month, and therefore legally due on the 3d of the following month. For instance, a note dated November 30th, payable 3 months after date, falls due on the last day of February, and three days of grace make it payable on March 3d. Less than a month is reckoned at the rate of 30 days to the month.

154. When it is required to find the difference between two dates in years, months, and days, it may be done as in Subtraction of Co npound Numbers.

EXAMPLE.

What is the difference in time between July 15th, 1865, and September 19th, 1862?

The earlier date is placed under the later, and the numbers of the months are written instead of their names.

Yr.	mo.	da.
1865	7	15
1862	9	19
2	9	26

155. As the number of days in the different months varies, counting time by days is the only exact method, when the dates are less than a year apart.

From Jan. 1, 1867,	to July 1, 1867,	is 6 mos.,	containing	181 days.
" Sept. 1, "	" Mar. 1, 1868,	" 6 "	"	182 "
" Apr. 1, "	" Oct. 1, 1867,	" 6 "	"	183 "
" Mar. 1, "	" Sept. 1, "	" 6 "	"	184 "

156. The number of days between two given dates may be found as in the following example:—

What is the number of days between January 5th and July 3d?

Add the number of days in January after the 5th to the days in the intervening months, and the three days in July.

In Jan.	26	days.
" Feb.	28	"
" Mar.	31	"
" Apr.	30	"
" May	31	"
" June	30	"
" July	3	"
Total,	179	

157. Or, call each month 30 days, and correct by adding one for every month intervening which contains 31 days, and subtract two for February, except in leap-years; then but 1. In the example already given, from Jan. 5th to July 3d, there are five whole months, two of which contain 31 days, and one, February, contains but 28. They consequently average 30 days each, making 150, which, with 26 days in January and 3 days in July, make a total of 179.

Time Tables will be found useful for ascertaining the time between different dates. (See TIME TABLE, page 114.)

158. It is sometimes desirable to know for what time to draw a note so that it will not fall due on a Sunday or a holiday. After finding the number of days, divide by 7 to obtain the number of weeks and days, then count the odd days from the day of the week on which the note is dated. In the example given, 179 days = 25 weeks and 4 days. If January 5th was on Monday, then July 3d will be four days from Monday, or on Thursday.

159. The following may be useful to those who have frequent occasion to draw notes:—

33 days = 4 weeks and 5 days, 63 days = 9 weeks, 93 days = 13 weeks and 2 days: therefore,

A note at *thirty* days will fall due *five* days later than the day of the week on which it was given.

A note at *sixty* days will fall due on the *same day* of the week.

A note at *ninety* days will fall due *two* days later.

160. It is customary among business men, in reckoning interest, to consider the year as consisting of 12 months of 30 days each, or 360 days. As there are 365 days in a year, this gives $\frac{5}{365}$, or $\frac{1}{73}$, too much. The difference is so small, however, that in ordinary transactions it is not noticed. The mercantile custom has in many cases been sanctioned by law. In New York, the law on this subject (Rev. Stat. vol. ii. p. 182) reads as follows:—

"For the purpose of calculating interest, a month shall be considered the twelfth part of a year, and as consisting of thirty days; and interest for any number of days less than a month shall be estimated by the proportion which such number of days shall bear to thirty."

INTEREST AT 6 PER CENT.

161. The interest on $1 for one year or

12 months	=	6 cents.
2 "	=	1 cent.
1 month or 30 days	=	½ cent, or 5 mills.
6 "	=	1 mill.

Therefore, *one-half* the number of months equals the interest on 1 dollar, in *cents;* and *one-sixth* the number of days equals the interest on 1 dollar, in *mills.*

162. To compute interest at 6 per cent.

If the time is in months or years.

RULE.—*Multiply the principal by one-half the number of months, and point off two decimals. If there are cents in the principal, point off four decimals; the remaining figures will be the interest, in dollars.*

If the time is in days.

RULE I.—*Multiply the principal by one-sixth the number of days, and in the product point off three decimals. If there are cents in the principal, point off five; the remaining figures will be the interest, in dollars.*

Or, to avoid multiplying by fractions:—

RULE II.—*Multiply the principal by the number of days, and divide the product by 6; then point off as in the preceding rule.* (See CANCELLATION, Art. 19.)

163. When the time is less than 1 month, the cents in the principal may be disregarded; when less than 2 months, all under 50c.; when less than 3 months, all under 33c.

EXAMPLES.

1. What is the interest on $1875 for 7 months?
   $1875 \times 3\frac{1}{2} = 6562\frac{1}{2}$ Ans. $65.62½.
2. What is the interest on $4250 for 24 days?
   $4250 \times 4 = 17000$ Ans. $17.
3. What is the interest on $5650.37 for 27 days?
4. " " $7250.45 " 3 mos. 29 days?
5. " " $364.50 " 1 yr. 4 mos. 12 da.?
6. " " $1575.25 " 9 mos. 17 days?

The notes, accounts-current, interest accounts, in another part of the book, will afford additional examples for practice.

164. To compute interest at any given rate.

RULE I.—*Find the interest at six per cent., and divide it by 6; the quotient will be the interest at one per cent.; then multiply this interest by the given rate.* Or,

RULE II.—*Find the interest at six per cent., and add to it or subtract from it in the same ratio as the given rate is greater or less than 6.*

For 7% add $\frac{1}{6}$.
" 8% " $\frac{1}{3}$.
" 9% " $\frac{1}{2}$, or divide by 4 instead of 6.
" 10% take $\frac{10}{6}$ by annexing one cipher and dividing by 6.
" 12% multiply by 2, or divide by 3 instead of 6.

For 3% take $\frac{1}{2}$, or divide by 12 instead of 6.
" 4% subtr. $\frac{1}{3}$, or divide by 9 instead of 6.
" $4\frac{1}{2}$% " $\frac{1}{4}$.
" 5% " $\frac{1}{6}$.

NOTE.—As the interest for 60 days at 6 per cent. equals 1 cent for every dollar, interest at that rate can be found by adding or subtracting as the time is more or less than 60 days.

EXAMPLES.

1. Find the interest on $1285. for 33 days at 7%.
2. " " $4825.60 " 90 " " 9%.
3. " " $2726.35 " 3 mos. 18 da. " 10%

ACCURATE INTEREST.

165. To compute accurate interest.

RULE.—*Find the interest as in the preceding rules, and subtract from it $\frac{1}{73}$ part of itself; in leap-year subtract $\frac{1}{61}$.*

NOTE.—$\frac{1}{73}$ *equals a little less than $1\frac{1}{2}$ cents for each dollar of interest.*

Or, Multiply the interest on the given sum for 1 year by the number of days for which interest is required, and divide by 365. The quotient will be the required interest. This rule is equivalent to the following formula:—

As 365 : {The number of days for which int. is required} :: {The int. on the given sum for 1 year} : {The required int.}

INTEREST ON GOVERNMENT BONDS.

166. By the ordinary method of computing interest at 6%, the interest on $6000 is $1 per day, and the principal will double itself in 200 months. The difference to the United States Government between paying interest at the rate of 360 days to the year, and paying accurate interest, or at the rate of 365 days to the year, is $5 per year for every $6000

The *Five-Twenty* Loan is over $950,000,000, and the interest on it more than $155,000 per day. The difference, on this loan, between usual interest and accurate interest, is nearly $2250 per day. The formula under the preceding rule is employed in the Treasury Department at Washington.

EXAMPLES.

1. What is the interest on U. S. Bonds of $15000 from May 1st to July 17th, at 6%?

From May 1st to July 17th = 77 days.
Int. on $15000 for 1 year = $900; 900 × 77 = 69300.
69300 ÷ 365 = $189.86 Ans.

2. What is the interest on a Five-Twenty U. S. Bond of $1000 from Nov. 1st to Feb. 3d? Ans. $15.45.

3. What is the interest on a Ten-Forty U.S. Bond of $1000, bearing 5% interest, from March 1st to Aug. 10th? Ans. $22.19.

INTEREST IN ENGLAND.

167. The legal rate of interest in England is 5 per cent., and parts of a year are counted in days at the rate of 365 days to the year. To compute English interest:—

RULE.—*Reduce the shillings and pence, if any, to the decimal or fraction of a pound (see Art. 72); then—*

FOR YEARS—*Multiply the principal by the number of years, and the product will be the interest, in shillings.*

FOR MONTHS—*Multiply the principal by the number of months, and the product will be the interest, in pence.*

FOR DAYS—*Multiply the principal by the number of days, divide the product by 73, and point off two decimals: the quotient will be the interest, in the denomination of the principal.*

EXAMPLE.—What is the interest on £425 for 1 year, 3 months, and 10 days, at 5%?

425s., interest for 1 year.
106.25 " " 3 months.
11.64 " " 10 days.
542.89s. = £27 2s. 11d. Ans.

PROBLEMS IN INTEREST.

168. To find the *principal*, when the time, rate per cent., and interest are given.

RULE.—*Divide the given interest by the interest on* ONE DOLLAR *for the given rate and time.*

EXAMPLES.

1. What sum invested at 6% for one year will produce $360?

Interest on $1, for 1 year, at 6% = .06.
.06)360.00 = 6000   Ans. $6000.

2. What principal in 2 years at 7% will give $3556?
3. " " 3 " 6 mos. at 6% will give $470?
4. " " 6 " 8 " " 8% " $540?
5. " " 3 " 4 " " 6% " $540?
6. What must I pay for real estate, producing $750 per year, that I may receive 6% on my investment?
7. What must I pay for stocks, paying a dividend of $345 yearly, that I may gain 9%?
8. What reduction must I obtain that I may purchase stocks of the par value of $8000, paying 6% dividend yearly, to receive 8% on what I invest?

169. To find the *rate* per cent., when the principal, time, and interest are given.

RULE.—*Divide the given interest by the interest on the principal at* ONE *per cent.*

EXAMPLES.

1. A house which cost $4800 rents, above expenses, for $264 per year. What per cent. does it pay on the investment?

Interest on 4800 at 1% = 48.
264 ÷ 48 = 5½   Ans. 5½%.

2. If I invest $3500 for 1 year, 2 months, and receive $490, what rate do I receive per year?   Ans. 12%.

170. To find the *time*, when the principal, rate, and interest are given.

RULE.—*Divide the given interest by the interest on the principal for* ONE DAY; *the quotient will be the required time, in days.*

EXAMPLES.

1. In what time will \$5530.42 produce \$30.42 interest at 6%?

Interest on \$5530.42 for 1 day = .921+

```
.921)30.42(33+.
     2763
     ----
      2790
      2763
      ----
```

Ans. 33 days.

2. How long will it take a sum of money to double itself at 6% simple interest? At 7%? At 8%?

3. Invested \$6000 at 6%, for which I received \$750.42. How long was it invested?

171. To find the principal, when the time, rate per cent., and amount are given.

RULE.—*Divide the given amount by the amount of* ONE DOLLAR *for the given rate and time.*

EXAMPLES.

1. What principal will amount to \$1120 in 2 years, at 6%?

Amount of \$1 for 2 years at 6% = \$1.12.

1120 ÷ 1.12 = 1000 Ans. \$1000.

2. What principal will amount to \$1500 in 1 year, 3 mos., at 5%? At 7%?

TRUE DISCOUNT.

172. Discount, as usually calculated, is the same as Simple Interest; but *true discount* is a deduction from an amount which is equal to the interest on the remainder at the same rate and for the same time for which the deduction was made.

173. The **Present Worth** is the sum paid, or the value of the note, or debt, after the discount has been deducted.

174. To find the Present Worth.

RULE.—*Divide the given sum by the amount of* ONE DOLLAR *for the given rate and time.*

To find the discount, subtract the present worth from the given sum.

EXAMPLES.

1. What is the present worth of $1360, due 6 years hence, @ 6%?

Int. on $1 for 6 yrs. = .36
1.00

Amount, 1.36)1360.00(1000

Ans. $1000.

2. What is the present worth of $1248, due 8 months hence, @ 6%? What is the true discount?

3. What is the present worth of $162.50, due 6 months hence, @ 7%, and what the discount?

BANKING.

175. Bank Discount is computed in the same manner as simple interest. It is deducted from the amount or face of the note when the note is discounted, and the remainder, called the proceeds, is placed to the credit of the person for whom the note is discounted. As the person offering the note can obtain the money immediately, and the note may remain unpaid until three o'clock on the day of its maturity, banks, generally, in reckoning time, include the day on which the note is discounted, as well as the day on which it matures. This, with the *three days of grace*, for which discount is also taken, makes *four* more days than the time mentioned in the note.

See, also, TRANSACTIONS WITH BANKS.

176. To compute Bank Discount.

RULE.—*Multiply the amount by* ⅙ *the number of days, including the day of discount and the three days of grace, and in the product point off three decimals.*

The above will give the interest at 6%. For any other rate, add or subtract in proportion as the given rate is greater or less than 6%, as in Art. 164.

EXAMPLES.

1. Robert F. Hay, on May 2d, offered the following note, properly indorsed, for discount:—

$525. PHILADELPHIA, March 29, 1867.

Sixty days after date, we promise to pay to Robert F. Hay, or order, at the Union National Bank, Five Hundred and Twenty-Five Dollars, without defalcation. Value received. R. J. BIRNEY & Co.

How much will he receive as the net proceeds of the note?

60 days from March 29th is May 28th, which, with the three days of grace added, gives May 31st. From May 2d to May 31st, including the day of discount, is 30 days.

Interest on $525 for 30 days = 2.63 discount.
525 — 2.63 = 522.37 net proceeds.

Face of the note, $525.00

2. On Nov. 4th, offered for discount a note for $350, dated Oct. 15th, payable 3 months after date. How much cash will I receive?

Find the time, discount, and proceeds of the following notes:—

3. Discounted Nov. 4th, at 6%.

$750. PITTSBURGH, Oct. 15, 1866.

Three months after date, I promise to pay to the order of Jas. Dunlap & Co. Seven Hundred and Fifty Dollars, at the Citizens' National Bank, without defalcation. Value received. JOHN F. CHASE.

4. Discounted Jan. 12th, at 7%.

$1250.$\frac{75}{100}$. NEW YORK, Dec. 10, 1865.

Sixty days after date, I promise to pay to S. H. Crittenden & Co., or order, Twelve Hundred and Fifty $\frac{75}{100}$ Dollars, for value received. HENRY T. STEWART.

5. Discounted July 6th, at 6%.

$450.$\frac{50}{100}$. TRENTON, N.J., May 10, 1866.

Four months after date, I promise to pay at the First National Bank, to the order of Samuel T. Brown, Four

Hundred and Fifty $\frac{50}{100}$ Dollars, without defalcation or discount. Value received.

HAYWARD, GLEASON & Co.

---

6. Discounted Sept. 18th, at 6%.

$1875. CHICAGO, Aug. 15, 1866.

Ninety days after date, we promise to pay to the order of Charles Manning & Co. Eighteen Hundred and Seventy-Five Dollars, for value received.

H. EVANS & Co.

---

177. To find how large a draft, at a given premium, may be purchased for a certain amount.

RULE.—*Divide the given amount by $1, increased by the rate of premium.*

NOTE.—To find how large a draft may be purchased, when sold at a discount, divide the given amount by $1, less the rate of premium.

EXAMPLES.

1. How large a draft may be purchased for $2020, at a premium of 1%?

1.01)2020(2000. Ans. $2000.

2. What is the face of a draft on New York to cost $18500, at 1½% premium?

3. For what amount may a draft on Cuba be purchased with $6430.77, at a premium of 4½%?

4. A commission merchant wishes to invest the proceeds of a sale, amounting to $4840, in a draft on St. Louis, which can be purchased at a discount of ¾%. How large a draft can he obtain?

178. To find the amount of a note that shall produce a given sum when discounted at bank.

RULE.—*Divide the given sum by the proceeds of $1 for the given rate and time.*

EXAMPLES.

1. For what sum must a note be drawn so that the discount for 63 days at 6% may be deducted and the proceeds will be $1295?

Interest on $1 for 63 days = .0105.

$$\begin{array}{r} \$1.0000 \\ .0105 \\ \hline .9895)1295(1308.74 \text{ Ans.} \end{array}$$

2. Required the amount of a note that may be discounted for 33 days, at 6%, and $5500 received as the proceeds.

3. How large must a note be made to obtain $425.50 from a bank, for 42 days; discount @ 6%?

179. Banks, by deducting the interest in advance, obtain a larger rate per cent. than they would by taking true discount; and this rate increases in proportion to the time for which the discount is taken. The advantages of short credits, however, are generally considered to be more than an equivalent for any such excess that might be gained by extending the time.

The following table shows the rates of interest obtained by banks, including the advantage from compounding the interest, when they discount notes at 6 and at 7 per cent., for any number of months from one to twelve. It will be seen that when the time is less than two months—the usual limit for which notes are discounted in cities—the excess is inconsiderable.

RATE.	1 mo.	2 mos.	3 mos.	4 mos.	5 mos.	6 mos.	7 mos.	8 mos.	9 mos.	10 mos.	11 mos.	12 mos.
6 per cent.	6.200	6.216	6.232	6.248	6.264	6.281	6.298	6.315	6.332	6.349	6.366	6.383
7 " "	7.272	7.295	7.317	7.339	7.362	7.385	7.408	7.432	7.456	7.480	7.503	7.527

At the nominal rate of 6 per cent., a bank receives, when it discounts a note for 1 month, $\frac{5}{995}$, or $.5\frac{25}{995}$ of 1 per cent. ($\frac{25}{9950}$ of 1 per cent. more than 6 per cent. per annum $= \frac{1}{4}$ of ONE CENT on $99.50); when for 2 months, $\frac{1}{99}$, or $1\frac{1}{99}$ per cent.; when for 1 year, $\frac{6}{94}$, or $6\frac{18}{47}$ per cent.

INTEREST ACCOUNTS.

180. In the settlement of mercantile accounts, interest is calculated or not, according to custom or the agreement of the parties. Amounts are considered due at the time they should be paid in cash, or when they are equivalent to cash.

181. Bankers, Saving Funds, &c., charge and allow interest on dealers' accounts according to regulations which vary in different places. After the time is adjusted, interest is generally calculated by one of the following methods:—

FIRST METHOD.

By Interest on each amount to the time of settlement.

SECOND METHOD.

By Product of Days.

THIRD METHOD.

By Daily Balances.

182. By the FIRST METHOD, interest is reckoned on each amount from the day it is due to the day of settlement, and the balance between the debit and credit interest is added to that side of the account on which the amount of interest is the largest.

When an amount is not due until after the day of settlement, a discount is allowed, and entered on the opposite side of the account in the interest column.

The labor of making out such accounts is much lessened by the use of Interest Tables, such as Price's and others.

183. By the SECOND METHOD, each amount is multiplied by the number of days from the time it is due to the day of settlement. The interest on the sum of the products for *one day* equals the sum of the interest on each amount taken separately. The interest on the balance of products for one day equals the balance of interest.

When an amount is not due until after the day of settlement, it is multiplied by the number of days from the day of settlement to the day when it becomes due, and the product is placed in the column of products on the opposite side, in the same manner as discount is treated in the first method.

184. By the THIRD METHOD, the balance existing at any time is multiplied by the number of days it remains unchanged. The interest on the product for *one day* equals the interest on the balance for the number of days it continues; and the interest on the difference between the total daily balances for one day equals the balance of interest between the debit and credit sides of the account, calculated on each amount separately, as by the first method.

When the rate of interest on one side of the account is different from the rate on the other, the interest is calculated on the total daily products of each side separately for one day, and the balance of interest is taken. If the rate of interest on both sides of the account is the same, the difference between the footings of the debit and credit sides of the total daily balances may be taken first, and the interest reckoned on that for one day.

This method is used by many bankers. Besides saving much labor, the total daily balances may be entered without delaying for any particular day, and can therefore be kept in readiness, and the account completed with very little additional trouble, whenever the day of settlement is determined.

For practice, all the accounts given may be made out in each of the different methods, and may also be averaged by Compound Average with the same results as above.

FIRST METHOD.—BY INTEREST ON EACH AMOUNT TO THE TIME OF SETTLEMENT.

JOHN C. BENNETT & Co. *in Account Current and Interest Account with* GEORGE D. PATTEN & Co. *to January 1, 1867.*

Date.	When due.		Amt.	Days.	Int.	Date.	When due.		Amt.	Days.	Int.
1866. July 31	1866. Oct. 31	To Mdse. at 3 mos., as per bill rendered, . . .	1200 00	62	12 40	1866. July 31	1866. Sept. 29	By Invoice of Coffee, at 60 days, shipped per Str. "Wm. P. Clyde," . .	1575 00	94	24 68
Aug. 5	Nov. 5	" Mdse. at 3 mos., as per bill rendered, . . .	1542 00	57	14 65	Oct. 15	Nov. 12	" Net Proceeds of sales of Sugar and Rice, as per Acc't Sales rendered, ...	1256 00	50	10 47
Sept. 10	Sept. 10	" Mdse. (Net), as per bill rendered, ...	750 00	113	14 13	" 23	" 25	" Draft on P. R. Brown & Co. at 30 days, . .	1000 00	37	6 17
Oct. 15	1867. Feb. 15	" Net Proceeds of sales of Flour, as per your Account Sales.	1830 00			Nov. 30	1867. Mar. 3	" Note of H. Y. King & Co. at 3 months, your favor, ...	500 00		
Nov. 20	1866. Nov. 20	" Cash paid your Draft on us at sight, favor J. Grant & Co., ...	640 00	42	4 48	1867. Jan. 1		" Discount on $1830, per contra, ...		45	13 73
1867. Jan. 1		" Discount on $500, per contra, ...		61	5 08						
		Credit Bal. of Interest,			*4 31*				4331 00		55 05
			5962 00		55 05			Add Bal. of Interest, .	4 31		
						July 1		*Bal. carried down,* . .	*1626 69*		
			5962 00		55 05				5962 00		55 05
1867. Jan. 1		To Balance due, ...	1626 69					E. E.			
		NEW YORK, Jan. 1, 1867.						GEO. D. PATTEN & Co.			

SECOND METHOD.—BY PRODUCT OF DAYS.

MESSRS. L. & B. CURTIS *in Account Current and Interest Account with* MESSRS. FIELD & COGLEY *to July 1, 1867.*

Date.	When due.		Amt.	Days.		Date.	When due.		Amt.	Days.	
1867.	1867.					1867.	1867.				
Jan. 1	Jan. 1	To Bal. due from old acc't	375 00	181	67875	Feb. 5	Feb. 5	By Cash, ...	300 00	146	43800
Feb. 10	May 10	" Mdse. @ 3 mos., as per bill rendered, . . .	450 00	52	23400	May 10	May 23	" Draft on Drexel & Co. at 10 days' sight, . .	500 00	39	19500
Mar. 25	" 24	" Mdse. @ 60 days, as per bill rendered, . . .	268 00	38	10184	June 2	July 5	" Note at 30 days, . . .	250 00		
May 24	Aug. 24	" Mdse. @ 3 mos., as per bill rendered, . . .	150 00			July 1		" Discount on $150, per contra, ...		54	8100
July 1		" Discount on $250, per contra, ...		4	1000						
			1243 00		102459				1050 00		71400
		Add Bal. of Interest,	5 18					*Balance of Products,*			*31059*
								31059÷6=5.176 Bal. of Int.			
								Balance of Account,	*198 18*		
			1248 18		102459				1248 18		102459
1867.											
July 1		To Balance due, ...	198 18								
								E. E.			
								FIELD & COGLEY.			
		PHILADA., July 1, 1867.									

THIRD METHOD.—BY DAILY BALANCES.

THE WESTERN SAVING FUND

In account with HENRY J. RODGERS.

Interest to Feb. 28th, 1867.

1867.			$	cts.	1867.			$	cts.
Jan.	2	To Cash,	100	00	Jan.	7	By Check,	50	00
"	12	" "	250	00	"	22	" "	100	00
Feb.	11	" "	30	00	Feb.	1	" "	40	00
"	21	" "	200	00	"	21	" "	50	00
"	28	" Int. to Feb. 28, '67,	1	62	"	28	" Cash on settlement of acct.	341	62
			581	62				581	62

Balances.					Time.		
100,	from Jan. 2	to Jan. 7,	5	days	=	500	for 1 day.
50,	" " 7	" " 12,	5	"	=	250	" "
300,	" " 12	" " 22,	10	"	=	3000	" "
200,	" " 22	" Feb. 1,	10	"	=	2000	" "
160,	" Feb. 1	" " 11,	10	"	=	1600	" "
190,	" " 11	" " 21,	10	"	=	1900	" "
340,	" " 21	" " 28,	7	"	=	2380	" "
						11630	

Total daily balance = $11630 for 1 day.

Which, at 5% interest = $1.62.

3. What is the balance due on March 1st of the following account:—

THE NATIONAL SAVING INSTITUTION

In account with PORTER A. FLORENCE.

			Dr. Amts.		Cr. Amts.		Days.	Daily Balance.			
1867.											
Jan.	2	To Cash	300	00							
"	17	By "			100	00					
"	27	To "	250	00							
"	"	By "			150	00					
Feb.	6	" "			350	00					
"	7	To "	250	00							

George M. Grant *In acct. with* Brownson & Co., *to July 1st, 1867.*

Days.		Dr.	Cr.	Daily Balance.		Days.	Total Daily Balance.	
1867.								
Jan.	7		1000 00		1000 00	10		10000 00
"	17		250 00		1250 00	7		8750 00
"	24	1500 00		250 00		7	1750 00	
"	31		500 00		250 00	6		1500 00
Feb.	6	1000 00		750 00		10	7500 00	
"	16		850 00		100 00	24		2400 00
Mar.	12	1250 00		1150 00		30	34500 00	
Apr.	11		1000 00	150 00		65	19750 00	
June	15		3000 00		2850 00	16		45600 00
		3750 00	6600 00				53500 00	68250 00
								53500 00
Bal. Int. to July 1st,			2 46					6)14750 00
							Credit Bal. of Int.	2.458 33
		3750 00	6602 46					
Bal. of a/c,		*2852 46*						
		6602 46	6602 46					
Bal. of a/c,			$2852 46					

Cincinnati, July 1st, 1866.

Brownson & Co.

PARTIAL PAYMENTS.

185. Partial Payments are payments made at different times of part of a Note, Bond, or other obligation, and should be indorsed upon the back of it.

186. When a partial payment is made *before the debt is due*, it cannot be apportioned part to the debt and part to the interest; but interest is allowed on the payment as well as on the principal to the time the debt becomes due.

187. Interest is not allowed to form part of the principal, so as to carry interest.

188. The following rule for computing interest when partial payments have been made has been adopted by the Supreme Court of the United States, and by New York, Massachusetts, and most of the other States of the Union, and is called

THE UNITED STATES RULE.

I. The rule for casting interest when partial payments have been made, is to apply the payment, in the first place, to the discharge of the interest due.

II. If the payment exceeds the interest, the surplus goes towards discharging the principal, and the subsequent interest is to be computed on the balance of principal remaining due.

III. If the payment be less than the interest, the surplus of interest must not be taken to augment the principal; but interest continues on the former principal until the period when the payments, taken together, exceed the interest due, and then the surplus is to be applied towards discharging the principal, and interest is to be computed on the balance as aforesaid.

Decision of Chancellor Kent, Johnson's Chancery Rep., vol. i. p. 17.

Or,

189. *Apply whatever payments may be made to the discharge of the interest then due, and the surplus, if any, to the discharge of the principal.*

NOTE.—The principal remains unaltered when the payment is less than the interest at the time due.

190. It will be perceived that, by the above rule, if a person owing the debt makes a payment less than the interest, he loses the use of it until the time when the sum of the payments exceeds the interest.

For instance, the interest on $1000 is $5 per month. If $5 per month is paid, at the end of the year $1000 would still be due, while the interest on the payments, $1.65, would be lost.

191. The Connecticut rule differs from the United States rule only in this respect, that if a payment greater than the interest at the time due be made before the principal has been on interest one year, the person making it is allowed interest on it to the end of the year. If settlement be made within one year, interest is allowed on the payments from the time they are made to the time of settlement.

EXAMPLES.

1. A bond was given for $1500, dated July 1st, 1863, payable 1 year after date, with interest. The following indorsements appear on the bond:—

July 1st, 1864, Received Fifty Dollars.
Jan. 1st, 1866, " One Thousand Dollars.

How much was due at the time of settlement, July 1st, 1866?

Original sum named in the bond,		$1500.00
Interest from July 1st, 1863, to July 1st, 1864,	$90.	
First payment, a sum less than interest,	50.	
	40.	
Interest from July 1st, 1864, to Jan. 1st, 1866,	135.	
	175.	
Second payment, a sum greater than interest,	1000.	825.00
Balance for new principal,		675.00
Interest from Jan. 1st, 1866, to July 1st, 1866,		20.25
Amount of principal and interest due July 1st, 1866,		$695.25

2. $3500. NEW YORK, Aug. 17, 1862.

For value received, I promise to pay to Henry L. Barnes, or order, on demand, Three Thousand Five Hundred Dollars, with interest. ROBT. H. WILSON.

Indorsements. March 17th, 1863, One Hundred Dollars. July 17th, 1863, Fifty Dollars. Nov. 17th, 1863, Three Hundred Dollars Feb. 17th, 1864, Fifteen Hundred Dollars.

How much remains due August 17th, 1864?

192. As it is customary among merchants to settle their accounts yearly, or oftener, the following rule is much used by them, and is called•

THE MERCHANTS' RULE.

I. *First find the interest on the principal from the time it becomes due to the time of settlement, and add it to the principal.*

II. *Find the interest on each payment from the time it was made to the time of settlement, and add the sum of the interest thus found to the sum of the payments.*

III. *Deduct the sum of the payments and interest thereon from the amount of principal and interest, and the difference will be the balance due.*

NOTE.—This is substantially the same as the First Method for finding interest on Accounts Current. (See Art. 92.)

EXAMPLES.

1. $600. PHILADELPHIA, June 12, 1865.

For value received, on demand, I promise to pay to the order of Andrew W. Dawson, Six Hundred Dollars, with interest, without defalcation.

CHAS. C. RUNYON.

Indorsements.

August 12th, 1865, Received One Hundred Dollars.
November 12th, 1865, " Two Hundred and Fifty Dollars.
January 12th, 1866, " One Hundred and Twenty Dollars.

How much was due February 12th, 1866?

Principal,		$600.00
Int. from June 12th, 1865, to Feb. 12th, 1866, 8 mos.,		24.00
Amount of note to Feb. 12th, 1866, ...		624.00
First payment, Aug. 12th, 1865,	$100.00	
Interest 6 months,	3.00	
Second payment, Nov 12th, 1865,	250.00	
Interest 3 months,	3.75	
Third payment, Jan. 12th, 1866,	120.00	
Interest 1 month,	.60	
Amount of payments and interest,	477.35	477.35
Balance due February 12th, 1866,		$146.65

2. $350. CLEVELAND, May 9, 1865.

Six months after date, I promise to pay to the order of James Brown & Co., Three Hundred and Fifty Dollars, value received. EDWARD S. LONG.

Indorsements.

July 12th, 1866, Received Seventy-Five Dollars.
Oct. 27th, 1866, " Two Hundred Dollars.

How much was due Jan. 3d. 1867?

TABLE

Showing in how many YEARS *a given principal will double itself.*

RATE.	AT SIMPLE INTEREST.	AT COMPOUND INTEREST.		
		Compounded Yearly.	Compounded Half-Yearly.	Compounded Quarterly.
1	100.	69.666	69.487	69.400
1½	66.66	46.556	46.382	46.298
2	50.00	35.004	34.830	34.743
2½	40.00	28.071	27.899	27.812
3	33.33	23.450	23.278	23.191
3½	28.57	20.150	19.977	19.890
4	25.00	17.673	17.502	17.415
4½	22.22	15.748	15.576	15.490
5	20.00	14.207	14.036	13.946
5½	18.18	12.946	12.775	12.686
6	16.67	11.896	11.725	11.639
6½	15.38	11.007	10.836	10.750
7	14.29	10.245	10.075	9.989
7½	13.33	9.585	9.914	9.328
8	12.50	9.006	8.837	8.751
8½	11.76	8.497	8.346	8.241
9	11.11	8.043	7.874	7.788
9½	10.52	7.638	7.468	7.383
10	10.00	7.273	7. +	7. +

AVERAGE OF PAYMENTS.

193. The average of several numbers is that number each would be if their sum was divided equally. Thus, the average number of yards in four pieces of cloth, one containing 24 yards, one 36 yards, one 38 yards, and one 42 yards, is 35 yards. The total number of yards equals 140, which, divided by the number of pieces, equals 35,—the average number of yards in each piece.

194. Average or Equation of Payments is the method of finding the time when the payment of several sums, due at different times, may be made at once, without loss of interest to either party.

195. Accounts are settled both by the methods given in Interest Accounts and by averaging. When several bills of goods are sold on credit, and become due on different dates, instead of settling each bill separately as it becomes due, it is customary to average the time, and settle the amount of all the bills at the averaged time. This saves the labor of computing interest on the several bills.

196. When all the amounts are alike, the average time is found by adding the different terms of credit together and dividing their sum by the *number* of the amounts. This, however, is seldom the case, and other rules have been found necessary.

197. To find the average time when all the terms of credit begin at the same time.

RULE.—*Multiply each amount by its term of credit, and divide the sum of the several products by the sum of the debts; the quotient will be the average time of credit.*

EXAMPLES.

1. A merchant purchases goods, January 6th, amounting to \$900: \$300 payable in 6 months, \$300 in 8 months, \$300 in 10 months. When may the whole be paid without loss to either party?

\$300 for 6 months	= 1800 for 1 month,	
300 " 8 "	= 2400 " "	
300 " 10 "	= 3000 " "	
900	)7200 " "	Ans. 8 months.

\$900 at the different terms of credit equals \$7200 for 1 month, or as many months as \$900 is contained times in \$7200, which is 8 times. Therefore, if the merchant gives his note payable 8 months after January 6th, it will be equivalent to giving three notes payable according to the terms of credit first proposed.

NOTE.—If the result contains a fraction less than a day, reject it; if it is more, add one to the number of days. Also, when the cents are less than 50, disregard them; when more, call them \$1.

198. The accuracy of the above rule has been questioned. The author of this book has in his possession eighteen different Arithmetics, some of them excellent ones, in which the rule is stated to be erroneous. The following example is generally used to illustrate its inaccuracy:—

"If a man owes me \$200, \$100 payable now and \$100 payable in 2 years, what is the equated time? Ans. 1 year."

It is said that this is incorrect, because I lose the interest on \$100 for 1 year, which is \$6; but for the other hundred I gain only the true discount, \$5.66+, making a difference of nearly 34 cents.

Or, for the first payment I should receive \$100 and interest for 1 year, which is \$106; and for the \$100 paid 1 year before it is due, I should receive the present worth of \$100, which is \$94.33$\frac{51}{53}$, making a total of \$200.33$\frac{51}{53}$, or 34 cents more than I receive by the usual method.

The fallacy is in supposing that \$5.66 is all that I gain for the \$6 which I lose; for if I receive the discount 1 year before it is due, it is clear that I gain the interest on it for 1 year; and the interest on true discount is always equal to the difference between true discount and interest. Interest on \$5.66 for 1 year = 34 cents; \$5.66 + .34 = \$6.00.

Again, if I am not paid the \$100 due now until 2 years have elapsed, I ought to receive as interest \$12; if I receive \$200 at the end of the first year, I gain the interest on \$200 for 1 year, which is \$12, the same as before. Interest on \$200 for 1 year is the same as interest on \$100 for 2 years.

199. The following has been given as the true rule for the Equation of Payments:—

"*Find the present worth of each debt, then find the time at which the sum of the present worths will amount to the sum of the debts; this gives the true time.*"

EXAMPLE CALCULATED BY THE "TRUE RULE."

Interest at 4 per cent.

Amount.	Time.	Present Worth.
1080	2 years	1000
6960	4 "	6000
8040		7000
7000		
1040 disc't.	Interest on \$7000 for 1 year, \$280.	

280) 1040 (3 yrs. $8\frac{4}{7}$ mos.

For \$7000 to gain \$1040 will require 3 yrs. 8 mos. $17\frac{1}{7}$ days.

SAME EXAMPLE.

Interest at 40 per cent.

Amount.	Time.	Present Worth
1080.	2 years	600.
6960.	4 "	2676.92
8040.		3276.92
3276.92		
4763.08 disc't.	Interest on \$3276.92 for 1 year = 1310.77.	

1310.77) 4763.08 (3 yrs. 7 mos. 18 days.

Difference in results, *29 days.*

As the rate of interest ought not to affect the result, the accuracy of this "true" rule is questionable. Even if it were correct, the amount of labor required to find the average time by this method is sufficient to prevent it from coming into general use.

The present worth is not in exact proportion to the time and amount due. The true discount of $500 for 1 year is not the same as the discount of $100 for 5 years.

MISCELLANEOUS EXAMPLES.

1. If A lends B $300 for 4 months, how long ought B to lend A $600, to equal the favor? Ans. 2 months.

2. If I owe $400, payable in 6 months, and pay $100 immediately, how long may I keep the balance as an equivalent? Ans. 8 months.

3. A man bought goods at different times to the amount of $10,000, which are due per average July 1st. He wishes to give 4 notes in payment, due 1 month apart. When ought they to mature, to equal the average?
Ans. May 15th, June 15th, July 15th, Aug. 15th.

200. To find the average time when the credits begin at different times.

RULE I.—*Find the date when each debt becomes due.* (See Time Tables.)

Find the time intervening between the earliest of these dates and the date of each succeeding amount.

Multiply the amount first due by 0.

Multiply each succeeding amount by the time intervening between the earliest date and the time the amount becomes due.

Divide the sum of the products by the sum of the debts; the quotient will be the average time required.

Add this average time to the day of maturity of the amount first falling due, for the day of payment.

Taking the time from the date of maturity of the amount first due, and the terms of credit as extending to the dates when actually due, makes the process similar to that of the preceding rule.

NOTE.—When a purchase is made for cash, it is due on the day of the purchase.

When the term of credit is the same for each amount, labor may be saved by averaging the dates of the purchase and adding the term of credit to the average date so found. When all the debts have the same term of credit except one or two amounts which have no credit, add interest to those amounts for the general term of credit, and then average as before. For finding the time, see INTEREST; also TIME TABLE.

EXAMPLES.

1. Required the time when the amount of the debts as below stated becomes due per average.

Date of Purchase.	Amount.	Time Credit.	When due.	Time from.
Jan. 6,	$300	6 mos.	July 6.	July 6 to Aug. 7,
Apr. 10,	200	6 "	Oct. 10.	32 days.
May 7,	400	3 "	Aug. 7.	July 6 to Oct. 10,
				96 days.

Statement arranged.

Due.	Amount.		Time (in days).	Product.
July 6,	300		0	00000
Aug. 7,	400	×	32	12800
Oct. 10,	200	×	96	19200
	900			)32000($35\frac{5}{9}$

Ans. 36 days from July 6th is August 11th.

201. ABBREVIATED METHOD.

The cents and dollars may be disregarded, in averaging, without any important change in the result.

EXAMPLE.

Due.	Amount.	Time.		Amount, omitting dolls. and cents.		Product.
Jan. 5,	$372.50	0	×	$37	=	000
" 15,	264.25	10	×	26	=	260
" 25,	227.50	20	×	23	=	460
" 30,	329.10	25	×	33	=	825
				119		)1545($12\frac{117}{119}$.

USUAL METHOD.

$$
\begin{array}{rcl}
372.50 \times 0 & = & 000000 \\
264.25 \times 10 & = & 264250 \\
227.50 \times 20 & = & 455000 \\
329.10 \times 25 & = & 822750 \\
\hline
1193.35 & &)1542000(12\tfrac{109980}{119335}.
\end{array}
$$

Ans. *Jan. 18th*, by both methods, the difference being only about $\frac{8}{119}$ of a day.

202. BY INTEREST.—*Find the interest on each amount for the time obtained as before; then*

Find how long it will take for the whole debt to gain that amount of interest; the result will be the average time.

NOTE.—The equated time will be the same, whatever may be the rate of interest: we can, therefore, take that rate which is most convenient. Interest tables can also be profitably used.

EXAMPLE UNDER RULE I.

Due.	Amount.	Days.	Int. at 6%.
July 6,	300	0	000
Aug. 7,	400	32	2.133
Oct. 10,	200	96	3.200
	$900		$5.333

Interest on $900 for 1 day = .150.

For $900 to gain 5.333 requires ($5.333 ÷ 150) $35\frac{83}{150}$ days.

36 days from July 6th = Aug. 11, Ans. as before.

2. Calculate the above at the rate of 12 per cent.

3. When shall a note to settle the following account be made payable?

HENRY FIELD

To JAMES L. EDWARDS *Dr.*

1867.				
Mar.	8	To Mdse @ 3 mos., as per bill rendered,	250	00
Apr.	4	" " 30 days, " " "	100	00
"	16	" " 60 " " " "	300	00
May	1	" " 60 " " " "	420	00
			1070	00

Due.	Amount.	Time.	Int. at 12 per cent.
May 4,	100	0	000
June 3,	250	30	2.500
June 15,	300	42	4.200
June 30,	420	57	7.980
	1070		14.680

For $1070 at 12% to gain 14.680 will require 41 days; 41 days from May 4th is June 14th.

By taking ⅓ of the number of days as a multiplier, interest at 12% for 1 day on $1070 = .356⅔.

203. ABBREVIATED METHOD, BY INTEREST.

Labor is saved by the use of the following rule in finding the time when due.

RULE.—*Count the time from the* FIRST *day of the first month given.*

Set opposite each month the number of months intervening between it and the first month.

This number added to the term of credit, with the day of the month opposite to which it is set, will give the time for which to calculate interest.

Then calculate interest for the months and days thus found, at 12 per cent., in the same manner as in the previous rule.

EXAMPLE.

Date of Sale.	Time of Credit.	Amount.
Jan. 6,	3 mos.	$300
Feb. 12,	4 "	400
Mar. 18,	3 "	250

STATEMENT.

Amount	No. of Months from 1st mo.	Total Time, mos. days.	Int. at 12 per cent.
$300	0	3 6	.600 = Int. 6 days. 9.000 = " 3 mos.
400	1	5 12	1.600 = " 12 days. 20.000 = " 5 mos.
250	2	5 18	1.500 = " 18 days. 12.500 = " 5 mos.
$950		Total Int.	45.200

Interest on amount of debt, \$950, for 1 mo. @ 12% = \$9.50.

```
9.50)4520(4 mos.
     3800
     ----
      720
       30 days in a month.
    -----
950)21600(22 14/19 days.
```

Average time, 4 mos. 23 days, which, counted from Jan. 1st, gives May 23d, Ans.

BY USUAL METHOD.

Amount.	When due.	Days.	Product.
\$300	Apr. 6	0	000
400	June 12	67	26800
250	" 18	73	18250
950			950)45050(47 days.

47 days counted from April 6th, gives May 23d, as before.

By the abbreviated method, all the labor performed appears in the operation; but in the usual method only a part of the work is written.

The abbreviated method is used to a considerable extent in New York, Philadelphia, and Boston, on account of the labor saved in counting time and in reckoning interest. Some have claimed that results may be obtained by this method with greater facility than by the use of Equation Tables.

In some instances, the result will not exactly agree with that obtained by the use of days for the time between the dates when due, from the fact that some months contain more days than others; but in ordinary cases the difference will be but a trifle, while the labor of averaging is very much diminished. The correct time may be obtained by adding to the total time one day for every month intervening between the first day and the day of maturity which contains 31 days.

2. Bought goods as follows:—

Jan. 8, 1867,	\$250 @ 3 mos.	credit.
Feb. 13, "	360 " 4 "	"
Mar. 6, "	125 " 60 days	"

What is the average date of payment?

Average the following examples by each of the preceding rules.

3. A merchant bought goods as follows:—

Sept. 5, 1867,	a bill of	$200	on a credit of	6 mos.
Oct. 10,	"	"	500	"	3 "
Nov. 11,	"	"	350	"	60 days.
Dec. 5,	"	"	425 for cash.		

What is the average date for the payment of the whole?

4. John E. Lewis purchased goods of Isaac S. Smyth & Co. to the amount of $5000, $1250 to be paid June 2d, 1868, $1000 to be paid July 5th, $2000 to be paid Aug. 15th; the balance, $750, will become due Aug. 30th. At what date must a single note for the whole amount be drawn, payable in 3 mos., that it may become due at the average date?

5. Purchased goods of Cragin & Co., as stated below:—

Jan. 3, 1868,	a bill of	$375.25	on 3 mos. credit.		
" 10,	"	"	562.25	"	"
" 15,	"	"	250.00	"	"
" 20,	"	"	100.00	"	"
" 24,	"	"	225.75	"	"
" 29,	"	"	322.50	"	"

When shall a note for the whole be made payable?

6. Bought of Woodman and Hammett as follows:—

Dec. 10, 1867,	a bill of	$175.25	@ 4 mos.		
" 15,	"	"	237.50	"	"
" 31,	"	"	150.00	"	"
Jan. 4, 1868,	"	325.00 for cash.			

What is the average date of payment? Ans.

7. Purchased goods as follows:—

Dec. 10, 1867,	a bill of	$325.00 at 3 mos.	
Jan. 15, 1868,	"	450.75 at 60 days.	
Jan. 20,	"	"	500.00 at 3 mos.
Feb. 2,	"	"	750.25 at 3 mos.
Feb. 15,	"	"	600.00 at 3 mos.

What is the average date, and what are the dates of 4 notes drawn at 60 days each, payable one month apart, to be equivalent to the average date? Ans.

AVERAGE OF ACCOUNTS,

OR COMPOUND EQUATION.

204. In the settlement of accounts it is frequently desirable to know when the balance of an account may be paid, so that no interest need be calculated and yet have neither party suffer loss. For instance, a commission merchant sells, at a credit of 6 months, goods for a consignor amounting to $2000, the charges on which are $500, due at the time of sale. Instead of remitting $1500, the balance of account, as soon as the cash for the goods is received, the commission merchant retains it until the interest on $1500 is equal to the interest on $500 for 6 months; and as $1500 is three times as large as $500, he retains the balance $\frac{1}{3}$ of 6 months, which is 2 months. This, added to the 6 months' credit, gives 8 months from the day of sale to the time when the balance of account should be paid.

205. To find the equated time for the settlement of an account when there are both debit and credit amounts.

RULE I.—1. *Find the time when due for each side of the account separately.*

2. *Multiply the* SMALLER *side of the account by the time between the two dates thus found, and divide the product by the balance of the account. The quotient will be the time to be counted from the date of the larger side.*

If the LARGER *side of the account falls due* LATEST, *count* FORWARD *from the* LATER *date.*

If the LARGER *side of the account falls due* EARLIEST, *count* BACK *from the* EARLIER *date.*

EXAMPLES.

1. When shall a draft for the settlement of the following account be made payable?

DR.		James B. Chauncey.						CR.	
1866. July	16	To Cash,	600	00	1866. Aug.	15	By Mdse.,	1800	00

$600 \times 30 = 18000$ $\qquad 18000 \div 1200 = 15$

15 days counted forward from the later date, on which the larger amount falls due, gives August 30th.

The interest on $600 for 30 days equals that on $18000 for 1 day; as many days are required, therefore, as 1200 is contained times in 18000, which are 15. Then, as Mr. Chauncey has retained $600 for 30 days, to get an equivalent, we retain the balance of account, $1200, after it has become due, for fifteen days, which brings us to August 30th.

2. Find the time when the balance of the following account becomes due:—

DR.		James B. Chauncey.						CR.	
1866. Jan.	16	To Mdse.,	1800	00	1866. Feb.	15	By Cash,	600	00

From January 16th to February 15th = 30 days.

1800 — 600 = 1200, Bal. of account. Smaller side, $600 × 30 = 18000
18000 ÷ 1200 = 15

15 days counted back from January 16th, the earlier date, gives January 1st.

In the above account, as the larger sum is due first, it is evident the balance, $1200, should be paid long enough before January 16th to produce interest equal to the interest on $600 for the time between January 16th and February 15th, viz., 15 days before January 16th; or, $30 + 15 = 45$ days before February 15th. When the balance becomes due in time past, interest is added to obtain the amount to be paid at the time of settlement.

3. The following account appears on my Ledger:—

DR.		Samuel T. Hanson.						CR.	
1859. Jan.	11	To Mdse. at 6 months,	171	24	1859. Jan.	11	By Cash,	100	00

When should the balance be paid, or draw interest?

From January 11th to July 14th, counting 3 days of grace, the time when the debit amount is due, is 184 days.

$100 \times 184 = 18400$ $\quad 171.24 - 100 = 71.24$, Bal. of account.

$18400 \div 71.24 = 258+$

Then 258 days counted forward from July 14th, the later date, is March 29th. Ans. March 29, 1860.

4. Find the average of the following account:—

Dr.		Charles D. Carlton.						Cr.	
1867. Mar.	31	To Charges,	31	31	1867. Mar.	3	By Mdse. @ 8 mos.,	323	00
					"	4	" " " 6 "	263	00
					"	24	" " " 6 "	241	00

Credits due October 3d.

Ans. Oct. 10/13.

206. Rule II.—*Multiply each sum by the number of days intervening between the date of its maturity and the earliest day on which any sum on either side of the account becomes due.*

Then divide the difference between the sum of the products on the debit and the sum of the products on the credit side, by the balance of the account.

The quotient will be the time to be counted FORWARD *from the date on which the first amount becomes due, when the balance of the account and the difference of the sums of the products are* BOTH ON THE SAME SIDE *of the account, but* BACKWARD *from the same date if they are on* OPPOSITE SIDES *of the account.*

EXAMPLE I.

BY PRODUCTS.

Due.	Amt.	Days.	Product.	Due.	Amt.	Days.	Product.
May 22,	300	0		May 27,	200	5	1000
June 1,	150	10	1500	June 6,	100	15	1500
July 11,	200	50	10000	July 10,	120	40	4800
	650		11500		420		7300
	420		7300				
	230		) 4200($18\frac{6}{23}$				

18 days counted forward from May 22d gives June 9th.—Ans.

The discount on the debit side of the account equals the interest of $650 for the time which is equivalent to $11500 for 1 day, and, starting at the same date, the discount on the credit side will equal the interest on $420 for the time equivalent to $7300 for 1 day. The balance of the account can remain unpaid as long after May 22d as the time required for it to equal $4200 for 1 day, which is 18 days.

EXAMPLE II.

BY INTEREST.

Due.	Am't.	Days.	Int. 12 per cent.	Due.	Am't.	Days.	Int. 12 per cent.
May 15,	2500	0		May 21,	400	6	.800
" 24,	1300	9	3.900	" 30,	1200	15	6.000
June 14,	400	21	2.800	June 2,	800	18	4.800
	4200		6.700		2400		11.600
	2400						6.700
	1800						4.900

For $1800 to gain $4.90 will require $8\frac{1}{6}$ days.
Eight days counted backwards from May 15th is May 7th.

If the above account were settled May 15th, $11.60 should be charged as interest, and $6.70 allowed as discount. Instead of adding $4.90 to the balance of the account, time is counted back to a date from which the interest on the balance of the account will equal the balance of interest.

EXAMPLE III.

BY ABBREVIATED INTEREST METHOD.

CREDIT SIDE OF THE ACCOUNT.

Date. 1866.	Time of Credit.	Am't.	No. mos. from earliest mo.	Total Time. mos.	days.	Int. at 12 per cent.
July 12,	3 mos.	$100	1	4	12	$4.000 int. 4 mos. 400 " 12 ds.
Aug. 15,	Cash	250	2	2	15	5.000 " 2 mos. 1.250 " 15 ds.
Oct. 10,	3 mos.	350	4	7	10	24.500 " 7 mos. 1.050 " 9 ds. .117 " 1 day.
		$700				

Total credit interest, $36.317

DEBIT SIDE OF THE ACCOUNT.

Date.	Time of Credit.	Am't.	No. mos. from earliest mo.	Total Time. mos. days.	Int. at 12 per cent.
1866. June 15,	3 mos.	$200	0	3 15	6.000 int. 3 mos. 1.000 " 15 ds.
Aug. 9,	3 "	400	2	5 9	20.000 " 5 mos. 1.200 " 9 ds.
Sept. 18,	1 "	300	3	4 18	12.000 " 4 mos. 1.800 " 18 ds.
		900	Total debit int.		42.000
		700	" credit "		36.317
	Bal. of account,	$200	Bal. of interest,		$5.683

Interest on $200 for 1 month = $2.

5.683 ÷ 2 = 2 months 25 days.

2 months 25 days forward from June 1st is Aug. 25th, Ans.

For additional practice, average the examples already given by each of the different methods.

Average the following Account Sales:—

Account Sales of Merchandise for joint account of Newhall, Hart & Co., H. Foster & Co., *and Ourselves.*

1866. April	9	Sold Leonard Barker & Co., @ 6 mos.:—			
		Ⓐ 15 hhds. Cuba Sugar, 25,422 lbs., @ 16c.		$4067	52
		Ⓐ 32 half-chests Oolong Tea, 1805 lbs., tare 480 = 1325, @ 1.10		1457	50
				$5525	02
		—— CHARGES. ——			
		Fire Ins. on $6000 @ 1½%,	$90.00		
		Cooperage, Weighing, Labor, &c.,	17.37		
		Com. and Guar. on $5525 @ 5%,	276.25	383	62
		Net proceeds due per average,		$5141	40

Paul & Thompson.

E. E. New York, April 9th, 1866.

Note 1.—Take the sales as the credit side, and the charges as the debit side.

2. Accounts Sales are averaged to know when the proceeds may be paid without charging interest to either party.

Average the following accounts :—

DR. **Parker Burton.** CR.

1866.					1866.				
May	22	To Mdse. at 3 mos.,	500	00	May	25	By Cash,	300	00
"	29	" " " "	250	00	June	9	" Sundries,	400	00
June	10	" " " 30 days,	150	00	July	2	" Cash,	100	00

Ans. Balance $100, due per average,

DR. **R. P. Lossing & Co.** CR.

1866.					1866.				
Mar.	10	To Mdse. (net)	250	75	Mar.	20	By Cash,	250	75
"	15	" " @ 3 mos.,	187	50	"	2	" Draft @ 30 days,	120	00
Apr.	14	" " 4 "	262	25	Apr.	26	" Cash,	150	00
May	24	" " 3 "	465	60	May	24	" Sundries,	50	00

The following table will be found useful when averaging accounts.

To find the time between two dates :—Look on the left for the month containing the earlier date, and on the same line, to the right, for the month containing the later date: the number of days under the name of the month, or the number of months at the top of the column, will give the required time, if both dates are on the same day of the month. If the day of the month of the later date is different from that of the earlier date, add or subtract, as the case may be.

To find the day which is a given number of days after a certain date :—Find the number of days in the table, opposite the month, containing the given date which is next larger than the given number of days; subtract the given number of days, and count back from the same day of the month above the number taken, as the day of the month of the given date.

For example, to find the day which is 144 days after June 28th, look opposite June for the number next greater than 144. which is 153 in Nov. 144 from 153 = 9; and 9 days back from Nov. 28th brings us to Nov. 19th, the required date.

TIME TABLE.

Showing the time, in months and in days, from any day in one month to the same day in any other month, and also what month is a given number of days from another month.

No. days.	No. of mo.	From	1 mo.	2 mos.	3 mos.	4 mos.	5 mos.	6 mos.	7 mos.	8 mos.	9 mos.	10 mos.	11 mos.	12 mos.
31	1	January to	Feb. 31 days.	March, 59 days.	April, 90 days.	May, 120 ds.	June, 151 ds.	July, 181 ds.	August, 212 ds.	Sept., 243 ds.	Oct., 273 ds.	Nov., 304 ds.	Dec., 334 ds.	Jan., 365 ds.
28	2	February "	March, 28 days.	April, 59 days.	May, 89 days.	June, 120 ds.	July, 150 ds.	August, 181 ds.	Sept., 212 ds.	Oct., 242 ds.	Nov., 273 ds.	Dec., 303 ds.	Jan., 334 ds.	Feb., 365 ds.
31	3	March "	April, 31 days.	May, 61 days.	June, 92 days.	July, 122 ds.	August, 153 ds.	Sept. 184 ds.	Oct., 214 ds.	Nov., 245 ds.	Dec., 275 ds.	Jan., 306 ds.	Feb., 337 ds.	March, 365 ds.
30	4	April "	May, 30 days.	June, 61 days.	July, 91 days.	August, 122 ds.	Sept., 153 ds.	Oct., 183 ds.	Nov., 214 ds.	Dec., 244 ds.	Jan., 275 ds.	Feb., 306 ds.	March, 334 ds.	April, 365 ds.
31	5	May "	June, 31 days.	July, 61 days.	August, 92 days.	Sept., 123 ds.	Oct., 153 ds.	Nov., 184 ds.	Dec., 214 ds.	Jan., 245 ds.	Feb., 276 ds.	March, 304 ds.	April, 335 ds.	May, 365 ds.
30	6	June "	July, 30 days.	August, 61 days.	Sept., 92 days.	Oct., 122 ds.	Nov., 153 ds.	Dec., 183 ds.	Jan., 214 ds.	Feb., 245 ds.	March, 273 ds.	April, 304 ds.	May, 334 ds.	June, 365 ds.
31	7	July "	August, 31 days.	Sept., 62 days.	Oct., 92 days.	Nov., 123 ds.	Dec., 153 ds.	Jan., 184 ds.	Feb., 215 ds.	March, 243 ds.	April, 274 ds.	May, 304 ds.	June, 335 ds.	July, 365 ds.
31	8	August "	Sept., 31 days.	Oct., 61 days.	Nov., 92 days.	Dec., 122 ds.	Jan., 153 ds.	Feb., 184 ds.	March, 212 ds.	April, 243 ds.	May, 273 ds.	June, 304 ds.	July, 334 ds.	August, 365 ds.
30	9	Septemb'r "	Oct., 30 days.	Nov., 61 days.	Dec., 91 days.	Jan., 122 ds.	Feb., 153 ds.	March, 181 ds.	April, 212 ds.	May, 242 ds.	June, 273 ds.	July, 303 ds.	August, 334 ds.	Sept., 365 ds.
31	10	October "	Nov., 31 days.	Dec., 61 days.	Jan., 92 days.	Feb., 123 ds.	March, 151 ds.	April, 182 ds.	May, 212 ds.	June, 243 ds.	July, 273 ds.	August, 304 ds.	Sept., 335 ds.	Oct., 365 ds.
30	11	November "	Dec., 30 days.	Jan., 61 days.	Feb., 92 days.	March, 120 ds.	April, 151 ds.	May, 181 ds.	June, 212 ds.	July, 242 ds.	August, 273 ds.	Sept., 304 ds.	Oct., 334 ds.	Nov., 365 ds.
31	12	December "	Jan., 31 days.	Feb., 62 days.	March, 90 days.	April, 121 ds.	May, 151 ds.	June, 182 ds.	July, 212 ds.	August, 243 ds.	Sept., 274 ds.	Oct., 304 ds.	Nov., 335 ds.	Dec., 365 ds.

MONEY, WEIGHTS, AND MEASURES.

MONEY.

207. Money is value, or its representative, used as a medium of exchange and as a standard of measure.

208. The word money is derived from the Latin *monetas*, which some derive from *monere*, to "admonish," to "inform," —the stamp on a coin informing the holder of its value. The Latin word *pecunia*, "money," is supposed to be derived from *pecus*, "a sheep," because in early times sheep, or stamped skins, were used in place of money.

209. In different countries, and in different conditions of society, various articles have been made to serve as money. Homer tells us the armor of Diomede cost nine oxen, while that of Glaucus cost one hundred; and the oldest Greek coins were stamped with an ox,—intimating the previous employment of cattle as money. The laws of the ancient Germans imposed penalties for offences, to be paid in cattle; while slaves and cattle—or "living money," as it was then called —were in common use among the Anglo-Saxons. The Carthaginians and Spartans employed for this purpose skins and pieces of leather marked with a stamp. In Hindostan, small shells called *cowries* are used in the smaller payments; they also circulate widely in Africa. In Abyssinia, rock-salt, in Iceland, dried fish, and among the North American Indians, the *belt of wampum*, is used as money. In 1776, according to Adam Smith, the workmen of a certain Scottish village carried nails as money to the baker's and to the ale-house.

210. Various metals have been used: the Spartans adopted iron; the ancient Romans, copper; the Russians, at one time, platinum; but gold and silver have been preferred by modern nations, as best adapted for the purposes of money, for the following reasons:—

I. Their value is comparatively uniform, and less subject to variations, and they may be kept or used without much deterioration.

II. Their nature is such that they can easily be identified.

III. They are capable of division or combination without loss of value.

IV. They possess great value in small compass, and are capable of being easily transported from place to place.

Gold and silver, in their purity, are soft, easily bent or injured, and exposed to rapid wear: they are therefore moderately hardened by the admixture of an alloy. For gold coin both copper and silver are employed as an alloy; and the color of the coin inclines to yellow or red, as the silver or copper may predominate.

211. Money is either *real* or *imaginary*. Real money includes all coins,—such as dollars, sovereigns, and the like; imaginary, or nominal money, is that which does not exist in specie,—such as mills, pounds, &c.

212. The Moneys of Account are those in which accounts are kept, and include imaginary as well as real money; but the relations of the denominations are not susceptible to fluctuations, like currency.

213. *Paper money* is a substitute for metallic currency.

214. Aside from the amount in actual existence, *the rapidity and value of exchanges* affect the abundance or scarcity of money. Any thing which dispenses with its use diminishes the amount of circulating medium necessary for a community, and in effect is the same as adding so much to the currency. The accounts of merchants, notes, bills of exchange, and credits generally, are of this nature.

215. When two kinds of money are in circulation, the one of least value will displace the other.

216. The term **Bullion** is applied to uncoined gold or silver, and includes gold dust, amalgamations, and ingots, or bars.

217. Coin, or **Specie,** is metal of known weight and fineness, stamped for the purpose of being used as money.

218. The smallest coin is believed to be the Turkish *para*, weighing from 1½ to 2½ grains, containing a small portion of silver, and its value is one-thirtieth of our cent. The smallest copper coin of Europe is the *centime* of Genoa, weighing fourteen grains, and worth one-twelfth of our cent. The ten-copeck piece of Russia is equal in weight to 4⅛ copper cents; a copper piece of 1795 weighs 890 grains; about as heavy as 5⅓ copper cents.

219. Currency is money in common circulation, whether coin or paper. *Agio* is the difference between currencies.

220. Billon (from the French, signifying base coin) is the name of a mixture having a small proportion of silver combined with some base metal.

221. Tokens are coins whose intrinsic value is below that assigned to them by law, and are not a legal tender above certain small amounts. Coins in *billon*—the nickel cent, and the one, two, three, and five cent pieces of 1866—are tokens. (See VALUE OF U. S. COINS.)

RELATIVE VALUES OF GOLD AND SILVER.

222. In the United States, as 15.988 to 1.
" England, " 14.287 " 1.
" France, " 15.50 " 1.
" Spain, " 16.00 " 1.
" China, " 14.25 " 1.

223. In America and Great Britain, gold is the standard of value. Silver is the standard of value in France, Belgium, Holland, Austria, and the Zollverein States, Russia, and the East Indies. Payments made in China are either in silver dollars or silver ingots.

224. In Great Britain,

A pound of standard gold $\frac{11}{12}$ fine is coined into £46 14*s.* 6*d.* = £3 17*s.* 10½*d.* per ounce, which is the mint price for standard gold, and is equivalent to $18.94 per ounce.

A pound of silver ($\frac{37}{40}$ fine) is coined into 66 shillings = 5*s.* 6*d.* per ounce. The mint price is 5*s.* per ounce, $\frac{37}{40}$ fine.

A pound of copper is coined into 24 pence.

A pound of bronze of 1860, 95 parts of copper, 4 of tin, and 1 of zinc, is coined into 48 penny pieces, or 80 half-pennies, or 160 farthings.

225. In France,

A kilogramme of gold is coined into 155 napoleons, or 3100 francs.

A kilogramme of silver is coined into 200 francs.

226. The standard of the various moneys in the north of Europe and Germany is the Cologne mark weight, Hamburg standard of fine silver; that is, 3608 grains Troy.

In Sweden, Norway, Denmark, and Mecklenburg, it is coined, when alloyed with copper, into 9¼ silver-species, dalers or thalers.

In Russia, into 13 silver roubles.

In Prussia and Hanover, into 14 thalers.

In the Southern States of the Zollverein, into 24½ gulden.

In Austria, into 20 gulden.

In Hamburg and Lubeck, into 35 marks current.

The acts of Congress of 1834 and 1843, fixing the value of certain foreign coins, and declaring the same as legal tender, were repealed by act of February 21, 1853.

It will be seen in the following table that the half-dollar, and smaller silver coins issued since 1853 are worth less, in proportion, than the silver coins issued before that time.

The smaller coins are designed chiefly for the purpose of making change, and are not a legal tender above certain small sums. (See Legal Tender.)

TABLE

Showing the weight and fineness of the Coins of the United States, as given by acts of Congress.

GOLD.

11/12 or .913⅓ FINE.	Standard Weight.	Pure Gold.	Coml. Val
Eagle, coined before 1834	270 grains	247.5 grains	$10.62
½ " " " "	135 "	123.75 "	5.31
¼ " " " "	67.5 "	61.87 "	2.65
.900 FINE.			
Eagle coined since 1834	258. "	232.2 "	10.00
½ " " " "	129. "	116.1 "	5.00
¼ " " " "	64.5 "	58.05 "	2.50
1 Dollar piece,	25.8 "	23.22 "	1.00
1 Double Eagle,	516. "	464.4 "	20.00
3 Dollar piece,	7.74 grains	69.66 "	3.00

SILVER.

	Standard Weight.	Pure Silver.	Coml. Val.
Dollar before 1837, and shares in proportion, 892.4 fine,	416. grs.	371.25 grs.	$1.05
Dollar since 1837, 900 fine,	412.5 "	371.25 "	1.05
½ " '37 to June, '53, " "	206.25 grs.	185.625 grs.	.52½
¼ " " " " "	103.125 "	92.8125 "	.26
Dime " " " "	41.25 "	37.125 "	.10½
½ " " " " "	20.625 "	18.5625 "	.05
3 Cent piece, March, 1851, to March, 1853, ¾ fine,	12.375 "	10.8 "	.03
½ Dollar since June, 1853,	192. "	172.8 "	.50

(And smaller coins in proportion.)

Old Cent, 178 grains copper.

Cent of 1866, 48 grs. 95% copper, 3% zinc, and 2% tin.
2 " piece " 96 " 95 " 5% nickel.
3 " " " 32 " 75 " 25% "
5 " " " 5 grams, or 77$\frac{16}{100}$ grs., 75% copper, 25% nickel.

A STATEMENT OF FOREIGN GOLD AND SILVER COINS.

(Prepared by the Director of the United States Mint.)

Explanatory Remarks.—The first column of the Tables of Foreign Coins embraces the names of the countries where the coins are issued; the second contains the names of the coin, only the principal denominations being given. The other sizes are proportional; and, when this is not the case, the deviation is stated.

The third column expresses the weight of a single piece in fractions of the troy ounce, carried to the thousandth, and, in a few cases, to the ten-thousandth, of an ounce. The method is preferable to expressing the weight in grains for commercial purposes, and corresponds better with the terms of the mint. It may be readily transferred to weight in grains by the following rule:—*Remove the decimal point; from one-half deduct four per cent. of that half, and the remainder will be grains.*

The fourth column expresses the fineness in thousands, *i.e.* the number of parts of pure gold or silver in 1000 parts of the coin.

The fifth and sixth columns of the first table express the valuation of gold. In the fifth is shown the value as compared with the legal content, or amount of fine gold in our coin. In the sixth is shown the value as paid at the mint after the uniform deduction of one-half of one per cent. The former is the value for any other purposes than recoinage, and especially for the purpose of comparison; the latter is the value in exchange for our coins at the mint.

For the silver there is no fixed legal valuation, the law providing for changing the price according to the condition of demand and supply. The present price of standard silver is 122½ cents per ounce, at which rate the values in the fifth column of the second table are calculated. In a few cases, where the coins could not be procured, the data are *assumed* from the legal rates, and so stated.

The silver purchased for coinage will be paid for in silver coins of the United States, of less denomination than the dollar; fine silver, 136⅛ cents per ounce; American plate, usual manufacture, 120 to 122 cents per ounce; genuine British plate, 125.8 cents per ounce.

FOREIGN GOLD COINS.

COUNTRY.	DENOMINATION.	Weight.	Fineness.	Value.	Value after Deduction of ½ per ct.
		Oz. Dec.	Thous.		Price paid at Mint.
Australia	Pound of 1852	0.281	916.5	$5.32.37	$5.29.71
"	Sovereign of 1855–60	0.256.5	916	4.85.58	4.83.16
Austria	Ducat	0.112	986	2.28.28	2.27.04
"	Souverain	0.363	900	6.75.35	6.71.98
"	New Union crown (assumed)	0.357	900	6.64.19	6.60.87
Belgium	Twenty-five francs	0.254	899	4.72.03	4.69.67
Bolivia	Doubloon	0.867	870	15.59.25	15.51.46
Brazil	Twenty milreis	0.575	917.5	10.90.57	10.85.12
Central America	Two escudos	0.209	853.5	3.68.75	3.66.91
Chili	Old doubloon	0.867	870	15.59.26	15.51.47
"	Ten pesos	0.492	900	9.15.35	9.10.78
Denmark	Ten thaler	0.427	895	7.90.01	7.86.06
Ecuador	Four escudos	0.433	844	7.55.46	7.51.69
England	Pound or sovereign, new	0.256.7	916.5	4.86.34	4.83.91
"	Pound or sovereign, average	0.256.2	916	4.84.92	4.82.50
France	Twenty francs, new	0.207.5	899.5	3.85.83	3.83.91
"	Twenty francs, average	0.207	899	3.84.69	3.82.77
Germany, North	Ten thaler	0.427	895	7.90.01	7.86.06
" "	Ten thaler, Prussian	0.427	903	7.97.07	7.93.09
" "	Krone (crown)	0.357	900	6.64.20	6.60.88
Germany, South	Ducat	0.112	986	2.28.28	2.27.14
Greece	Twenty drachms	0.185	900	3.44.19	3.42.47
Hindostan	Mohur	0.374	916	7.08.18	7.04.64
Italy	Twenty lire	0.207	898	3.84.26	3.82.34
Japan	Old cobang	0.362	568	4.44.0	4.41.8
"	New cobang	0.289	572	3.57.6	3.55.8
Mexico	Doubloon, average	0.867.5	866	15.52.98	15.45.22
"	Doubloon, new	0.867.5	870.5	15.61.05	15.53.25
Naples	Six ducati, new	0.245	996	5.04.43	5.01.91
Netherlands	Ten guilders	0.215	899	3.99.56	3.97.57
New Granada	Old doubloon, Bogota	0.868	870	15.61.06	15.53.26
" "	Old doubloon, Popayan	0.867	858	15.37.75	15.30.07
" "	Ten pesos, new	0.525	891.5	9.67.51	9.62.68
Peru	Old doubloon	0.867	868	15.55.67	15.47.90
"	Twenty soles	1.035	898	19.21.8	19.12.2
Portugal	Gold crown	0.308	912	5.80.66	5.77.76
Prussia	New Union crown (assumed)	0.357	900	6.64.19	6.60.87
Rome	Two-and-a-half scudi, new	0.140	900	2.60.47	2.59.17
Russia	Five roubles	0.210	916	3.97.64	3.95.66
Spain	One hundred reals	0.268	896	4.96.39	4.93.91
"	Eighty reals	0.215	869.5	3.86.44	3.84.51
Sweden	Ducat	0.111	975	2.23.72	2.22.61
Tunis	Twenty-five piastres	0.161	900	2.99.54	2.98.05
Turkey	One hundred piastres	0.231	915	4.36.93	4.34.75
Tuscany	Sequin	0.112	999	2.31.29	2.30.14

FOREIGN SILVER COINS.

COUNTRY.	DENOMINATION.	Weight.	Fineness.	Value.
		Oz. Dec.	Thous.	
Austria	Old rix dollar	0.902	833	$1.02.27
"	Old scudo	0.836	902	1.02.64
"	Florin before 1858	0.451	833	51.14
"	New florin	0.397	900	48.63
"	New Union dollar	0.596	900	73.01
"	Maria Theresa dollar, 1780	0.895	838	1.02.12
Belgium	Five francs	0.803	897	98.04
Bolivia	New dollar	0.643	903.5	79.07
"	Half dollar	0.432	667	39.22
Brazil	Double milreis	0.820	918.5	1.02.53
Canada	Twenty cents	0.150	925	18.87
Central America	Dollar	0.866	850	1.00.19
Chili	Old dollar	0.864	908	1.06.79
"	New dollar	0.801	900.5	98.17
Denmark	Two rigsdaler	0.927	877	1.10.65
England	Shilling, new	0.182.5	924.5	22.96
"	Shilling, average	0.178	925	22.41
France	Five franc, average	0.800	900	98.00
Germany, North	Thaler, before 1857	0.712	750	72.67
" "	New thaler	0.595	900	72.89
Germany, South	Florin, before 1857	0.340	900	41.65
" "	New florin (assumed)	0.340	900	41.65
Greece	Five drachms	0.719	900	88.08
Hindostan	Rupee	0.374	916	46.62
Japan	Itzebu	0.279	991	37.63
"	New Itzebu	0.279	890	33.80
Mexico	Dollar, new	0.867.5	903	1.06.62
"	Dollar, average	0.866	901	1.06.20
Naples	Scudo	0.844	830	95.34
Netherlands	Two-and-a-half guild	0.804	944	1.03.31
Norway	Specie daler	0.927	877	1.10.65
New Granada	Dollar of 1857	0.803	896	97.92
Peru	Old dollar	0.866	901	1.06.20
"	Dollar of 1858	0.766	909	94.77
"	Half-dollar, 1835–38	0.433	650	38.31
Prussia	Thaler before 1857	0.712	750	72.68
"	New thaler	0.595	900	72.89
Rome	Scudo	0.864	900	1.05.84
Russia	Rouble	0.667	875	79.44
Sardinia	Five lire	0.800	900	98.00
Spain	New pistareen	0.166	899	20.31
Sweden	Rix dollar	1.092	750	1.11.48
Switzerland	Two francs	0.323	899	39.52
Tunis	Five piastres	0.511	898.5	62.49
Turkey	Twenty piastres	0.770	830	86.98
Tuscany	Florin	0.220	925	27.60

WEIGHTS AND MEASURES.

227. The weights and measures used by the different nations throughout the world have been derived from very imperfect and variable standards. Thus, a foot was the length of a king's foot, and, consequently, varied as a king with a long foot or a short foot happened to reign. The *hand*, *span*, *cubit*, or fore-arm, and *fathom*, or length of the two arms extended, all varied with the size of the person. Henry I., King of England, declared that the ell, or ulna, or yard, should be the length of his own arm, from the extreme end of the longest finger to the middle of the breast, and that the other measures should be raised upon this. The old English pound, which was the legal standard of weight from the time of William the Conqueror to that of Henry VII., was derived from the weight of grains of wheat gathered from the middle of the ear, and well dried, 32 (changed in later times to 24) grains making a pennyweight, or the weight of a penny, 20 pennyweights an ounce, and 12 ounces a pound. Henry VII. introduced the troy pound. The avoirdupois pound was introduced during the reign of Henry VIII.

An acre was as much land as a yoke of oxen could plough in a day. A hyde was about 100 acres.

228. America, England, and France have endeavored to found their systems of weights and measures upon invariable or natural standards.

The standard units of linear, superficial, and solid measures of the United States are identical with those of Great Britain.

STANDARD OF LENGTH.

229. The standard unit of length is the *yard*, and is determined as follows:—

A pendulum vibrating *seconds* of mean time in the latitude of London, in a vacuum and at the level of the sea, is divided into 391,393 equal parts. 360,000 of these parts are equivalent to the length of the standard yard, or 36 inches.

STANDARD OF WEIGHT.

230. The standard unit of troy weight is the weight of 22.7944 cubic inches distilled water at its maximum density, or 22.8157 cubic inches at 62° Fahrenheit, barometer in both cases being at 30 inches. (See HEAT, page 237.)

The *avoirdupois* pound contains 7000 troy grains; the *troy* pound contains 5760 grains. The avoirdupois pound is equal to the weight of 27.7015 cubic inches of distilled water at its maximum density, or 27.7274 cubic inches at 62° Fahrenheit.

The English Imperial weights and those of the United States are identical.

STANDARDS OF CAPACITY.

231. The United States standard unit of liquid measure is the old English wine gallon of 231 cubic inches, and contains 8.3389 lbs. avoirdupois of distilled water of 39.83° Fahrenheit, the barometer at 30 inches.

The Imperial standard gallon, for liquids and all dry substances, contains 10 lbs. avoirdupois distilled water 62° Fahrenheit, barometer 30 inches, equal to 277.274 cubic inches.

The United States standard unit of dry measure is the British Winchester bushel, so called from the standard being kept at Winchester. It is a cylinder 18½ inches in diameter by 8 inches deep, and contains 2150.42 cubic inches, or 77.6274 pounds avoirdupois, of distilled water at its maximum density. A dry-measure gallon contains 268⅘ cubic inches.

The weights and measures of some of the States differ from those of the United States. For the French system of weights and measures, see FRANCE, page 132.

UNITED STATES.

MONEY.

10 mills (m.) = 1 cent, ct.
10 cents = 1 dime, d.
10 dimes = 1 dollar, $.
10 dollars = 1 eagle, E.

232. The origin of the symbol $, or the United States dollar mark, has been ascribed to several sources. By some it is supposed to represent the *U* written upon the *S*, denoting U. S. (United States). Some think it is a modification of the figure 8, having reference to 8 reals, or piece of Eight, as the dollar was formerly called; others, that it represents the "Pillars of Hercules," which were stamped on the Pillar Dollar; and others, still, that it is a combination of the initials P. and S., from the Spanish *Peso Duro*, signifying Hard Dollar. As it is used in Portugal to note the thousands' place, it is probable that it originated in that country: a Mil-reis, or thousand reis, is written thus, 1$000.

STATE CURRENCIES.

233. The money of this country before the adoption of the decimal currency by Congress in 1786 was in the denominations of pounds, shillings, and pence. The *Colonial notes* which were then in circulation had depreciated in value; and the number of shillings equivalent to a dollar at that time are given in the following table:—

NEW ENGLAND CURRENCY.

New England States, Virginia, Kentucky, and Tennessee, } $1 = 6*s.* = 72*d.*
1*s.* = 16⅔ cts.

NEW YORK CURRENCY.

New York, Ohio, Michigan, and North Carolina, } $1 = 8*s.* = 96*d.*
1*s.* = 12½ cts.

PENNSYLVANIA CURRENCY.

Pennsylvania, New Jersey, Delaware, and Maryland, } $1 = 7*s.* 6*d.* = 90*d.*
1*s.* = 13⅓ cts.

GEORGIA CURRENCY.

Georgia and South Carolina, $1 = 4*s.* 8*d.* = 56*d.*
1*s.* = 21$\frac{3}{7}$ cts.

WEIGHTS AND MEASURES.

LINEAR OR LONG MEASURE.

12 inches (in.)	= **1** foot (ft.).				
36 "	= **3** "	= 1 yard (yd.).			
198 "	= 16½ "	= **5½** "	= 1 rod (r.).		
1920 "	= 660 "	= 220 "	= **40** "	= 1 furlong (F.).	
63360 "	= 5280 "	= 1760 "	= 320 "	= **8** "	= **1** mile (m.)

69½ miles (nearly) = 1 degree (deg. °); 360 degrees = circumference of the earth: 6 feet = 1 fathom; 3.45 statute miles = 1 league; 1 knot or geographical mile = $1\frac{11}{72}$ statute miles; 4 inches = 1 hand. The earth revolves at about 1000 miles per hour.

SURFACE OR SQUARE MEASURE.

144 sq. inches	= 1 sq. foot.					
1296 "	= **9** "	= 1 sq. yard.				
39204 "	= 272¼ "	= **30¼** "	= 1 sq. rod.			
1568160 "	= 10890 "	= 1210 "	= **40** "	= 1 sq. rood.		
6272640 "	= 43560 "	= 4840 "	= 160 "	= **4** "	= 1 acre.	
4014489600 "	= 27878400 "	= 3097600 "	= 102400 "	= **640** sq. a.	= **1** sq. mile	

36 sections or square miles = 6 miles square = 1 township.

Carpenters' work is frequently computed by the square, containing 100 square feet; painters', by the square yard.

SURVEYORS' MEASURE.

792 inches	= 1 link (l.).			
198 "	= **25** "	= 1 rod (rd.).		
792 "	= 100 "	= **4** " or 66 ft.	= 1 chain (ch.).	
63360 "	= 8000 "	= 320 "	= **80** "	= **1** mile.

625 sq. links = 1 pole; 16 poles = 1 sq. chain; 10 sq. chains = 1 acre.

An acre is equal to 208⅔ feet square, nearly.

CUBIC OR SOLID MEASURE.

1728 cubic inches (cu. in.)	= 1 cubic foot (cu. ft.).	
27 " feet	= 1 " yard (cu. yd.).	
16 " "	= 1 cord foot.	

8 cord ft. or 128 cubic feet = 1 cord of wood.

A pile of wood 8 ft. long, 4 wide, and 4 high, = 1 cord.

24¾ cubic ft., or 16½ ft. long, 1½ feet high, and 1 ft. wide, = 1 perch.

Masons' work is frequently computed by the perch.

40 cubic feet of round timber, *i.e.* as much round timber as will make 40 feet hewn, = 1 ton or load.

50 cubic feet of hewn timber = 1 ton or load.

A cubic foot of distilled water, maximum density, weighs 62½ lbs. avoir.

LIQUID MEASURE.

WINE MEASURE.

4 gills (g.)	= 1 pint (pt.).			
8 "	= 2 "	= 1 quart (qt.).		
32 "	= 8 "	= 4 "	= 1 gallon (gal.) (231 cubic inches).	
2016 "	= 504 "	= 252 "	= 63 "	= 1 hogshead (hhd.).

In some States the barrel is estimated at 31½ gallons; in others, 32, 28, &c. Casks, called tierces, pipes, butts, hogsheads, and tuns, are usually gauged, and do not express any definite measures. The following table is sometimes used:—42 gallons = 1 tierce; 2 tierces = 1 puncheon; 2 hogsheads = 1 pipe; 2 pipes = 1 tun.

BEER MEASURE.

Used in measuring beer or milk, but becoming obsolete.

2 pints (pt.)	= 1 quart (qt.).	
8 "	= 4 "	= 1 gallon (gal.) = (282 cubic inches).

36 gallons = 1 barrel; 54 gallons = 1 hhd.

DRY MEASURE.

2 pints (pt.)	= 1 quart (qt.).		
16 "	= 8 "	= 1 peck (pk.).	
64 "	= 32 "	= 4 "	= 1 bushel (bus.) = 2150.42 cu. inches,

or a cylinder 18½ inches deep and 8 inches in diameter. 36 bushels = 1 chaldron. In a *heaped bushel* the cone is 6 inches above the brim of the measure. A heaped bushel contains 2747.70 cubic inches, or about five pecks, even measure. For weights of different grains, see table, page 228. 8 *struck* bushels = 1 English quarter.

WEIGHTS.

TROY OR MINT WEIGHT.

Used in weighing precious metals, jewelry, liquors, and in philosophical experiments,

24 grains (gr.)	= 1 pennyweight (pwt.).		
480 "	= 20 "	= 1 ounce (oz.).	
5760 "	= 240 "	= 12 "	= 1 pound (℔).

APOTHECARIES' WEIGHT.

Used in compounding medicines. In this weight, the pound, ounce, and grain are the same as in troy weight. The ounce is differently divided.

20 grains (gr.)	= 1 scruple (℈).			
60 "	= 3 "	= 1 drachm (dr. or ʒ).		
480 "	= 24 "	= 8 "	= 1 ounce (℥).	
5760 "	= 288 "	= 96 "	= 12 "	= 1 pound.

MEDICAL DIVISION OF THE GALLON

60 minims (♏)	= 1 fluidrachm,	f ʒ.	16 fluidounces	= 1 pint,	O.
8 fluidrachms	= 1 fluidounce,	f ℥.	8 pints	= 1 gallon,	Cong.

O. is an abbreviation of *octans*, the Latin for *one-eighth; Cong.* for *congiarium*, the Latin for gallon.

A single common teaspoonful, or 45 drops, makes about one fluidrachm. A common teacup holds about 4 fluidounces; a common tablespoon, about half a fluidounce; a pint of water weighs a pound.

℞ is an abbreviation for *recipe*, or take; ā., aa., for equal quantities; j. for 1; ij for 2; *ss.* for *semi*, or half; gr. for grain; P. for *particula*, or little part; P. æq. for equal parts; q. p., as much as you please.

AVOIRDUPOIS OR COMMERCIAL WEIGHT.

Used in almost all commercial transactions.

16 drams	= 1 ounce.				
256 "	= **16** "	= 1 pound (7000 grains).			
6400 "	= 400 "	= **25** "	= 1 quarter.		
25600 "	= 1600 "	= 100 "	= **4** "	= 1 hundredweight.	
51200 "	= 32000 "	= 2000 "	= 80 "	= **20** "	= **1** ton.

At the custom-house, and in some kinds of business, 28 lbs. = 1 quarter, 112 lbs. = 1 cwt., and 2240 lbs. = 1 ton.

The standard avoirdupois lb. = weight of 27.7015 cubic inches distilled water at maximum density.

TIME MEASURE.

60 seconds	= 1 minute.				
3600 "	= **60** "	= 1 hour.			
86400 "	= 1440 "	= **24** "	= 1 day.		
2592000 "	= 43200 "	= 720 "	= **30** "	= 1 month.	
31557600 "	= 525960 "	= 8766 "	= 365¼ "	= **12** "	= **1** year.

The time in which the earth revolves around the sun is 365 days, 6 hours, 9 minutes, $9\frac{6}{10}$ seconds. February has 28 days, except in leap-year, or years which may be divided by 4 without a remainder, when it has 29. Four months (April, June, September, and November) have each 30 days; all the others have each 31 days.

CIRCULAR MEASURE.

60 seconds (″)	= 1 minute (′).			
3600 "	= **60** minutes	= 1 degree (°).		
108000 "	= 1800 "	= **30** "	= 1 sign (S.).	
1296000 "	= 21600 "	= 360 "	= **12** "	= **1** circle (C.).

90° make a quadrant or right angle.

PENDULUMS.

6 points = 1 line; 12 lines = 1 inch.

SHOEMAKERS' MEASURE.

No. 1 small size is $4\frac{1}{3}$ inch, and every succeeding No. increases $\frac{1}{3}$ of an inch to 13.
No. 1 large " $8\frac{11}{24}$ " " " " $\frac{1}{3}$ " " 15.

DIAMOND WEIGHT.

16 parts = 1 grain.
4 grains = 1 carat.
1 carat = $3\frac{1}{5}$ grains troy, nearly.

ASSAYERS' WEIGHT.

1 carat = 10 pwts. troy.
1 carat grain = 2 pwts. 12 grains, or 60 grains troy.
24 carats = 1 lb. troy.

The term carat is also used to express the fineness of gold,—each carat meaning a twenty-fourth part.

MISCELLANEOUS TABLES.

BOOKS AND PAPER.

SIZE OF PAPER.

	Inches.		Inches.
Demy	17 by 22	Letter	10 by 15
Medium	19 " 24	Folio post	16 " 21
Double medium	24 " 38	Foolscap	14 " 17
Super-royal	21 " 27	Crown	15 " 20
Imperial	22 " 32	Double Elephant	26 " 40

A sheet (medium) folded in 2 leaves is called folio.
" " 4 " quarto or 4to.
" " 8 " octavo or 8vo.
" " 12 " duodecimo or 12mo.
" " 16 " 16mo.

24 sheets = 1 quire.
480 " = 20 " = 1 ream.
2 reams = 1 bundle; 5 bundles = 1 bale.

---

12 units = 1 dozen.
144 " = 12 " = 1 gross.
12 gross = 1 great gross.
20 units = 1 score.
56 lbs. = 1 firkin of butter.
100 " = 1 quintal of dried fish.

196 lbs. = 1 barrel of flour.
200 " = 1 " beef, pork, or fish.
280 " = 1 " salt.
100 " = 1 cask of raisins.
14 " iron or lead = 1 stone.
12 bbls. of wheat = 7 English quarters.

$21\frac{1}{2}$ stone = 1 pig; 8 pigs = 1 fother.

GREAT BRITAIN.

MONEY.

4 Farthings	= 1 Penny,	*d.*
12 pence	= 1 Shilling,	*s.*
20 shillings	= 1 Pound,	*£.*

234. The *Gold coins* are the sovereign, which represents the pound, and the half-sovereign. The guinea, of 21 shillings, and its subdivisions, have not been coined since 1816. The standard for gold is 11 parts fine gold and 1 part alloy. The sovereign weighs $123\frac{171}{623}$ grains, and contains $113\frac{1}{623}$ or 113.001 grains pure gold.

The *Silver coins* are crowns of 5*s.*, half-crowns, florins of 2*s.*, shillings, the 6*d.*, the 4*d.* or groats, and 3*d.* pieces. The *shilling* weighs $87\frac{3}{11}$ grains, and contains $80\frac{8}{11}$ grains pure silver.

The *Copper coins* are the penny, half-penny, and farthing, coined at the rate of 24 pence per pound avoirdupois.

235. *Bank-of-England Notes* are a legal tender for any sum over £5; silver is not a legal tender over 40*s.*; copper. for not more than 12*d.* in pennies or half-pennies; or 6*d.*, in farthings.

236. £ is a contraction of *libræ*, *s.* of *solidi*, *d.* of *denarii*, and *q.* of *quadrantes;* farthing is another word for *four-thing.*

In accounts, a straight line is written between shillings and pence when both are mentioned: thus, 2/6 for 2*s.* 6*d.*

The word sterling is supposed to be derived from the first coiners of English silver, who came into England from Germany in the reign of Richard I., and were called *Easterlings.* It is used to distinguish the currency of Great Britain from that of the Colonies, and from some continental money bearing the same denominations.

237. Intrinsic par value of £1 = \$4.866; U. S. Custom-House value, £1 = \$4.84. Freight bills are paid at the rate of \$4.80 per £1. In British America, £1 = \$4.

The English mint price of gold is £3 17*s*. 10½*d*. for standard gold, or $\frac{11}{12}$ fine. The mint price of silver is 5*s*. per ounce for standard silver, or $\frac{37}{40}$ fine.

238. The average yearly loss on the wear of gold is estimated at 1 in 950, and of silver 1 in 200.

WEIGHTS AND MEASURES.

239. Before 1826, the chief of the measures of capacity agreeing with those of the United States, were the wine gallon of 231 cubic inches, the beer gallon of 282 cubic inches, and the Winchester bushel of 2150.42 cubic inches.

240. By act of Parliament, which came into operation January 1, 1826, certain weights and measures, under the name of Imperial Weights and Measures, were declared to be the only lawful ones in the United Kingdom.

241. By this act, the imperial gallon, both Liquid and Dry Measure, contains 277.274 cubic inches, or 10 lbs. avoirdupois distilled water, the temperature 32°, barometer 30 inches. The imperial bushel contains 2218.192 cubic inches, or 8 imperial gallons; 8 bus. = 1 quarter; 10 qrs. = 1 last.

100 Imperial Bushels = 103.15 Winchester bushels.
100 Winchester " = 96.94 Imperial "

5 Imperial Gallons nearly equal 6 Wine Gallons.
59 " " 60 Ale "

144 lbs. Avoirdupois = 175 lbs. Troy.
192 oz. " = 175 oz. "

242. The standard avoirdupois pound of the United States and the imperial pound avoirdupois are alike.

The Troy pound = 22.815689 cubic inches distilled water

The linear, superficial, and cubic measures are the same in England as in the United States. (See COMPARATIVE TABLES.)

FRANCE.

243. The **Decimal** or **Metric System** of moneys, weights, and measures is now established in France, and has been adopted, to a greater or less extent, in Belgium, Spain, Portugal, Holland, Switzerland, Sweden, Austria, Turkey, Brazil, and several other countries.

244. MM. Delambre and Mechain estimated the length of the meridian from the Equator to the Pole by the measurement of an arc between Dunkirk and Barcelona, and the *ten-millionth* part of this meridian, or one-fourth of the circumference of the earth, was taken as the unit of *length*, and is termed a **Metre.**

245. The square of 10 metres is the unit of *surface measure*, and is called an **Are** (pronounced *air*).

246. The cube of the *tenth part of a metre* is the unit of capacity for either Liquid or Dry Measure, and is called a **Litre** (pronounced *le'-tur*).

247. A kil'olitre, the cube of a metre, is the unit of Solid Measure, and is known as the **Stere.**

248. A **Gramme** is the weight of a quantity of water, at 32° Fahr. (the temperature of melting ice), contained in a cube of the *one-hundredth part of a metre.*

249. The names of the *multiples* of these integers are derived from the Greek, and those of the *divisions* from the Latin language.

Deca	signifies	10 times.		Deci,	the	10th part.
Hecto	"	100 "		Centi,	"	100th "
Kilo	"	1000 "		Mille,	"	1000th "
Myria	"	10000 "				

MONEY.

10 Centimes = 1 Decime.
10 Decimes, or 100 Centimes = 1 FRANC.

250. The French coin is based upon the unit of weight,—the *gramme.*

251. Silver is the legal standard of value in France. The franc in silver is valued at 9.384 pence sterling. The value of the franc in gold is 9.516 pence sterling, giving fr.25.22 for £1 sterling. The United States Custom-House valuation of the franc is 18.6 cts.; United States Mint price, 19.6 cts.

252. The mint standard for both gold and silver is $\frac{9}{10}$ pure and $\frac{1}{10}$ alloy. The gold coins are the napoleon, of 20 francs, and the 100, 50, 10, and 5 franc pieces.

A kilogramme of standard gold is coined into 155 twenty-franc pieces.

The silver coins are the silver napoleon, of 5 francs, and the 2, 1, ½, and ¼ franc pieces.

The copper or bronze pieces are 10, 5, 2, and 1 centimes, weighing, respectively, 10, 5, 2, and 1 grammes.

253. Accounts were formerly kept in livres tournoise, with its subdivisions of the sou and denier. 12 deniers = 1 sou or sol, 20 sous = 1 livre tournoise, 24 livres = 1 louis-d'or, 3 livres = 1 ecu or crown, 81 livres = 80 francs.

WEIGHTS.

Gramme = 15.432349 grains Troy.

The kilogramme (1000 grammes) is the weight most frequently used in commerce, and is equal to 2.679227 lbs. (2 lbs. 8 oz. 3 dwt.) Troy; or, 2.204621 lbs. (2 lbs. 3 oz. 4.652 dr.) avoirdupois. A kilogramme is generally taken as $2\frac{1}{5}$ lbs.

373¼ grammes = 1 lb. Troy. 453⅗ grammes = 1 lb. avoirdupois.
1 cwt. = 50.80234 kilogrammes.
100 myriogrammes = 1 ton, $20\frac{1}{6}$ lbs.
1 quintal métrique = 100 kilogrammes.

NOTE.—At the U. S. Post-Office, 15 grammes are taken as ½ oz.

MEASURES OF LENGTH.

1 METRE = 39.371 English inches.
1 decimetre = 3.9371 " "
1 kilometre = 0.62138 miles.
1 Eng. mile = 1.609036 kilometres.

Old Measure.—1 aune = $1\frac{1}{4}$ yds. 1 brace = $\frac{5}{8}$ yds. See Art. 73.
Merchants usually reckon the metre as *one and one-twelfth* yards.

MEASURES OF SURFACE.

1 ARE = a square decametre = 119.6046 sq. yds.
1 centiare = 10.76441 sq. ft.
1 " = 1.196046 sq. yds.
1 hectare = 2 acres, 1 rood, 35 perches.
1 acre, Eng. = .40466 hectares.
100 sq. ft. = 9.28987 sq. metres.

MEASURES OF CAPACITY.

1 LITRE = 61.02803 cubic inches.
1 " = 2.1135 wine pints, or 1.7608 imperial pints, or 908 qts. dry measure.
1 hectolitre = 3.53171 cubic ft. = 22.01 imperial gals., or 26.419 wine gals., or 2.839 Winchester bus.

MEASURES OF SOLIDITY.

1 STERE or kilolitre = 35.31714 cubic feet = .2759 cord.
1 " = 1.308042 " yds.
100 cubic inches = 16.38592 " centimetres.

254. The terms of the Metric System are now generally used by scientific men. Congress, by act of July 27, 1866, made it lawful in contracts and in legal proceedings to employ the weights and measures of the Metric System; and Great Britain, in 1864, passed an act authorizing its use.

SYNOPSIS OF

FOREIGN MONEYS OF ACCOUNT.

Money at		Dolls. Cts.
Amsterdam, 5 cents = 1 stiver, 20 stivers = 1 guilder or florin.	1 florin	= .40
Berlin, 30 silver groschen = 1 thaler.	1 thaler	= .69
Bremen, 5 schwaren = 1 grote, 72 grotes = 1 rix-daler, 5 rix-dalers = 1 louis-d'or.	1 s. daler	= .79$\frac{7}{8}$
Calcutta, 12 pies = 1 anna, 16 annas = 1 rupee.	1 rupee	= .44$\frac{1}{2}$
Christiania, 120 skilling = 1 specie-daler. 1 banco rix-dollar = .39$\frac{3}{4}$.	1 s. daler	= 1.06
Constantinople, 40 paras = 1 piastre, 100 piastres = 1 medjidie.	1 medjidie	= 3.35
Copenhagen, 96 skilling = 1 rigsbank daler. 1 banco rix-dollar = .55.	1 s. daler	= 1.05
Frankfort, 60 kreutzer = 1 Zollverein florin or guilder.	1 florin	= .40
Genoa, 100 centesimi = 1 lira Italiana.	1 lira	= .18$\frac{6}{10}$
Hamburg, 12 pfenning = 1 schilling, 16 schilling = 1 mark.	1 m. banco	= .35$\frac{1}{2}$
Lisbon, 1000 reis = 1 milreis.	1 milreis	= 1.12
London, 240 pence = 12 shillings = 1 pound.	1 pound	= 4.86
Madrid, 34 maravedis = 1 real, 20 reals = 1 duro.	1 duro	= 1.00
Naples, 10 grani = 1 carlino, 10 carlini = 1 ducat.	1 ducat	= .80
New York, 100 cents = 1 dollar.		
Palermo, 20 grani = 1 taro, 30 tari = 1 onza.	1 onza	= 2.40
Paris, 100 centimes = 1 franc.	1 franc	= .19$\frac{6}{10}$
Pekin, 1 tael = 10 mace = 100 candareens = 1000 cash.	1 tael	= 1.48
Rio de Janeiro, 1000 reis = 1 milreis.	1 milreis	= .51$\frac{1}{4}$
Rome, 10 bajocchi = 1 paolo, 10 paoli = 1 scudo Romano.	1 s. Romano	= .99$\frac{1}{2}$
St. Petersburg, 100 copeck = 1 silver rouble.	1 s. rouble	= .75
Stockholm, 12 runstyken = 1 skilling, 48 skillingar = 1 daler in banco.	1 daler	= 1.06
Venice, 100 centesimi = 1 lira Austriaca, 3 lire Austriache = 1 florin Austriaco.	1 lira	= .16
Vienna, 100 kreutzer = 1 gulden or florin.	1 florin	= .48$\frac{1}{2}$

COMPARATIVE TABLES OF WEIGHTS AND MEASURES.

1 Imperial Gallon = 277.274 cubic inches = 1.2 Wine Gallons.

Wine Measure,	1 quart = 57¾	"	1 gall. = 231 cubic inches.
Dry "	1 " = 67⅕	"	1 " = 268 "
Beer "	1 " = 70½	"	1 " = 282 "

Troy Weight, Apothecaries' Weight, } 1 pound = 5760 grains.
Avoirdupois " 1 " = 7000 "
175 lbs. Troy = 144 lbs. Avoirdupois.

Dry Measure,	1 Bushel of U. S. (Winchester bu.)	= 2150.42 cub. in.
"	1 Imperial Bushel of Great Britain	= 2218.192 "
"	1 Bushel U. S. heaped measure	= 2747.7167 "

FOREIGN WEIGHTS AND MEASURES

FREQUENTLY MET WITH IN REPORTS OF MARKETS.

Ahm, in Rotterdam . (nearly) . .	40 gallons.
Almude, in Portugal	4.37 "
Almude, in Madeira	4 to 8 gallons.
Alquiere, in Madeira	1⅝ to 2 pecks.
" in Bahia	1 bushel.
" in Maranham	1¼ "
" in Rio Janeiro	1 to 1¼ bushels.
" in Pernambuco	1 to 1¼ "
Anna of rice, in Ceylon	260.4 lbs.
Arroba, in Portugal	32 "
" in Spain	25 "
" of wine, in Spain (large) . .	4.246 gallons.
" " " (small) . . .	3.34 "
Arroba, in Malaga	4¼ "
Arsheen, in Russia	28 inches.
Bahar, in Batavia (large)	4½ piculs.
" " (small)	3 "
Bale of cinnamon, in Ceylon (net) . .	104⅝ lbs.
Barilla, in Naples	11 gallons.
Cantar, in the Levant	118.8 lbs.
" of oil, in Leghorn	88 "
" of brandy "	120 "
" in Malta	174½ "
" (grosso) in Naples	196½ "
" (piccolo) "	106 "
" (grosso) in Sicily	192½ "
" (sottile) "	175 "
Carro, in Naples	52.2 bushels.
" of wine, in Naples	264 gallons.

Catta of tea, in China	1⅓ lbs.
Cayang of rice, in Batavia	3581 lbs.
Chetwert, in Russia	5.95 bushels.
Fanega, in Spain	1.6 “
Hectolitre, in France	2.84 bus. or 26.42 gallons
Kilogramme, in France and Netherlands	2⅕ lbs.
Last of grain, in Amsterdam	85¼ “
“ “ in Bremen	80⅔ “
“ of salt, in Cadiz	75⅘ bushels.
“ or moyo of salt, in Portugal	70 “
“ of grain, in Dantzic (nearly)	93 “
“ “ in Flushing	92½ “
“ “ in Hamburg	89.7 “
“ “ in Lubeck	91 “
“ “ in Rotterdam	85$\frac{3}{16}$ “
“ in Sweden	75 “
“ Utrecht	59+ “
Lispound, in Hamburg	14 lbs.
Mark, in Holland	9 ounces.
Maund (factory), in Calcutta	74⅝ lbs.
“ (bazaar), 10% heavier	82.4 “
Mina of grain, in Genoa	3.43 bushels.
Moyo, of Lisbon	23+ “
“ in Oporto	30 “
Oke, in Smyrna	2.83 lbs.
Orna (or eimer) of wine, in Trieste	14.94 gallons.
“ of oil “	17 “
Palmo, in Naples	10⅓ inches.
Picul, in Batavia and Madras	136 lbs.
“ in China and Japan	133⅓ “
Pipe of wine, in Spain	160+ gallons.
Pood, in Russia	36 lbs. 1 oz. 10 drs
Quintal, in Portugal	89.05 lbs.
“ in Smyrna	127.2 “
“ (of 4 arrobas), in Spain	100 “
“ in Turkey	124½ “
“ of cotton (45 okes), in Turkey	127.3 “
Rottolo, in Portugal	12¼ “
Rottolo, in Genoa	24 “
“ in Leghorn	8 “
Salma of grain, in Sicily	9.77 bushels.
“ (general) “	7.85 “
“ of wine “	23.06 gallons.
Scheffel, in Germany	1½ to 3 bushels.
Ship pound, in Denmark	352 lbs.
“ “ in Hamburg	299½ “
Staro (or stajo), in Trieste	2.34 + bushels.
Tale, in China	1⅓ ounces
Vara, in Rio Janeiro (nearly)	1¼ yards.
“ in Spain	9⅕ “

EXCHANGE.

255. The term Exchange, in commerce, signifies the giving or receiving of one currency for its value in another; or, the method of making payments by means of written orders without the transmission of money. See Bills of Exchange.

256. Exchange is of two kinds, *Domestic* or *Inland*, and *Foreign*.

257. Domestic Exchange includes the exchanges made within the limits of one country.

258. Foreign Exchange relates to the transactions between different countries.

Foreign Exchange comprises *Nominal Exchange* and *Real Exchange*.

259. Nominal Exchange has reference to the comparative market value of the currencies of different countries.

260. Real Exchange is that which relates to the inter change of commodities without reference to the precious metals.

261. The **True** or **Intrinsic Par of Exchange** between two countries is the *exact equivalent of pure metal* in the coined piece which forms the unit of price of one country compared with the currency of the other. The alloy is reckoned of no value.

262. "Thus, according to the mint regulations of Great Britain and France, £1 sterling is equal to 25 fr. 20 cent., which is said to be the par between London and Paris. Exchange between the two countries is said to be at par when bills are negotiated at this rate; that is, when a bill for £100 drawn in London is worth 2520 francs in Paris, and conversely. When £1 in London buys a bill on Paris for more than 25 fr. 20 cent., the exchange is said to be in favor of London and against Paris; when £1 in London will not buy a bill on Paris for 25 fr. 20 cent., exchange is against London and in favor of Paris.

263. "Exchange is made to diverge from par by any discrepancy between the actual weight or fineness of the coins and the mint standard, and by the variations in the demand and supply of bills of exchange.

"The cost of conveying bullion or coin forms the limit within which the rise and fall of real exchange is confined; for if a merchant can send a bill for less than the expense of sending gold, he will send a bill, but if sending a bill would cost more than the expense and risk of sending gold, then he will send gold."

264. The **Commercial Par of Exchange** is the market value of the currency of one country when sold for the currency of another.

265. The **Course** or **Rate of Exchange** is the current prices of exchanges, or the *variable* price of the money of one country which is paid for a *fixed* amount of that of another country.

DOMESTIC EXCHANGE.

266. The calculations connected with Domestic Exchange require only the ordinary applications of Percentage.

EXAMPLES.

1. What is the cost of a bill for $240 on New York, purchased at 1¼% premium? Ans. $243.

2. What is the cost of a draft on New Orleans for $1800, at 1¾% premium?

3. Sold $375 uncurrent money at 2¼% discount. How much did I receive? How much did I lose?

4. Exchanged $600 in bank notes for gold at 5% premium. How much did I receive?

5. Bought goods, $1250, and sold them at a profit of 25%; purchased a draft on St. Louis, with the proceeds, at a discount of ¾%. What was the amount of the draft?

6. Shipped goods to Havana, and received a draft for $2500, which gave me a profit of 20%; sold the draft at 4½% premium. How much did I gain by both transactions?

7. A commission merchant sold goods, the net proceeds of which were $2750. How large a draft can he buy to remit to his consignor, if he pays $\frac{1}{2}$% premium for the draft? How large a draft if he purchases at $\frac{1}{2}$% discount?

FOREIGN EXCHANGE.

267. In Foreign Exchange it is usual to reckon the money of one country as fixed, and the other as variable. The country whose money is calculated at a fixed price is said to receive the variable price, while the other country is said to give the variable price. Thus, if I buy a bill of exchange on Paris, I receive so many francs per dollar,—the dollar is the fixed price, and the francs the variable price. If I buy a bill on Hamburg, I pay so many cents per marc banco; the marc banco is called the fixed price, and the cents the variable price. In quotations of exchange rates, it is usual to give only the variable prices.

268. Nearly all the bills of exchange drawn in this country are drawn and negotiated on one of the following places: viz., London, Paris, Bremen, Hamburg, Cologne, Leipsic, Frankfort, and Amsterdam.

QUOTATION OF FOREIGN BILLS OF EXCHANGE,

BY DREXEL & CO., BANKERS, *Philada., June 1, 1866.*

Exchange.			*Explanation.*
On London,	60 days,	109 @ 109$\frac{5}{8}$	Premium (on old par of 4.44$\frac{4}{9}$), from 9 to 9$\frac{5}{8}$ per cent. on bills at 60 days' sight.
" "	3 "	109$\frac{3}{4}$ @ 110$\frac{1}{2}$	Premium from 9$\frac{3}{4}$ to 10$\frac{1}{2}$ per cent. on bills at 3 days' sight.
" Paris,	60 "	5.11	At 5 francs, 11 centimes per dollar.
" "	3 "	5.08	" 5 " 8 " " "
" Bremen,	60 "	.80	" 80 cents per rix-dollar.
" Hamburg,	60 "	.37	" 37 " " marc banco.
" Cologne,	60 "	.73$\frac{1}{2}$	" 73$\frac{1}{2}$ " " thaler.
" Leipsic,	60 "	.74	" 74 " " "
" Frankfort,	60 "	.42	" 42 " " guilder or florin.
" Amsterdam,	60 "	.42 @ .42$\frac{3}{4}$	From 42 to 42$\frac{3}{4}$ cts. per guilder.

See, also, LONDON COURSE OF EXCHANGE.

269. Bills of exchange are drawn in the money of the country in which they are made payable (See FORMS OF BILLS OF EXCHANGE.)

Exchange on England.

270. By the usage of bankers for ages, the pound sterling has been valued by the old Spanish Carolus pillar dollar, now entirely out of circulation in Europe and America; of these, 4.44\frac{4}{9}$ were equivalent to the pound sterling.

This rate originally represented the true par of exchange between the two countries. In 1834 the eagle was reduced in weight to 258 grains (see TABLES OF COINS OF U. S.), and now contains 232.2 grains pure gold.

The English sovereign is the coined piece of which the pound sterling is the money of account, and contains 113.001 grains pure gold.

Standard weight of sovereign, grains	123.274
Alloy, $\frac{1}{12}$ part	10.273
Fine gold in the sovereign . .	113.001

By the proportion—

232.2 grains : 113.001 grains : : $10,

we find that the equivalent of the pound sterling is $4.8665; and, allowing for the wear of coin, we have $4.84, the value established by Congress in 1842, and the rate at which duties are estimated in the Custom-Houses.

It has been found convenient to retain the *old* value as the basis of exchange, and to express the present exchangeable value by a *premium* on this basis. It requires the addition of 9% to make the Custom-House value, and the addition of about 9½% to equal the intrinsic value, of a pound sterling in our currency.

Old par value of £1.	= $4.444	Old par value,	$4.4444
9% premium,	= .399	9½% premium,	.4222
Custom-House value,	$4.8443	Intrinsic value,	$4.8666

Exchange quotations refer to the old par. When, therefore, exchange is quoted at about 9½% premium, there is in fact no real premium, but the true par has been attained. When nothing is said to the contrary, the quotations are for bills at *usance*, or 60 days' sight and 3 days of grace, which, at 6% interest, involves a loss of more than 1% besides the time of transportation. On the other hand, 1% is about the cost, including freight, insurance, &c., of shipping gold; and as one of these items balances the other, the real par of exchange on England is 9½%, at which rate it is as well, or better, to remit good 60-day bills as specie.

PRO FORMA ACCOUNT OF A SHIPMENT OF MEXICAN DOLLARS FROM NEW YORK TO LONDON.

10000 dollars purchased in New York at 1¾ prem. . .	10175.00
Packing Charges, Shipping, &c.	7.50
Insurance at ½% on 10175.00, and Policy $1 . .	51.87
Total cost in New York	$10234.37

	£	s.	d.	£	s.	d.
Value in London, 10000 dollars weighing 8660 ounces, and sold at 58⅛ pence per ounce				2097	6	11
Charges in London, Freight, ¼% . .	5	4	9			
Primage, 5%		5	2			
Landing Charges, Postage, &c. . .		13	9			
Brokerage, ⅛%, Com. ½% = ⅝% =	13	2	2	19	5	11
Net Proceeds, Cash, in London . . .				2078	1	0
Add Interest for 63 days, at 4%				14	10	11
				£2092	11	11

Par of £2092 11*s.* 11*d.* = $9300.43. This amount drawn at 60 days' sight, to produce the above $10234.37, would establish the rate of exchange on London at 110.04 per cent.

Gold is sometimes exported when exchange is quoted below the true par, by bankers who have branch-houses and therefore no commissions to cover, and who insure their own risks; by those who can save a guaranty commission on commercial bills, and by those who are compelled to procure specie.

Exports of Specie from New York for the week ending June 2, 1866, to Liverpool, Southampton, Havre, Bremen, and Hamburg.

May 30,	American Gold,	$2,715,700
" "	French "	6,208
" "	Spanish "	9,492
" 31,	American "	485,000
June 1,	" "	1,645,197
" "	Gold and Silver bars,	14,800
" "	Sovereigns,	62,920
" 2,	Gold and Silver bars,	82,500
		5,021,817
	Amount bro't forwa d,	$5,021,817
June 2,	Foreign Coin and American Gold,	1,179,468
" "	German Silver,	2,000
" "	Mexican "	40,828
" "	Silver Coin,	20,000
" "	American Gold,	606,834
" "	Foreign Coin,	5C
	Total for the week,	$6,870,997

RULES FOR COMPUTING STERLING EXCHANGE,

USED BY BANKERS AND DEALERS IN EXCHANGE.

271. The par value of a pound sterling, 4.44\frac{4}{9}$, equals 4\frac{4}{9}$, or $\frac{40}{9}$ dollars; and as there are 40 sixpences in a pound, 1 sixpence is equal to $\frac{1}{9}$ of a dollar. To find the real value, a premium must be added.

272. TO FIND THE VALUE OF STERLING MONEY.

RULE I.—*Reduce the pounds and shillings to sixpences, by multiplying the pounds by 40 and the shillings by 2; to their sum add 1, if the pence equal or exceed 6; divide by 9, and to the quotient add the given premium, and 2 cents for every penny exceeding 6 in the given number of pence.*

EXAMPLE.

1. What is the value in U. S. Currency of £540 7*s.* 7*d.*, at a premium of 9½ %?

```
540 × 40 =   21600
  7 ×  2 =      14
 7 = 6 + 1 =     1
           9)21615
             2401.6667
                   9½%
             216150003
              12008333
             228.158336 Premium.
            2401.6666
            2629.824936
Value of 1d.,       2
           $2629.84
```

RULE II.—*Reduce the pounds and shillings to sixpences, and to their sum add ⅙ the number of pence; then divide by 9, and to the quotient add the given premium.*

EXAMPLE GIVEN UNDER RULE I.

```
  7 ÷  6 =      1.166
  7 ×  2 =     14
540 × 40 =  21600
           9)21615.166
              2401.685  Par value
                    9½  per cent.
            216.15165
             12.00842
            228.16007   Premium.
           2401.685
   Ans.   $2629.845
```

2. Reduce £1872 11*s.* 5*d.* to dollars at par. Ans. $8322.54.

3. Reduce £617 1*s.* 1*d.* to United States currency at 9% premium. Ans. $2989.28.

4. What is the value of £1500 at 8% premium?

5. What will be the cost of the following bill of exchange at 8¾% premium?

£150. NEW YORK, June 13, 1866.

Sixty days after sight of this FIRST of EXCHANGE (Second and Third of same tenor and date unpaid), pay to the order of R. J. Milligan One Hundred and Fifty Pounds, value received, and charge the same to account of

BROWN & BROS.

To BROWN, SHIPLEY & Co.,
Liverpool, England.

273. To reduce Federal money to Sterling.

RULE I.—*Divide the given amount by the value of £1 at the given premium.*

RULE II.—*Multiply the given amount by 9, and divide the product by 40; annex two ciphers to the quotient, and divide by 100 increased by the premium.*

EXAMPLES.

1. A commission merchant wishes to remit $7071.57 to

England. How large a bill of exchange can he purchase at 9% premium?

7071.57	1591.1033
9	100
40)63644.13	109)159110.3300
1591.1033	1459.7277
	20
	14.5540
	12
Ans. £1459 14*s.* 6½*d.*	6.6480

2. What amount of exchange can I buy for $3567 60 at 8½% premium? £739 16*s.* 6*d.*

3. Purchased a bill of exchange, at 9⅝% premium, which cost $4275. How large was the bill?

4. How large a bill of exchange can I buy for $2850, if I pay 9¼% premium?

The cost of goods imported from England is often estimated by adding the proportion of charges to the value of the pound or shilling. For example:—

An invoice amounts to £2400, which, with	
Exchange at 9% premium =	$11626.66
Duties, freight, and other charges, amount to	600.34
Making the total cost	$12227.00

Then, if £2400 cost $12227, one pound cost 12227 ÷ 2400 = $5.09½ nearly, and 1 shilling costs 25½ cts., 1 penny 2⅛ cts. Cloth at 16*d.* per yd. would cost 33 cents.

TABLE

Showing the value of £1 sterling from 4 to 12½ per cent. premium on the old par of $4.44⅘.

Old par	$4.444	7¾ per cent.	$4.789	9⅝ per cent.	$4.872
4 per cent.	4.622	8% (Eng. fr'ts)	4.800	9¾ "	4.878
4½ "	4.644	8¼ per cent.	4.811	9⅞ "	4.883
5 "	4.667	8½ "	4.822	10 "	4.889
5½ "	4.689	8¾ "	4.833	10⅛ "	4.894
6 "	4.711	9 (Cust.-House)	4.844	10½ "	4.911
6½ "	4.733	9⅛ per cent.	4.850	11 "	4.933
7 "	4.756	9¼ "	4.856	11½ "	4.956
7¼ "	4.767	9⅜ "	4.861	12 "	4.978
7½ "	4.778	9½ "	4.867	12½ "	5.000

STERLING TABLE.

Calculated at the Par Value of $4.444 to £1 Sterling.

£	$ cts. m.	£	$ cts. m.	£	$ cts. m.	Shill'gs.	$ cts. m
1	4.44.4	41	182.22.2	81	360.00.0	1	0.22.2
2	8.88.9	42	186.66.7	82	364.44.4	2	0.44.4
3	13.33.3	43	191.11.1	83	368.88.9	3	0.66.7
4	17.77.8	44	195.55.6	84	373.33.3	4	0.88.9
5	22.22.2	45	200.00.0	85	377.77.8	5	1.11.1
6	26.66.7	46	204.44.4	86	382.22.2	6	1.33.3
7	31.11.1	47	208.88.9	87	386.66.7	7	1.55.6
8	35.55.6	48	213.33.3	88	391.11.1	8	1.77.8
9	40.00.0	49	217.77.8	89	395.55.6	9	2.00.0
10	44.44.4	**50**	222.22.2	**90**	400.00.0	**10**	2.22.2
11	48.88.9	51	226.66.7	91	404.44.4	11	2.44.4
12	53.33.3	52	231.11.1	92	408.88.9	12	2.66.7
13	57.77.8	53	235.55.6	93	413.33.3	13	2.88.9
14	62.22.2	54	240.00.0	94	417.77.8	14	3.11.1
15	66.66.7	55	244.44.4	95	422.22.2	15	3.33.3
16	71.11.1	56	248.88.9	96	426.66.7	16	3.55.6
17	75.55.6	57	253.33.3	97	431.11.1	17	3.77.8
18	80.00.0	58	257.77.8	98	435.55.6	18	4.00.0
19	84.44.5	59	262.22.2	99	440.00.0	19	4.22.2
20	88.88.9	**60**	266.66.7	**100**	444.44.4	**20**	4.44.4
						Pence.	**$ cts. m.**
21	93.33.3	61	271.11.1				
22	97.77.8	62	275.55.6	200	888.88.9	1	0.01.9
23	102.22.2	63	280.00.0	300	1333.33.3	2	0.03.7
24	106.66.7	64	284.44.4	400	1777.77.8	3	0.05.6
25	111.11.1	65	288.88.9	500	2222.22.2	4	0.07.4
26	115.55.6	66	293.33.3	600	2666.66.7	5	0.09.3
27	120.00.0	67	297.77.8	700	3111.11.1		
28	124.44.4	68	302.22.2	800	3555.55.6	6	0.11.1
29	128.88.9	69	306.66.7	900	4000.00.0	7	0.13.0
30	133.33.3	**70**	311.11.1	**1000**	4444.44.4	8	0.14.8
						9	0.16.7
31	137.77.8	71	315.55.6	1100	4888.88.9	10	0.18.5
32	142.22.2	72	320.00.0	1200	5333.33.3		
33	146.66.7	73	324.44.4	1300	5777.77.8	11	0.20.4
34	151.11.1	74	328.88.9	1400	6222.22.2	**12**	0.22.2
35	155.55.6	75	333.33.3	1500	6666.66.7		
36	160.00.0	76	337.77.8	1600	7111.11.1		
37	164.44.4	77	342.22.2	1700	7555.55.6	¼	0.00.5
38	168.88.9	78	346.66.7	1800	8000.00.0	½	0.00.9
39	173.33.3	79	351.11.1	1900	8444.44.4		
40	177.77.8	**80**	355.55.6	**2000**	8888.88.9	¾	0.01.4

(See, also, IMPORTERS' ADVANCE TABLE.)

To find the value of any given amount not mentioned in the table, take the sum of those numbers that will equal the given amount.

London Course of Exchange.

274. London has been called the great clearing-house of the world. Nearly all the foreign trade of the United States is settled through England and France.

LONDON RECEIVES FROM, OR GIVES TO,

Variable, according to the exchanges,

Amsterdam	12 florins and 3 stivers	for	£1 sterling.	
Bremen	609¼ rix-dollars	"	£100 sterling.	
Berlin	6 dollars, 25 silver groschen	"	£1	"
Christiania	4 specie-daler, 30 skilling	"	"	"
Constantinople	140 piastres	"	"	"
Copenhagen	9 rigsbank daler, 10 skilling	"	"	"
Frankfort	121 Zollverein florins	"	£10	"
Genoa	25 lire, 35 centesimi	"	£1	"
Hamburg	13 marks, 12 schillings	"	"	"
Milan	25 lire, 40 cents	"	"	"
Leghorn	25 " 50 "	"	"	"
Paris	25 francs, 21 centimes	"	"	"
Rome	46 Paoli	"	"	"
Stockholm	12 dalers in banco, 1 skilling	"	"	"
Vienna	13 florins, 70 kreuzers	"	"	"

Calcutta	23	pence	sterling	for	1 Comp. rupee.
Gibraltar	48½	"	"	"	1 duro, or hard dollar, or Spanish dollar.
Lisbon	53¼	"	"	"	1 milreis.
Madrid	50¼	"	"	"	1 hard dollar.
Naples	39⅝	"	"	"	1 ducat.
New York	49½	"	"	"	1 U. S. dollar.
Palermo	119½	"	"	"	1 onza.
Pekin	78¼	"	"	"	a thousand cash.
Rio Janeiro	30	"	"	"	1 milreis.
St. Petersburg	38¼	"	"	"	1 silver rouble.
Venice	47	"	"	"	6 lire Austriache.

(See, also, SYNOPSIS OF MONEYS OF ACCOUNT.)

Exchange on France.

100 Centimes make 1 Franc.

1. What is the cost of a bill of exchange on Paris for fr.10277.76—exchange at fr.4.89 per dollar?

Ans. $2101.79.

2. What must be paid for a bill on Paris for fr.3875.50, at fr.5.19 per dollar?

3. What is the difference between the Custom-House value of 18.6 cts. per franc, and exchange at fr.5.19 per dollar, on a bill for 58000 francs?

4. Estimating fr.5.21 to be the par value of $1, what is the premium on gold when exchange for currency is quoted at fr.3.45 per dollar?

PRO FORMA ACCOUNT OF A SHIPMENT OF MEXICAN DOLLARS FROM NEW YORK TO PARIS.

10000 dollars purchased at $1\frac{3}{4}$ premium,				10175.00
Packing Charges, Shipping, &c.,				7.50
Marine Insurance, at $\frac{1}{2}$% on $10175.00,			50.87	
Policy,			1.	51.87
Total cost in New York,				$10234.37
Value in Paris 10000 dollars sold at fr.5.34				fr.53400.00
Charges in Havre:—				
Import Duty and Permits,		fr.6.40		
Cartage, Cooperage, &c.,		10.10		
Freight, $\frac{1}{4}$% on $10000,	25.00			
Primage, 10%,	2.50			
At fr.5.25,	$27.50 =	144.37	160.87	
Charges in Paris:—				
Freight,	fr.72.25			
Viewing and Delivering,	3.25			
Brokerage $\frac{1}{8}$%, Com. $\frac{1}{2}$% = $\frac{5}{8}$%,	333.75		409.25	570.12
Net proceeds, cash, in Paris,				fr.52829.88
Add Interest for 63 days, at 4%,				369.80
Total,				fr.53199.68

This amount drawn at 60 days' sight, to realize the above $10234.37, will require the rate of exchange to be fr.5.20 per dollar. Without commission in Paris, the rate would be fr.$5.22\frac{1}{3}$, or $\frac{1}{2}$% lower.

CUSTOM-HOUSE BUSINESS.

275. **Custom-Houses** are houses or offices established by government for the collection of duties on commodities entered for importation or exportation, where bounties and drawbacks upon such importations or exportations are paid or received, and where vessels are entered and cleared, &c.

276. **Ports of Entry** are places at which custom-houses are established; and it is lawful to introduce merchandise into a country only at these places.

277. Vessels arriving at any port of the United States must report at the Custom-House within twenty-four hours after their arrival, and within forty-eight hours must enter, or make a further report, which shall contain all the particulars required to be inserted in a manifest.

278. Manifests, or invoices, must be produced, containing particulars of goods, with their cost in the currency of the country from whence imported. When no invoice has been received, and the owner or consignee has testified under oath that such is the case, the goods are entered by appraisement. When the value exceeds $100, permission must first be obtained from the Secretary of the Treasury to enter in this manner. If the invoice or entry does not contain the right gauge or measurement of the goods, they must be weighed, gauged, or measured at the expense of the importer. When the value of the foreign currency is not fixed by any law of the United States, the invoice must be accompanied by a consular certificate, showing its value in specie, or United States dollars; and in default thereof, a bond for the production of such certificate will be required.

279. **Specific Duty** is rated at a specified amount upon each article, ton, yard, ℔., &c., without regard to its value.

280. **Ad-Valorem Duty** is rated at a certain per cent.

upon the cost of the goods in the country from which they were imported.

281. In estimating duties, certain allowances are made for the package, waste, or damage, as it is the design of the government to tax only so much of the goods as may actually arrive and be available in the market.

282. **Tare** is the allowance made for the weight of the package containing the goods, in the manner prescribed by law. In some cases it is reckoned at so much per package, sometimes at a certain percentage, and sometimes by actual weight or measurement.

283. **Draft** is the allowance made for waste or impurities.

284. **Leakage** is an allowance made for waste on liquids. Breakage is an allowance on liquors imported in bottles.

285. **Gross Weight** is the entire weight of goods and packages combined.

286. **Net Weight** is the weight after all allowances have been deducted.

287. **Tonnage** is the amount paid per ton on the vessel for permission to enter port.

288. **Warehousing** is the placing of goods in public store, or bonded warehouse, in charge of the government, when the importer does not wish to withdraw the goods or pay the duties immediately. All goods so deposited must be withdrawn, or the duties thereon paid, within one year; and all goods remaining beyond three years are regarded as abandoned to the government, and sold under regulations prescribed by the Secretary of the Treasury.

289. **A Custom-House Broker** is one who attends to making the proper entries of goods at the custom-house, for merchants. As there is a great variety of points involving special questions for each separate invoice, style of merchandise, and form of entry, the services of a responsible custom-house broker will materially aid those who are inexperienced

TABLE OF FOREIGN MONEYS,

As fixed by law for estimating duties at the United States Custom-House.

For all others a consular certificate is required.

	$. cts.	Lower Denominations.	
Ducat of Naples	.80	10 carlini	each, 10 grani.
Florin or Guilder of Austria, Augsburg, and Bohemia	.48½	60 kreutzers	" 4 pfennings.
Florin or Guilder of Frankfort, Nuremberg, and Southern Germany.	.40	60 kreutzers	" 4 "
Florin of Netherlands	.40	100 centimes.	
Florin of Trieste	.48½	60 kreutzers	" 4 "
Franc of France and Belgium	.18$\frac{6}{10}$	100 centimes.	
Lira of Lombardo-Ven. Kingdom	.16	100 "	
Lira of Sardinia	.18$\frac{6}{10}$	4 reali	" 20 solidi.
Lira of Tuscany	.16	20 soldi	" 12 denari.
Livre of Leghorn	.16	20 "	" 12 "
Livre of Genoa	.18$\frac{6}{10}$	20 "	" 12 "
Livre Tournois of France	.18½		
Louis d'or, or Rix-dollar of Bremen.	.78¾	72 grotes	" 5 schwaren.
Marc Banco of Hamburg	.35	16 schillings	" 12 pfennings.
Milrea of Azores 83⅓, Madeira 1.00, Portugal 1.12		1000 reis.	
Onza or Ounce of Sicily	2.40	30 tari	" 20 grani.
Pagoda of India	1.94	36 fanams	" 48 jittas.
Pound sterling of Great Britain and Ireland, and Jamaica	4.84	20 shillings	" 12 pence.
Pound sterling of Canada, British Provinces, Newfoundland, Nova Scotia, and New Brunswick	4.00	20 "	" 12 "
Pagoda Star of Madras	1.84	42 fanams	" 80 cash.
Real Plate of Spain	.10	34 maravedis	
Real Vellon of Spain	.5	34 "	
Rouble (or Ruble) Silver, Russia	.75	100 copecks.	
Rupee of Company and of British India	.44½	16 annas	" 12 pyce.
Specie dollar of Denmark	1.05	6 marks	" 16 skilling.
Specie dollar of Norway	1.06	6 "	" 16 "
Specie dollar of Sweden	1.06	48 skilling	" 12 oefre.
Tael of China	1.48	10 mace	" 10 candareens.
Thaler or dollar of Bremen, of 72 grotes	.71	72 grotes	" 5 schwaren.
Thaler or Rix-dollar of Prussia, Berlin, Leipsic, Northern Germany, and Saxony	.69	30 groschen	" 12 pfennings.
Dollar of Mexico, Peru, Chili, Central America, and Cuba	1.00	8 shillings.	

290. The ton in all cases is taken at 2240 lbs. In weights and currencies, less than one-half a pound or one-half a dollar is disregarded; more than one-half is taken as one.

1. What is the duty to be paid on the following invoice, at the rate of 35 % ad valorem and 50 cents per lb. specific duty?

Invoice of Merchandise purchased by BELL & CO. *for account and risk of* CADE, BROTHERS & CO., *Philadelphia, forwarded to Liverpool for shipment per steamer "Persia."*

HUDDERSFIELD, ENG., 10th Dec. 1867.

Mark	Description	yds.	Rate	£	s.	d.
D ◇ P	7 pieces 56 inch Fancy Coatings (all wool).					
547	※1128 46¼ ※1136 43¾					
	1130 45 1138 45¾					
	1131 46¾ 1161 46¼	319¼				
	1137 45½ damage,	1½				
		317¾				
	Deduct $\frac{1}{37}$ overmeasure,	8½				
		309¼	11/3 6*d.*	173	19	1
	7 ps. making up,				3	6
	Sample Card, 3/-, Case, 23/-, Carriage, 5/-,			1	11	6
				175	14	1
	Commission, 2½ per cent.,			4	7	10
				180	1	11
	2½ per cent. discount on £173. 19. 1.,			4	6	11
				175	15	0
	Consul's certificate,				10	4
	Gross Weight, 654 lbs.			£176	5	4
	Net " 539 "					
	Cash, Dec. 10, 1867.					

Extract from Bill of Lading.

D ◇ P 547

Shipped by WESTON & Co., on "*Persia*," from Liverpool to New York, one Case, marked as pr. margin, and consigned to CADE, BROS. & CO., Philadelphia. LIVERPOOL, 13th Dec. /67.

Feet.	In.			£	s.	d.
35—	3	@ 45/- per ton,		£1.	9.	8
			Primage,		1.	11
				£2.	1.	7

NOTE.—The ton is a ton measurement, 40 cubic feet; the Case is 35 cubic feet 3 in. $\frac{35\frac{1}{4}}{40}$ of 45 shillings = £1. 9. 8. for freight.

Shipping Charges.

Charges on Case D ◇ P 547, shipped by WESTON & Co. pr. Persia for New York, consigned to CADE, BROS. & Co., by order of BELL & Co., Huddersfield.

Dues and entry at Customs,	1.	11
Bills of Lading,	1.	6
Cartage,	2.	9
Commission,	2.	6
	£8.	8

LIVERPOOL, 13th Dec. /67.

Duty.

Invoice Value,	£176. 5. 4	
Deduct Consul fee, not dutiable,	10. 4	
	175. 15. 0	
Liverpool charges,	8. 8	
	£176. 3. 8	
Woolens.		
£176. 3. 8., at $4.84, = $853, duty 35 per cent.,		$298.55
lbs.—539, " 50 cts.,		269.50
	Duty,	$568.05

2. Imported 25 bags canary-seed, weighing 5920 lbs., the tare of which was 75 lbs., and paid duty of $1 per bushel of 60 lbs. How much did I pay?

3. Imported from England, per brig Wellington, 24 sacks wool, weighing 2560 lbs., invoiced at 1*s*. 3*d*. per lb. How much duty did I pay, the rate being 10 cents per lb. and 11 per cent. ad valorem? 3% tare allowed. Ans. $333.50.

4. Paid duties, at 35% ad valorem, on goods imported from France at fr. 7325.25. How much did I pay?

5. H. J. Claflin & Co. imported 10 cases white muslins, 2055 ps. of 20 yds. each, 1¼ yds. wide, on which they paid duties at 4¼ cts. per square yard. The goods cost 2½*d*. pr. yard, and the charges in Manchester amounted to £49 16*s*. 6*d*. If they remitted bills of exchange purchased at 9½% premium in gold, and gold was at a premium of 33½%, what was the total cost? Ans. Duties, $1865.53; total cost, $4970.77.

6. Morse, Shepard & Co. received per "Aurora," from Paris, 5 cases shawls, weighing 1123 lbs. and invoiced at fr. 12,225, on which they paid duties at 22 cts. per lb. and 35 per cent. ad valorem. How much were the duties, and how much did a bill of exchange on Paris to pay for the invoice cost, if purchased at fr. 5.08?
Ans. Duties, $1142.91; Exch., $2406.50.

7. Imported 1 case shawls, weighing 220 lbs., which cost £110 10*s*., and paid as duty 40 cts. per lb. and 35 per cent. ad valorem; 2 cases white muslin, containing 6845 yds., and costing £105 15*s*., the duty on which was 3 cts. per square yard. How much did the goods cost me, if I paid 9½ per cent. exchange premium, and 41 per cent. premium in gold?

PROFIT AND LOSS.

291. The difference between the cost of an article and the amount received for it is the gain or loss.

292. The cost of goods consists of the price paid to the person from whom they were purchased, or the expense of producing them, and all charges, such as commissions, freight, packing, duties, exchange, insurance, drayage, &c., necessary to place the goods in a condition ready for use or sale.

TOTAL GAINS AND LOSSES.

293. The total gains or losses on goods may be easily ascertained, when all are sold, by taking the difference between the cost and selling price; but when part remains unsold—

RULE I.—*Add the value of the merchandise unsold to the amount received for sales, and take the difference between the sum thus obtained and the cost of the merchandise; the difference will be the gain or loss.* Or,

RULE II.—*Find the difference between the amount of sales and the cost of the merchandise;* then—

When there is an excess of COST over SALES—

If the value of the goods remaining unsold is more than this excess, the difference is a gain.

If the value of the goods is less, the difference is a loss.

When the SALES exceed the COST—

Add the value of the goods unsold to the difference between the SALES *and the* COST; *the result will be the gain.*

294. In estimating the value of goods remaining unsold, when an "account of stock" is taken, it is customary to use the invoice or purchase price; but if the market value of the goods has depreciated, either from the nature of the goods or the state of the market, or if there has been a decided advance in prices, an allowance must be made accordingly. A safe rule is, if they are salable goods, to estimate them at what it would cost to replace them.

GAINS AND LOSSES ON PARTICULAR GOODS.

295. CASE I.—To find the gain or loss, when the cost and rate per cent. are given.

RULE.—*Multiply the cost by the rate per cent., and divide by 100.*

NOTE.—The selling price is found by adding the gain to the cost, or deducting the loss.

EXAMPLES.

1. Bought broadcloth for $250, and sold it at 15% advance. How much did I gain?

$250 \times 15 = 3750$ $37.50, Ans.

2. How much do I gain per barrel, if I sell flour which cost $11 per bbl. at a profit of 25%? Ans. $2.75.

3. Bought a cargo of wheat for $11500, and sold it at a profit of 16½%. How much did I gain?

4. A merchant purchased a quantity of lumber for $2200. He paid for freight and drayage $75; commission for selling, $125. He gained 27% on the entire cost. How much was it sold for, and how much did he make?

5. Bought 100 barrels of sugar for $1500.75, which I sold at an advance of 12½%. How much did I gain, and how much did I receive?

6. What difference will it make in the cost per yard to the American merchant who buys his goods in England for $4 per yard, and pays a duty of 30% on them, if the price in England is reduced to $3 per yard?

EXAMPLES.

1. What is the selling price of the following goods at 25% above the given price?

5 gross steel pens, gr. $\frac{1}{.60}$, $\frac{2}{\$1.00}$, $\frac{2}{\$1.20}$. (See ABBREVIATIONS.)
20 diamond satin bonnets, @ 30c.
50 doz. tassels, @ $1.50 per doz.
1 case, 12 pairs men's calf sewed boots, @ $4.
3 " 60 " misses' lasting gaiter boots, @ $1.40.
8 ps. mousseline de laine, 240 yds., @ 60c.
12 doz. bl'k Italian cravats, @ doz. $\frac{3}{\$12}$, $\frac{2}{\$15}$, $\frac{7}{\$16}$.

296. CASE II.—To find the rate per cent., when the gain or loss, or cost and selling price, are given.

RULE.—*Multiply the gain or loss by 100, and divide the product by the cost.*

EXAMPLES.

1. Sold a house for $7995, which cost me $6500. What per cent. did I gain?

$7995 - 6500 = 1495 \qquad 1495 \times 100 = 149500$
$149500 \div 6500 = 23.$ Ans. 23%.

2. Bought a cargo of flour for $18000, and sold it for $20000. What per cent. did I gain?

3. If by a decline of prices I was obliged to sell a lot of coffee for $2200 which cost me $2500, what per cent. did I lose?

4. A merchant bought a quantity of silks at $2.50 per yard, and sold them at $2.87½. What per cent. did he make?

297. CASE III.—To ascertain the cost, when the selling price and rate per cent. gained or lost are given.

RULE.—*Multiply the selling price by 100, and divide the product by 100 increased by the gain per cent. or diminished by the loss per cent.*

EXAMPLES.

1. An invoice of goods purchased in England was sold for $3600, realizing a gain of 20%. What was the cost?

$100 + 20 = 120 \qquad 360000 \div 120 = 3000.$
Ans. $3000.

2. A merchant sold sugar for $1260, by which he lost 10%. What was the cost?

$100 - 10 = 90 \qquad 126000 \div 90 = 1400.$
Ans. $1400.

298. CASE IV.—To find the cost, when the gain or loss and the rate per cent. are given.

RULE.—*Multiply the gain or loss by 100, and divide the product by the rate per cent.*

EXAMPLES.

1. I gained $2250 by selling goods at a profit of 15%. What did they cost?

225000 ÷ 15 = 15000. Ans. $15000.

2. How large sales must I make, at a profit of 12½ per cent., to clear $3000? Ans. $27000.

3. Sold flour at an advance of 20%, and gained $136. What did it cost?

299. CASE V.—To find the rate, when the cost and gain or loss are given.

RULE.—*Multiply the gain or loss by 100, and divide by the cost.*

EXAMPLES.

1. Bought goods for $1875, and sold them so as to gain $468.75. What was the rate per cent.?

46875 ÷ 1875 = 25. Ans. 25%.

2. Sold teas which cost me 45 cts. per pound, and gained 9 cts. per pound. What was the rate of gain?

3. A merchant sold corn which cost him $325, and gained $48.75. What was the gain per cent.?

4. If the United States wine gallon contains 231 cubic inches, and the beer gallon 282 cubic inches, what per cent. is the latter larger than the former?

5. What per cent. do I gain if I sell cloth which cost $2.50 for $3.75 per yard?

300. To find what the gain or loss per cent. would be if sold at another price, the selling price and rate per cent. of gain or loss being given.

RULE.—*Multiply the proposed selling price by 100, increased by the given rate per cent. gained, or diminished by the given per cent. of loss, and divide the product by the actual selling price, and take the difference between the quotient and 100.*

EXAMPLES.

1. If by selling cloth at $5 per yard I gain 25%, what per cent. will I gain if I sell it at $6 per yard?

100 + 25 = 125   125 × 6 = 750
750 ÷ 5 = 150   150 — 100 = 50. Ans. 50%.

2. Sold flour for $10, and lost 20%. What per cent. would I have lost if I had sold it for $8? Ans. 36%.

PREMIUM AND DISCOUNT.

301. Premium is the percentage by which an amount is increased. **Discount,** the percentage by which an amount is diminished.

302. In purchasing one currency with another of different value, the discount on that of the highest value is not the same as the premium on that of the lowest at the same rate.

$100 in currency, at a discount of 5%, is worth $95 in gold. $95 in gold, at a premium of 5%, is worth 95 + 4.75 = 99.75.

303. Merchants are usually allowed a discount of 5% on invoices and bills purchased at 6 months' credit, for cash payment within 30 days. The 5% is allowed on the amount of the bill or invoice; but often, when part is paid, the discount is calculated on the cash payment, instead of on the proportion of the bill settled, which causes a loss to the purchaser. If an invoice costs $2500, and $1900 is paid, it will cancel $2000, thus saving to the purchaser $100; but if the 5% is calculated on $1900, the amount paid, the payment will cancel only $1995, making a difference of $5 between the two methods.

304. To find what amount is settled when part only is paid, a discount on sales being allowed for prompt payment.

RULE.—*Annex two ciphers to the cash payment, and divide by 100 less the rate per cent. of discount.*

100 — 5 = 95 190000 ÷ 95 = 2000. Ans. $2000.

BY ANALYSIS.—If 5% discount is allowed, $95 will pay a bill of $100, and $1900 will pay as many hundreds as 95 is contained times in it, = 2000, the answer.

BY PROPORTION.—95 : 100 : : 1900 : 2000.

The difference between 5% on the amount of invoice and 5% on the amount of cash paid equals 25 cents for every $100 of the invoice; at 6%, the difference equals 36 cts.; at 3%, 9 cts.

TABLE

Showing the Comparative Value of Gold and Currency.

When $1 in Gold is sold for Currency at	The Discount on Currency is	The Amount in Gold which can be bought for $100 in Currency.
1.05 or 5 per cent. Prem.	4.77 per cent.	$95.23 or $95\frac{25}{105}$ accurately.
1.10 " 10 " "	9.10 "	90.90 " $90\frac{10}{11}$ "
1.15 " 15 " "	13.04 "	86.96 " $86\frac{22}{23}$ "
1.20 " 20 " "	16.67 "	83.33 " $83\frac{1}{3}$ "
1.25 " 25 " "	20.00 "	80.00 " 80 "
1.30 " 30 " "	23.08 "	76.92 " $76\frac{12}{13}$ "
1.40 " 40 " "	28.58 "	71.42 " $71\frac{3}{7}$ "
1.50 " 50 " "	33.33 "	66.66 " $66\frac{2}{3}$ "
1.60 " 60 " "	37.50 "	62.50 " $62\frac{1}{2}$ "
1.70 " 70 " "	41.18 "	58.82 " $58\frac{14}{17}$ "
1.80 " 80 " "	44.45 "	55.55 " $55\frac{5}{9}$ "
1.90 " 90 " "	47.37 "	52.63 " $52\frac{12}{19}$ "
2.00 " 100 " "	50.00 "	50.00 " 50 "
2.50 " 150 " "	60.00 "	40.00 " 40 "
5.00 " 400 " "	80.00 "	20.00 " 20 "
7.50 " 650 " "	86.67 "	13.33 " $13\frac{1}{3}$ "
10.00 " 900 " "	90.00 "	10.00 " 10 "
50.00 " 4900 " "	98.00 "	2.00 " 2 "
100.00 " 9900 " "	99.00 "	1.00 " 1 "

The accuracy of the above figures can be tested by simply adding to those in the last column that per cent. of each which is designated in the column containing the rate of premium.

The above Table may also be used for finding what rate taken off the selling price is equivalent to a certain rate added to the cost or purchase price. For instance, 20%, as shown in the discount column, deducted, is equivalent to 25% added to the remainder, as shown in the premium column.

To find how much gold can be bought for a given amount of currency. *Multiply the amount of currency by 100, and divide the product by 100 increased by the rate of premium on gold.*

DISCOUNTING BILLS AND INVOICES.

305. In discounting Bills and Invoices, losses sometimes occur when they are not suspected. If an article is sold at a profit of 40%, and 10% be deducted from the selling price, the gain is not 30%, but 26%, because the discount is calculated on the first cost and also on the profit, whereas the profit is calculated on the first cost only. So, also, if 40% be added, and then 30% deducted, the apparent profit is 10%, but the *real loss* is 2%.

Cost,	$200	Cost,	$1.00
40 per cent.,	80	40 per cent.,	.40
Advanced price,	280	Advanced price,	1.40
Less 10 per cent.,	28	Less 30 per cent.,	.42
Cash price,	252	Cash price,	.98
26 per cent. profit.		2 per cent. loss.	
10 per cent. of $200 (cost)	= $20	30 per cent. of $1.00 (cost)	= .30
10 per cent. of $80 (profit)	= 8	30 per cent of .40 (profit)	= .12
	$28		.42
= 14 per ct. of cost.		or 42 per ct. of cost.	

Ex. 3.—What is the difference between discounting a bill of $1200 at 40%, and then taking a discount off the remainder of 5% for cash payment, and discounting the whole bill at 45%?

Ex. 4.—If a merchant buys a book at a discount of 20% on the retail price, and sells it at the retail price, what per cent. on the purchase-price does he gain? What per cent. does he gain if he buys at 33⅓% discount and sells it at the retail price?

306. To find the selling price from which a certain per cent. may be deducted and the goods sold at cost, or a given per cent. above or below cost.

RULE.—To sell at cost.

Multiply the cost by 100, and divide the product by 100 diminished by the rate per cent. to be deducted.

To sell at a given rate per cent. above or below cost.

Multiply 100 increased by the per cent. to be gained or diminished by the per cent. to be lost, by the cost, and divide the product by 100 diminished by the rate to be deducted from the selling price.

EXAMPLES.

1. Bought goods for $100 : for how much shall I sell them that I may deduct 20% and yet obtain what they cost?

$100 \times 100 = 10000$
$10000 \div 80 = 125.$ Ans. $125.

2. For what must I sell goods worth $100, so that I may deduct 45% and yet gain 30%?

$100 + 30 = 130$ $100 \times 130 = 13000$
$13000 \div 55 = 236.31.$ Ans. $236.31.

NOTE.—236.31 = 136.31% advance on 100. When a long list is to be made out at a uniform rate of profit, labor may be saved by adding the total advance at once.

3. If I buy cloth for $1.90 per yard, at what price must I mark it, that I may deduct 5% for my cash customers from the marked price, and yet gain 20%? Ans. $2.40.

4. A bookseller wishes to increase the price of a book which he now sells for $2, so that he can deduct 20% and yet receive the present price. What must be the advanced price?

5. A dry-goods merchant sells cloths for $168, by which he gains 20%. What must be the advanced price so that he can deduct 5% and still make the same profit?

6. What must be the price from which 20% may be deducted and leave 40 cts.?

7. Bought cassimeres for $1.20 per yard: at what price must they be sold that 5% may be deducted for cash payment and leave a profit of 25%?

8. Find the selling price of French plate glass that cost $60 per light, from which 45% may be deducted and 30% gained on cost.

What is the selling price of the goods in the following invoice, so that 25% may be gained on the prices given, and yet allow a discount of 5% for cash payment?

PHILADELPHIA, April 20, 1867.

MR. CHAS. P. GREGORY

Bo't of J. J. BAILEY & Co.

1 doz. long shawls,	@ $6 75	81	00
2 pieces sheeting, 30.35 yds.,	" .15		
6 doz. linen hdkfs.,	" 3.00		
3 pieces twilled muslin, 84 yds.,	" .20		
1 piece mousseline de laine, 32 yds.,	" .24		

PHILADELPHIA, March 12, 1867.

J. HARRIS BROWN

Bo't of MYERS & CLAGHORN.

240 yds. ingrain carpet, @ $1.20,	288	00
Less 5%,	14	40
	$273	60
Rec'd payment, MYERS & CLAGHORN, per J. B. JONES.		
Freight and other expenses to Madison,	21	89
	$295	49

At what must I sell the carpeting per yard, to gain 20% and allow a discount of 10% from selling price?

SOLUTION.—5% of $1.20 = 6¢. 1.20 — 6 = 1.14, net cash price per yard in Philadelphia. Charges, 21.89 = 8% of total cost in Philadelphia. 8% of 1.14 = 9+. 1.14 + 9 = $1.23, advanced cost per yard.

Proof.—240 yds. @ $1.23 = $295.20, which, allowing for fractions, is the cost of the invoice.

20% of $1.23 = 25¢, nearly; adding this to the cost, we have $1.48 as the amount to be received. Then, to obtain the selling price, 100 — 10 = 90   148 ÷ 90 = 1.64+.   Ans. $1.64 per yd.

Proof.—10% of 1.64 = 16+   1.64 – 16 = 1.48.

PRICE LISTS.

307. Price Lists are made out by manufacturers and dealers, as prices to be charged, subject to the deductions of certain rates per cent., which fluctuate according to the cost of manufacturing, demand for the goods, etc. By changing the rate of discount, the prices are changed without altering the price lists.

EXTRACT FROM PRICE-LIST OF CLARKSON & CO.,

MANUFACTURERS AND IMPORTERS OF BRUSHES.

Terms, net cash. *PHILADELPHIA.* *January 1, 1868.*

Ground Paint Brushes.

Wire Bound.

No. 6,	per doz.,	$2.00
" 5,	" "	2.50
" 4,	" "	3.00
" 3,	" "	3.50

Kalsomine Brushes.

5 in.,	per doz.,	$24.00
6 in.,	"	33.00
7 in.,	"	42.00
8 in.,	"	48.00
9 in.,	"	57.00

HOOPES & TOWNSEND'S CARRIAGE-BOLT WORKS.

PRICE LIST PER HUNDRED.

1 in.,	$\frac{1}{4}$ in.	diameter,	$2.50
2 "	" "	"	3.10
3 "	" "	"	3.65
2 "	$\frac{7}{16}$ "	"	4.55
3 "	" "	"	5.25
2 "	$\frac{1}{2}$ "	"	7.64
3 "	" "	"	8.48

20 per cent. discount to the trade.

Tire Bolts.

$\frac{3}{16}$ in.,	$1.50
$1\frac{1}{4}$ "	1.68
$2\frac{3}{4}$ "	1.75
$2\frac{5}{16}$ "	2.41

Wrought Axle Clips.

Size,	0.	1.	2.	3.	4.
Price,	$1.05.	1.05.	1.05.	1.10.	1.20.

If a discount of 20% on the above prices is allowed, leaving a net gain of 10%, what is the cost of manufacture?

Find the selling price of the following goods, so that a discount of 10% may be deducted and leave a gain of 15%. The prices annexed show the cost.

100 Amer. Glass, $1.40 each.
100 Tire Bolts, $\frac{3}{16}$ in., $1.00.
200 yards Muslin, 20¢.
100 gross Pens, @ 90¢.
25 ounces Carmine Ink, $2.00.
50 yards Broadcloth, $2.40.
75 Amer. Cyclopedias, $60.00.
80 packs Enamelled Cards, 40¢.
25 gross Lead Pencils, $3.00.
400 lbs. Letter Paper, 35¢.

Invoice of Merchandise, marked as in the margin, and forwarded by J. Powers & Co., *Philadelphia, per Penna. R.R., to Messrs.* Brown & Gregg, *Chicago, as per their order and at their risk.*

Mark	Description		$	cts.
B. & G.	25 Boxes Valencia Raisins,			
	Gross weight,	710 lbs.		
	Tare, 4½ lbs. per box,	112½ "		
		597½ @ 15 cts.	89	62½
B. & G.	5 Bags Canary Seed,			
	1184 lbs. — 15 lbs. tare = 1169 net,			
	$19\frac{29}{60}$ bushels @ 4.85,		94	49
B. & G.	10 Bbls. Currants, 266, 254, 236, 264, 244, 243, 260, 260, 260, 243,			
	Total,	2530		
	Tare, 26 lbs. per bbl.	260		
		2270 @ 18c.	408	60
B. & G.	10 Boxes Castile Soap, 406 lbs.			
	Tare, 8 lbs. per box, 80			
	326 lbs. @ 14c.		45	64
B. & G.	5 Cases ½ Sardines,			
	500 boxes @ 35c.		175	00
			813	35
	Cartage,	3.00		
	Ins. on $900 @ ½ per cent.	4.50	7	50
			820	85
	Rec'd Payment,			
	J. Powers & Co.			

Charges in Chicago:—

Freight on 4050 lbs. @ $1.10 per h'd.	44.55
Cartage,	3.00
	47.55

Total charges equal 7%, nearly, of first cost of goods.

What must be the selling prices in the above invoice, that I may gain 30%?

SOLUTION.

Total invoice price,		$813.35
Charges in Philada.	$7.50	
Chicago,	47.55	55.05
Total cost,		$868.40

55.05 = 7%, nearly, of $813.35.

	Invoice Price.			Selling Price
Raisins,	15c. + 7%	= 16c.,	increased 30%	= .21
Canary Seed,	4.85 + "	= 5.19	" "	= 6.75
Currants,	.18 + "	= .19	" "	= .25
Castile Soap,	.14 + "	= .15	" "	= .20
Sardines,	.35 + "	= .37	" "	= .48

The above is given simply as an exercise in calculation. Goods are not generally sold at a uniform rate of profit.

Invoice of Queensware shipped by GEORGE HAMMERSLY, *Liverpool, Eng., per "Emily Augusta," and consigned to* MESSRS. FIELD & COGLEY, *Philadelphia, for their account and at their risk.*

			£.	s.	d.	£.	s.	d.
◇ F. & C. 15	36 Teapots, $\frac{18}{18}$ $\frac{18}{24}$, "Niagara" F. Gold Band	27/-	2	7	3			
	18 Sugars, 24 "Niagara" F. Gold Band .	"	1		3			
	18 Creams, 24 " "	6		9				
	20 Bowls, 30 " "	8/-		5	4			
	14 doz. Teas unhd. " "	5/-	3	10				
	27 " Plates, $\frac{4}{5}$ @ 2/-, $\frac{20}{7}$ @ 3/-, $\frac{3}{8}$ @ 3/6, "Niagara" F. Gold Band		3	18	6			
	5 " Dishes, $\frac{2}{10}$ @ 9/-, $\frac{2}{12}$ @ 15/-, $\frac{1}{14}$ @ 21/-, "Niagara" F. G'd Band		3	9				
	5 " Bakers', $\frac{2\frac{1}{2}}{7}$ @ 6/-, $\frac{2\frac{1}{2}}{8}$ @ 9/-, "Niagara" F. Gold Band . . .		1	17	6			
	6 Cover dishes, 92, "Niagara" F. Gd. Bd.	2/3		13	6			
	4 Sauce Tureens Comp., " "	2/6		10				
	10 Pickles, " "	6		5		18	5	4
	25 per cent. discount, . . .					4	11	4
						13	14	
	Crate and Straw						13	6
	Shipping Charges						9	10
						14	17	4

Ft. In. 65 11 Freight 13/-	$3	12
£14. 17*s.* 4*d.* at par = ...	66	08
Exchange, 10½ per cent.	6	76
Insurance, 1¼ per cent. on $5	1	12
Duties and Entry	18	70
Interest from Shipment, ...		54
	$96	32

What is the value of a shilling in the above invoice at the advanced cost price?

Find the percentage of the particular charges and of the general charges of the following invoice; and, also, find the percentage to be added to allow a discount of 5% from the selling price and retain a profit of 25%.

BIRMINGHAM, ENG., April 30, 1867.

Invoice of Hardware purchased by order and for account and risk of H. L. HARRISON & BRO., *Philadelphia, and forwarded to* MESSRS. ALFRED FIELD & CO., *Liverpool, for shipment.*

		£.	s.	d.			
H. L. H. 170 F.	13/6 ½ doz. Jap'd Oval Trays, 10883, 24 in. . . .		6	9			
	11/- 8/- ½ " " " " ea. 10882, 10778, 20 in.		9	6			
	7/3 8/6 10/- 11/6 2 " Oval Trays, 7128, ea. 18, 20, 22, 24, in ¼ dozs.	3	14	6	4	10	9
	Extra pap'g 2 parcels ½*d*., and 1 @ 8*d*. . .						9
	Case, &c., 5/6; Freight to Liverpool, 4/- . .					9	6
					5	1	0
	171						
	9/9 12 doz. Painted Scale Beams, No. B, 12 in. . .	5	17				
	65 per cent. discount . .	3	16	1	2	0	11
	8/- 9/- 10/6 14/- 10 gro. Tin'd Kettle-Ears, ea. A, B, 0, 1, 16/- 20/- 23/6 2, 3, 4, ...	50	10				
	77½ per cent. discount . .	39	2	9	11	7	3
	Cask, &c., 7/6; Freight to Liverpool, 12/3 .					19	9
					14	7	11
	169						
	4/- 2/- 4 doz. Brt. Ov. Bake Pans, ea. 1.3 } cwt. qr. lb. 5 1 5 3 " " " " 4.5 } @ 7*d*. ℔ lb.	17	5	11			
	40 per cent. discount . .	6	18	4	10	7	7
	Cask, &c., 6/-; Freight to Liverpool, 6/6 . .					12	6
					11	0	1
	Amount of Case, 170				5	1	00
	" " Cask, 171				14	7	11
	" " " 169				11	0	1
					30	9	0
	Commission, 4 per cent. . .				1	5	2
	Dock and Town Dues, 1/3; Cartage, Porterage, &c., 4/6; Shipping, 3/-		8	9			
	Bills of Lading, 1/6; Canal Ins. ⅛ per cent., 3/2; Consul's fee, 11/-		15	8	1	4	5
	E. E.				32	18	7

pro ALFRED FIELD & CO.
W. MINCHER.

Charges on arrival in Philadelphia:—

Duties on case 170, $24, @ 40%,	9.60	
" " cases 171, 169, $123, @ 35%,	43.05	52.65
Brokerage,		2.00
Fees, &c., 2.75, Triplicate Invoice, 1.25,		4.00
Cartage,		3.00
Bonded Warehouse Fees,		7.00
Freight from Liverpool,		18.35
		87.00

In reckoning the cost of goods, the amount of all the charges is found, and then the invoice price of each article is increased in the proportion that the charges bear to the purchase price of the goods. The profits are to be added after finding the total cost.

In foreign invoices, when the prices are in pounds, shillings, or francs, it is frequently found convenient to increase the true value of the pound or franc in the proportion that the charges bear to the purchase price, and then obtain the total cost of each article by taking the currency at this increased valuation. For instance, if the charges were equal to 20% of the first cost of the goods, the shilling would be estimated at an advance of 20% on 22.2c.,—the par value of a shilling,—or at the valuation of 26.6c. Then, 300 yards extra ticking, @ 2 shillings per yard, would be marked as costing 53$\frac{1}{5}$c. per yard.

A franc, in an invoice on which the charges are equal to 66% of the invoice, would be reckoned at 66% advance on he exchange value of a franc. Or, the total cost of the invoice in United States currency may be divided by the number of shillings or francs in the total purchase price of the goods.

In the invoice on the next page, the cost is calculated in this manner, no account being taken of the particular discounts or charges, although for strict accuracy this should be done. The entire cost of each item is reckoned at 42$\frac{1}{3}$c. per franc. Thus, 4 gross combs, @ 36 fr. per gross, cost 36 × 42$\frac{1}{3}$ = $15.24 per gross.

PARIS, October 16, 1865.

Invoice of One Package Merchandise purchased by J. GLAENZER & VESSEPUY, JR., *of Paris, for account and risk of* MESSRS. E. CLINTON & Co., *of Philadelphia, and shipped at Havre by* SHERBETTE, KANE & Co. *on board the Steamer Bosphorus, bound for New York, and consigned to themselves.*

E. C. & Co. ※134	1 CASE.				
	※ 6. 13 kilo. Beau Blanc Bristles, @ fr.11.^{50} . .	149	50		
	7. 12 " " " " " 12.^{50} . .	150	00		
		299	50		
	3 per cent. discount . .	8	95	290	55
	※ 3233. 4 gro. Buffalo Tuck Combs, @ fr.36 net . .	144			
	3234. 3 " " " " " 42 " . .	126			
	3235. 2 " " " " " 48 " . .	96			
	3331. 36 doz. Hair Brushes, " 6 " . .	216		582	00
	2899. 5 gro. Tooth Brushes, 4 R, @ fr.51 . . .	255			
	2900. 5 " " " 5 R, @ fr.63 . . .	315			
		570			
	4 per cent. discount . .	22	80	547	20
	※ 2911. 4 gro. Tooth Brushes, @ fr. 21	84			
	2913. 3 " " " " 33	99			
	" bis 3 " " " " 33	99			
	2919. 3 " " " " 45	135			
	" bis 1 " " " "	45			
		462			
	2 per cent. discount . .	9	20	452	80
				1872	55
	Commission 3 per cent. on fr. 290.55 = 8.70				
	" 5 " " 1582. = 79.10			87	80
	Packing 20. Boxes 15. Visa 13.40 Postage 5.25			53	65
	Freight from Paris to Havre			10	80
				2024	80
	15 days' interest, @ 6 per cent. . . .			5	05
				2029	85

Charges and Duties paid in New York for account of invoice consigned to E. CLINTON & CO., *Nov. 15/65.*

25 kilos. = lbs. 55, @ fr.15 per lb.,	8	25		
Francs, 290.55 = $54.00				
366. = 68.00 @ 35%,	23	80		
1216. = 226.00 " 40%,	90	40	122	45
1872.55				
Entry Bond, @ $0.50				
Oath, Transfer Order, &c., 1.25				
Postage, .15				
Cartage, .75				
Bond for Triplicate Invoice, .65				
Premium on Gold, @ $47\frac{5}{8}$%, 58.00				
Contingent Exp. 50¢, Com. 3.50, 4.00	65	30		
Insurance, fr.2024.80, @ 40¢ pr. fr. = $810, @ $2\frac{1}{4}$%,	18	22		
Freight from Havre to New York, per "Scotland," £1 9*s.* 11*d.* @ $145\frac{1}{2}$,	9	67		
	215	64		
Freight and Drayage from New York to Philadelphia,	2	00	217	64
Francs 2029.86, @ 5.20,	390	86		
Gold Premium @ $47\frac{5}{8}$%,	184	93	575	29
			792	93

1872.55 fr. cost $792.93.
Cost of 1 franc, $41\frac{5}{8}$¢.

NOTE.—25 kilogrammes B. B. Bristles pay a specific duty.

For entire accuracy, omit duties and particular charges until the average, without them, is found. Then add the charges and duties per franc on any lot to the average already found for the value per franc on that particular lot.

The duties per franc may be found by dividing the amount of duties by the number of francs which the lot cost.

IMPORTERS' ADVANCE TABLE,

Showing the value of Sterling Money from 1 penny to £5, at par, and at an advance from 7½ to 50 per cent.

Invoice price.	ADVANCE PER CENT.										
	Par.	7½	10	12½	15	20	25	30	33⅓	40	50
s. d.	$ cts.	$ cts.	$ cts.	$ cts.	$ cts.	$ cts.	$ cts.	$ cts.	$ cts.	$ cts.	$ cts.
1d.	.0185	.0199	.0204	.0208	.021	.0222	.0231	.0241	.0261	.0259	.0278
6	.11	.12	.13	.13	.13	.13	.14	.14	.15	.15½	.16¾
7	.13	.14	.14	.15	.15	.16	.16	.17	.17	.18¼	.19½
8	.14¾	.16	.16	.17	.17	.18	.19	.19	.20	.20¾	.22½
9	.16¾	.18	.18	.19	.19	.20	.21	.22	.22	.23¼	.25
10	.18½	.20	.20	.21	.21	.22	.23	.24	.25	.26	.27¾
11	.20¼	.22	.22	.23	.23	.24	.25	.27	.27	.28½	.30½
1s.0	.22¼	.24	.24	.25	.26	.27	.28	.29	.30	.31	.33¼
1 1	.24	.26	.26	.27	.28	.29	.30	.31	.32	.33¾	.36
1 2	.26	.28	.29	.29	.30	.31	.32	.34	.35	.36¼	.39
1 3	.27¾	.30	.31	.31	.32	.33	.35	.36	.37	.39	.41¾
1 4	.29½	.32	.33	.33	.34	.36	.37	.39	.40	.41½	.44½
1 5	.31½	.34	.35	.35	.36	.38	.39	.41	.42	.44	.47¼
1 6	.33¼	.36	.37	.38	.38	.40	.42	.43	.44	.46¾	.50
1 7	.35¼	.38	.39	.40	.40	.42	.44	.46	.47	.49¼	.52¾
1 8	.37	.40	.41	.42	.43	.44	.46	.48	.49	.51¾	.55½
1 9	.39	.42	.43	.44	.45	.47	.49	.51	.52	.54½	.58¼
1 10	.40¾	.44	.45	.46	.47	.49	.51	.53	.54	.57	.61
1 11	.42½	.46	.47	.48	.49	.51	.53	.55	.57	.59½	.64
2 0	.44½	.48	.49	.50	.51	.53	.56	.58	.59	.62¼	.66¾
3	.66¾	.72	.73	.75	.77	.80	.83	.87	.89	.93¼	1.00
4	.89	.96	.98	1.00	1.02	1.07	1.11	1.16	1.19	1.24½	1.33¼
5	1.11	1.19	1.22	1.25	1.28	1.33	1.39	1.44	1.48	1.50	1.66¾
6	1.33¼	1.43	1.47	1.50	1.53	1.60	1.66	1.73	1.78	1.86¾	2.00
7	1.55½	1.67	1.71	1.75	1.79	1.87	1.94	2.02	2.07	2.17¾	2.33¼
8	1.77¾	1.91	1.96	2.00	2.04	2.13	2.22	2.31	2.37	2.49	2.66¾
9	2.00	2.15	2.20	2.25	2.30	2.40	2.50	2.60	2.67	2.80	3.00
10	2.22¼	2.39	2.44	2.50	2.56	2.67	2.78	2.89	2.96	3.11	3.33¼
£1	4.44½	4.78	4.89	5.00	5.11	5.33	5.56	5.78	5.93	6.22¼	6.66¾
2	8.89	9.56	9.78	10.00	10.22	10.67	11.11	11.56	11.85	12.44½	13.33½
3	13.33½	14.33	14.67	15.00	15.33	16.00	16.66	17.33	17.78	18.66	20.00
4	17.77¾	19.11	19.56	20.00	20.44	21.33	22.22	23.11	23.70	24.89	26.66¾
5	22.22¼	23.89	24.44	25.00	25.56	26.67	27.78	28.89	28.63	31.11	33.33¼

EXPLANATION.—Find the value of an article invoiced at 2 shillings, when the charges on the invoice are 33⅓ per cent. on the cost of the goods:—Look under 33⅓, and opposite 2 shillings, and we have 59,—the advance cost of the article. When the invoice price is not in the table, take the sum of such numbers as will equal the required cost. When the rate of advance is not given, add the required rate to the value in the par column.

308. The length of credit has much to do with the accumulation of profits. The difference between long credits and short credits is shown in their effects in the following example :—

If a young man commences business with a capital of $1000, and is able to turn it over every *three* months at 10% profit, in five years it will

Amount to	**$6727.50**	If every 3 mos. at 8%,	**$4660.96**
If every 4 mos. at 10%,	4177.25	" 4 " "	3172.17
" 6 " "	2593.74	" 6 " "	2158.93
" 7½ " "	2143.59	" 7½ " "	1850.93
" 10 " "	1771.56	" 10 " "	1586.87
" 12 " "	1610.51	" 12 " "	1469.33
" 2½ yrs. "	1210.00	" 2½ yrs. "	1166.40

309. One of the practical questions to be determined when reducing prices, is, Can enough more goods be sold at the reduced price to compensate for the reduced profits?

QUICK SALES AND SMALL PROFITS.

A man commenced business on a borrowed capital of $4000, and paid interest monthly at the rate of 6% per annum,—that is, $20 per month. His expenses were $180 per month additional. He invariably paid cash, thereby saving 5% discount on the invoice price. He sold his entire stock every month at an advance of 5% on the invoice price, and immediately reinvested the proceeds. What profit did he make by the end of the year? Ans. $4879.18.

ECONOMY THE SOURCE OF WEALTH.

AT COMPOUND INTEREST, IN TEN YEARS,

2¾ cts. a day, or	$10 a year, will become	$130.
11 "	40 " "	520.
27½ "	100 " "	1300.
50 "	182.50 " "	2305.
100 "	365 " "	4814.

MARKING GOODS.

310. It is customary in many mercantile houses to use a private mark, which is placed on the goods to denote their cost and selling price. A word or phrase containing ten different letters is taken, the letters of which are written instead of figures. For instance, the word "Cumberland" is selected; then the letters represent the figures as follows:—

C	u	m	b	e	r	l	a	n	d
1	2	3	4	5	6	7	8	9	0

If it is required to mark 1.50, it is done thus, *ced;* 75 would be *le;* 37, *ml,* &c.

Blacksmith, Importance, Republican, Perth Amboy, Fair Spoken, Now be sharp, Noisy Table, and Cash Profit, are among the words and phrases which can be used in this manner.

311. It sometimes happens that the selling price contains three figures, while the buying price contains but two. To prevent this difference from being noticed, the letter denoting the cipher is prefixed to the buying price. For instance, if the buying price was 87, it would be marked *dal;* and the selling price, 1.25, *cue;* thus giving each price three letters.

312. An extra letter, called a "Repeater," is used to prevent the repetition of a figure. Instead of writing *cdd* for 100, which would show at once that the two right-hand figures were alike, and thus aid in giving a clue to the key-word, some additional letter would be selected for a repeater,—*y*, for instance,—and then the price would be written *cdy;* 225 would be written *uye.*

313. Instead of letters, arbitrary characters are frequently used, something like the following:—

┘	Z	T	⊐	◺	□	×	‡	⊥	⊓
1	2	3	4	5	6	7	8	9	0

Fractions may be designated by additional letters or characters. Thus, *f* may represent ½, *w* ⅜, &c.; or ½ may be written ⌒, ½ +, &c.

314. The marks on packages, barrels, &c. are often some arbitrary mark, or letter selected at random, or the initials of the purchaser placed there for the purpose of showing that the goods belong to some particular lot, and are put on for the sake of distinction merely.

What is the profit, and what the selling price, of the following?—

		Gain.	Selling Price.
First cost, $1.10,	Freight, 10%,	20%,	
" .50,	" 20%,	10%,	
" 1.00,		30%,	
" 4.80,		15%,	
" 2.50,	" 10%,	20%,	
" 1.75,		5%,	
" 3.00,	Charges, 7½%,	25%,	

Mark the selling price of the above, using the word "Cumberland" instead of figures.

Annual Production of the Gold and Silver Mines of the World before 1865. (Value in Francs.)

	Silver.	Gold.
United States and British America	92,888,000	227,333,000
Mexico	103,444,000	14,500,000
New Granada	1,333,000	17,222,000
Peru	28,889,000	4,133,000
Bolivia	13,333,000	2,067,000
Brazil	....	10,333,000
Chili	18,889,000	4,133,000
Other American Countries	5,556,000	3,617,000
	264,332,000	283,338,000
Europe and Australia	47,784,000	418,456,000
Africa, India, China, Japan, &c	111,111,000	275,555,000
	423,227,000	977,349,000

What is the value of the above in United States currency, estimating the franc at 5.18 per dollar, and specie at a premium of 30%?

PARTNERSHIP SETTLEMENTS.

315. Partnership is the association of two or more persons for the transaction of business. Such an association is called a firm, house, or company, and the members of the association are called partners. (See PARTNERSHIP, page 318, and ARTICLES OF AGREEMENT, page 320.)

316. The means contributed by the members of the firm are called its *Capital.* Money, property, notes and debts due from others, are called *Assets*, or *Resources.* Debts which the firm owe are called *Liabilities.* Amounts withdrawn affect the original investment. They are sometimes counted as resources; but what has been withdrawn can hardly be considered a resource, and settlements based upon such estimates are frequently erroneous. When it is desired to retain the net capital at starting unchanged, the amounts withdrawn may be treated as resources; but they must be taken from each partner's capital to obtain his true share. Obligations assumed by the firm for a partner are to be treated in the same manner as sums withdrawn by him; and additional sums invested, or to which he is entitled, increase his original investment.

317. If the Resources are greater than the Liabilities, the difference is termed the *Net Capital;* if the Liabilities are greater than the Resources, the difference is termed the *Net Insolvency.* The difference between the total gains and the total losses is called *Net Gains*, or *Net Losses.*

318. When the net capital at closing exceeds the net capital at commencing, the difference is the net gain. When the net capital at closing is less than at commencing, the difference is the net loss. When there is an insolvency at closing, the sum of the net capital at starting, and the net insolvency, is the net loss.

When there is a net insolvency at commencing business,

and a net capital at closing, the sum of both is the net gain; when the net insolvency at closing is greater than at commencing, the increase is the net loss.

319. The gains and losses of a firm are divided among the partners in accordance with the original agreement or contract between them. The division is seldom made in exact proportion to the amount invested: it is more customary to credit each partner with interest on his capital invested, less interest on sums withdrawn during the year.

Sometimes the skill of one partner is considered equivalent to another's capital; in some cases certain privileges are granted to him who invests most; and sometimes a stated salary is allowed each partner according to his ability, and is taken from the gains of the firm before they are divided.

EXAMPLES.

1. A merchant commenced business with $5000 in cash, $3000 worth of goods in store, and owing $1500. At the end of the year he had $2500 in cash, $4200 in goods, $3300 in notes, and he owed to various persons $1350. How much did he gain?

$5,000 Cash.	$2,500 Cash.
3,000 Mdse.	4,200 Mdse.
	3,300 Notes.
8,000 Assets at commencing.	
1,500 Liabilities.	10,000 Assets at closing.
	1,350 Liabilities at closing.
$6,500 Net cap. at commencing.	
	$8,650 Net capital at closing.

$8650 — $6500 = $2150, Net gain.

2. A firm on January 1st, 1865, had a capital consisting of $3200 in cash, $18,500 in merchandise, and $4600 in notes and debts due them; their debts amounted to $2100. At the end of the year their assets were $12,000 in merchandise, $5000 in cash, and $14,000 in notes and debts due them, 20% of which were considered worthless. Their liabilities were notes held by others against them, amounting to $18,000. How much did they gain or lose?

320. To find each partner's share of the gains or losses, when the shares are in proportion to the investments.

RULE.—*Place the amount invested by each partner as a numerator, and the whole capital of the firm as a denominator: the several fractions will express each partner's share.* Then, *Multiply the gain or loss by the fraction expressing each partner's share, and the product will be his share of the gain or loss.* Or,

By DISTRIBUTIVE PROPORTION (see page 48)

$$\left\{\begin{matrix}\text{The whole capital}\\ \text{of the firm}\end{matrix}\right\} : \left\{\begin{matrix}\text{Each partner's}\\ \text{capital}\end{matrix}\right\} :: \left\{\begin{matrix}\text{Whole gain}\\ \text{or loss}\end{matrix}\right\} : \left\{\begin{matrix}\text{Each partner's gain}\\ \text{or loss.}\end{matrix}\right.$$

Or, BY PERCENTAGE:

Multiply each partner's capital by the percentage which the gains or losses may be of the capital of the firm.

EXAMPLES.

1. A., B., and C. formed a partnership. A. invested $3000, B. $2500, and C. $1500. Their profits were $2800, to be divided in proportion to their capital. What was each partner's share?

FIRST METHOD.

$\$3000 + \$2500 + \$1500 = \$7000$, Firm's capital.

$\frac{3000}{7000} = \frac{3}{7}$, A.'s share. $2800 \times \frac{3}{7} = \$1200$, A.'s gain.
$\frac{2500}{7000} = \frac{5}{14}$, B.'s " $2800 \times \frac{5}{14} = \$1000$, B.'s "
$\frac{1500}{7000} = \frac{3}{14}$, C.'s " $2800 \times \frac{3}{14} = \$600$, C.'s "
$2800, Firm's gain.

SECOND METHOD.

$7000 : $3000 : : 2800 : $1200, A.'s gain.
$7000 : $2500 : : 2800 : $1000, B.'s "
$7000 : $1500 : : 2800 : $600, C.'s "
$2800, Proof.

THIRD METHOD.

$\$2800 = 40\%$ of $7000.
$\$3000 \times 40\% = \$1200$, A.'s gain.
$\$2500 \times 40\% = \$1000$, B.'s "
$\$1300 \times 40\% = \$600$, C.'s "
$2800

2. A. and B. speculated in grain. A. invested 1200 bushels of wheat, at $1.50 per bushel; B. invested 2000 bushels corn, at 80¢ per bushel. The gains and losses were shared in proportion to value of investment. Their net gains were $510. What was the share of each?

OPERATION.

1200 bus. at $1.50 = $1800. $\frac{1800}{3400} = \frac{9}{17}$ of 510 = 270, A.'s gain.
2000 bus. at .80 = $1600. $\frac{1600}{3400} = \frac{8}{17}$ of 510 = 240, B.'s gain.

3. Four men purchased a piece of land for $36,000. The first contributed $20,000, the second $10,000, the third $4000, and the fourth $2000. They sold the land at an advance of 50% on the purchase price. How much was each man's share of the gain?

4. A. and B. are partners. A. invested $15,000, and B. $6000. A.'s share of the gain or loss is $\frac{2}{3}$, B.'s $\frac{1}{3}$. At the end of the year their resources are $35,000 in goods and cash, and their liabilities consist of notes outstanding to the amount of $15,500. How much is the firm's net capital, and what is each partner's share of the gain or loss?

A.'s investment,	$15,000	Resources,	$35,000
B.'s investment,	6,000	Liabilities,	15,500
Firm's net cap. at commencing,	$21,000	Firm's net cap.,	$19,500
Deduct net capital at closing,	$19,500	A.'s $\frac{2}{3}$ loss,	$1,000
Firm's net loss,	$1,500	B.'s $\frac{1}{3}$ "	500
		Firm's net loss,	$1,500

321. To find each partner's interest at closing.

Rule.—I. *Find the firm's net capital or net insolvency at commencing and at closing.*

II. *Find the firm's net gains or net losses, and each partner's share.* Then,

III. *To each partner's original investment add any additional investments or sums to which he may be entitled, and his share of the net gains, if any; also, deduct the amounts withdrawn by him, and obligations assumed by the firm for him, and his share of the net losses, if any.*

If the original agreement entitle him to any other sum, or make him responsible to the firm for any sum, add or subtract, as the case may be.

EXAMPLES.

1. A. and B., having been in business 1 year, dissolve partnership. B. retires, leaving A. to continue the business and liquidate the debts of the firm. A. invested $12,000, B. $10,000. Each is to receive interest on his investment, and share the gains and losses equally. How much did each gain? what is A.'s capital at closing, and how much should he pay B. on retiring, the resources and liabilities being as follows?

Resources.

Cash on hand,		$5,000
Personal debts due firm, per Ledger,	$12,000	
Less 25 per cent. for bad debts,	3,000	9,000
Mdse., as per inventory,		16,530
Bills Receivable,		3,500
U. S. 5-20 bonds,		4,000
Accrued interest on 5-20 bonds,		120
Real Estate (store and lot),		6,500
Store fixtures,		350
Total Resources,		$45,000

Liabilities.

Personal debts firm owe per Ledger,	$8,170
Bills Payable,	4,200
Interest on notes and drafts,	130
Total Liabilities,	$12,500

OPERATION.

Total resources,	$45,000
" liabilities,	12,500
Firm's net capital at closing,	$32,500

Interest on A.'s investment, $12,000 for 1 year,	= $720
" B.'s " 10,000 "	= 600

Firm's net capital at closing,			$32,500
A.'s investment,	$12,000		
Interest for 1 year,	720	12,720	
B.'s investment,	$10,000		
Interest for 1 year,	600	10,600	23,320
Firm's net gains in business,			$9,180

A.'s investment,	$12,000	B.'s investment,	$10,000
Interest for 1 year,	720	Interest for 1 year,	600
His ½ net gains,	4,590	His ½ net gains,	4,590
A.'s net capital,	$17,310	B.'s net capital,	$15,190

A.'s net capital,	$17,310
B.'s "	15,190
Firm's net capital, as before,	$32,500

2. D. and E. are partners; each invested $3000, and agreed to share the gains and losses equally. During the year, D. drew out $600, and E. $500. What were their gains at the end of the year, their resources and liabilities being as follows?

Resources.

Cash on hand,	$3,500	
Mdse., as per inventory,	3,600	
Bills Receivable,	1,200	
Debts due firm, as per Ledger,	2,500	
Total resources,		$10,800

Liabilities.

Debts firm owe, as per Ledger,	$1,500	
Bills Payable,	800	
Total liabilities,		2,300
Firm's net capital at closing,		$8,500

D. invested	$3,000		
Less amount withdrawn,	600		
D.'s credit balance,		$2,400	
E. invested	3,000		
Less amount withdrawn,	500		
E.'s credit balance,		$2,500	
Balance of investments,			4,900
Firm's net gains,			$3,600

PROOF.

D. invested	$3,000	E. invested	$3,000
Withdrew	600	Withdrew	500
	2,400		2,500
½ net gains,	1,800	½ net gains,	1,800
D.'s net cap. at closing,	$4,200	E.'s net cap. at closing,	$4,300

D.'s net capital,	$4,200
E.'s "	4,300
Firm's net capital, as above,	$8,500

3. A., B., and C. form a partnership; A. invests $15,000, B. $12,000, and C. nothing. They share the gains and losses as follows,—viz.: A. ½, B. ⅓, and C. ⅙. A. draws out during the year $800, B. $900, and C. $400. What is each partner's

capital, and what are the gains at the end of the year, when their resources amount to $40,000, and their liabilities to $44,000?

OPERATION.

Liabilities,	$44,000	A.'s investment, $15,000	
Less resources,	40,000	Less am't withdrawn, 800	$14,200
Firm's net insolvency,	$4,000	B.'s investment, 12,000	
		Less am't withdrawn, 900	11,100
			25,300
A.'s ½ loss,	$14,450.00	Less am't withdrawn by C.,	400
B.'s ⅓ "	9,633.33	Firm's net investment,	24,900
C.'s ⅙ "	4,816.67	Add firm's insolvency,	4,000
Total losses,	$28,900.00	Firm's net loss,	$28,900

A.'s investment,	$15,000	A.'s ½ loss,	$14,450
Less amount withdrawn,	800	Net investment,	14,200
	$14,200	A.'s net insolvency,	$250

B.'s investment,	$12,000.00	C.'s ⅙ loss,	$4,816.67
Less am't withdrawn,	900.00	Add am't withdrawn,	400.00
	11,100.00	C.'s net insolvency,	$5,216.67
Less his ⅓ loss,	9,633.33		
B.'s net capital,	$1,466.67		

A.'s insolvency,	$250.00
C.'s "	5,216.67
	5,466.67
Deduct B.'s net capital,	1,466.67
Firm's net insolvency,	$4,000.00

4. *In which a salary is allowed each partner. No interest account kept.*

A., B., and C. entered into partnership January 1st, 1865. A. and B. each invested $7000, C. invested $14,000. A.'s share of the gains or losses was ¼, B.'s ¼, and C.'s ½. A. was to receive a salary of $1000 per year, B. $1500, and C. $500, for services. A. drew out $650, B. $450, and C. $900. What was each partner's interest in the firm January 1st. 1866, when their resources were $54,500, and their liabilities $13,500?

OPERATION.

Resources,			$54,500
Liabilities,			13,500
Firm's net capital,			$41,000
A.'s investment,	$7,000		
Add salary,	1000		
	8,000		
Less amount withdrawn,	650		
A.'s credit balance,		7,350	
B.'s investment,	$7,000		
Add salary,	1,500		
	8,500		
Less amount withdrawn,	450		
B.'s credit balance,		8,050	
C.'s investment,	$14,000		
Add salary,	500		
	14,500		
Less amount withdrawn,	900		
C.'s credit balance,		13,600	29,000
Firm's net gains,			$12,000

A.'s credit balance,	$7,350	B.'s credit balance,	$8,050	C.'s credit balance,	$13,600
" $\frac{1}{4}$ gain,	3,000	" $\frac{1}{4}$ gain,	3,000	" $\frac{1}{2}$ gain,	6,000
Net capital,	$10,350	Net capital,	$11,050	Net capital	$19,600

PROOF.—A.'s net capital,	$10,350
B.'s "	11,050
C.'s "	19,600
Firm's net capital, as above,	$41,000

5. *In which amounts withdrawn are averaged, and interest is charged and allowed.*

A. and B. entered into partnership January 1st, 1864. A. invested $12,000, and B. $14,500, the gains and losses to be shared equally; each partner to be allowed 6 per cent. on his investment, and to be charged at the same rate on sums drawn out. A. drew as follows:—March 1st, $300; July 9th, $250; September 10th, $200; December 16th, $150. B. drew, April 7th, $100; August 4th, $400; November 23d, $250. What was each partner's interest January 1st, 1865, their resources and liabilities being as follows?

Resources.		*Liabilities.*	
Cash,	$3,600	Personal debts firm owe,	$11,500
Personal debts due firm,	16,000	Bills Payable,	500
Bills Receivable,	1,400	Total liabilities,	12,000
Mdse., as per inventory,	26,000		
Penna. Central R.R. Stock	6,000	*Firm's net capital,*	*41,000*
Total resources,	$53,000		$53,000

Average date of amounts withdrawn by A., July 6th.
" " " B., Aug. 26th.

A.'s investment,	$12,000		B.'s investment,	$14,500.00	
Less amount withdrawn,	900	$11,100	Less am't withdrawn,	750.00	$13,750.00
Interest on investment, $12,000, for 1 year,	720		Int. on investment, $14,500, for 1 year,	870.00	
Less interest on $900 withdrawn, from average date, July 6th to Jan. 1st (178 days),	267	453	Less int. on $750 withdrawn, from average date, Aug. 26 to Jan. 1 (127 days),	158.75	711.25
A.'s credit balance,		$11,553	B.'s credit balance,		$14,461.25

Firm's net capital,		$41,000.00
A.'s credit balance,	$11,553.00	
B.'s "	14,461.25	26,014.25
Firm's net gains,		$14,985.75

A.'s investment, less amount withdrawn,	$11,100.00	B.'s investment, less amount withdrawn,	$13,750.00
Credit balance of int.,	453.00	Credit balance of int.,	711.25
His ½ gains,	7,492.88	His ½ gains,	7,492.87
A.'s net capital,	$19,045.88	B.'s net capital,	$21,954.12

Firm's net capital, as above, $41,000.

6. A., B., and C. commenced business with a capital of $6000 each. The gains and losses were to be shared equally, and each partner was to receive interest on his capital, and to pay interest on all sums withdrawn. At the close of the year they had—Cash on hand, $4250; Merchandise, $16,500; Bills Receivable, $1000; Personal debts due them, $4120.67. The firm owes—Bills Payable, $500; Personal debts, $630.35.

During the year, A. drew out $1007.57, the interest on which to the end of the year was $20.15; B. drew $2049.61, on which the interest was $20.50; C. drew $3213.92, the interest on which was $28.12. How much did they gain or lose, and what was each partner's capital at the end of the year?

NOTE.—When books are kept by Double Entry, the above results can be obtained with very little trouble.

7. When the capital of the firm or company is kept separate from the accounts of the partners, and the amounts withdrawn are to be considered as taken from the gains and not from the capital, the following forms of statement are generally adopted:—

Assets.		*Liabilities.*		
Real Estate,	$45,000	Bills Payable,		$15,750
Machinery and fixtures,	7,000	Debts, per Ledger,		14,250
Cash,	2,500	Capital Stock,		50,000
Mdse., as per inventory,	8,500	*Net gains,*		*22,900*
U. S. 5-20 Bonds,	6,000	Jas. L. Hart's ½ gain,	$11,450	
Accrued int. on do.,	120	Less am't withdrawn,	8,400	
Bills Receivable,	12,000	Balance,	$3,050	
Central Pacific R.R. Stock,	5,000	Robt. Hunter's ¼ gain,	$5,725	
Partners' withdrawals and interest,—		Less am't withdrawn,	4,880	
		Balance,	$845	
James L. Hart,	8,400	P. S. Weston's ¼ gain,	$5,725	
Robert Hunter,	4,880	Less am't withdrawn,	3,500	
Philip S. Weston,	3,500	Balance,	$2,225	
	$102,900			$102,900

8. A. and B. commenced business as partners. A. invested $20,000, and B. $10,000, A. sharing ⅔ and B. ⅓ of the gains and losses. No interest account was kept. A. drew out $1700, and B. $2150. Their assets at the close of the year consisted of—Cash, $4200; Bills Receivable, $8800; Mdse., $26,000; and Personal debts, $16,000. 10 per cent. of the personal debts are considered bad. Their liabilities are—Bills Payable, $3250; Personal accounts, $11,250. If B. should retire from the firm, how much ought he to receive?

Assets.		*Liabilities.*	
Cash,	$4,200	Bills Payable,	$3,250
Bills Receivable,	8,800	Personal accounts,	11,250
Mdse.,	26,000		$14,500
Personal accts., less 10%,	14,400	Capital invested,	30,000
	$53,400		$44,500
Add amount drawn out,	3,850	*Firm's net gain,*	*12,750*
	$57,250		$57,250

	Dr.			*Cr.*
A.'s Acct.	Drawn out,	$1,700	Capital,	$20,000
	Balance,	*26,800*	⅔ net gain,	8,500
		$28,500		$28,500
B.'s Acct.	Drawn out,	$2,150	Capital,	$10,000
	Balance,	*12,100*	⅓ net gain,	4,250
		$14,250		$14,250

DETECTING ERRORS IN TRIAL BALANCES.

322. The **Trial Balance** is the best short test of the correctness of account-books that has yet been devised. It is not, however, entirely reliable; because its equilibrium is not affected by posting into the wrong account, or omitting to post both a debit and a credit of equal amounts.

When the Trial Balance is not in equilibrium, to discover where the error exists,—

1. Ascertain the exact amount of the error. Omitting to do this has led to prolonged search for what did not really exist.

2. If the error is of large amount, examine whether the amounts have been entered in the Trial Balance correctly. Many mistakes are made in transferring amounts from one place to another. For this reason, some book-keepers always post with their Ledger on their right, to prevent reading the figures backwards.

3. Examine the Cash Balance: it can never be on the credit side, and should agree with the amount actually on hand. The balance of Bills Receivable should never be on the credit side, nor the balance of Bills Payable on the debit side of the account.

4. If posts are made directly from the Cash Book, see whether the balance brought down from the previous month has been deducted from the debit footing before posting to the debit of cash. The total debit footing, less the balance from the previous month, is the proper amount to post.

5. Examine the books, to find an amount corresponding with the error, or with half the error; an amount posted to the wrong side of an account will produce an error in balancing equal to twice the amount.

6. Divide the error by 9. It is a principle in figures that the difference between any number and the same number

transposed in whole, or in part, may be divided by 9 without a remainder, and the sum of the figures in the difference will make 9's. Thus, the difference between 753 and 735 = 18 ÷ 9 = 2, and 1 + 8 = 9.

9753	9753	9753	9753
7953	9573	9735	3579
1800	180	18	6174

Errors in transposition are among the most difficult of detection.

7. See whether the footings of the accounts and the balances are correct.

If the error is in one figure only, it is generally an error in adding, carrying, or transferring.

If the error is in the dollar column or cent columns only, the columns on the left need not be re-added.

8. If, after the above examinations, the error remains undiscovered, examine each post separately, and check the amounts both in the book from which postings are made and in the Ledger, and then examine the amounts to see if any remain unchecked. If the entries are made correctly, and the amounts are in equilibrium before posting, by following the above suggestions the error will soon be detected.

FRAUDULENT BALANCES.

323. To ascertain the true weight with fraudulent balances, when the weights are accurate.

RULE.—*Find what weights balance the substance to be weighed; then transpose them, and find the weight that will produce an equilibrium; then multiply together the two weights thus found, and extract the square root of the product.*

EXAMPLE.—If by the first weighing the article weighs 8 lbs., and by the second it weighs 10⅛ lbs., the product is 81, the square root of which is 9, the true weight.

DIVIDENDS AND INVESTMENTS.

324. Stocks is a general term applied to the bonds of the Government or State, and to the bonds and shares of incorporate companies. They are usually bought and sold, through the medium of brokers, at the Stock Exchange.

325. Bonds are obligations or deeds securing the payment of a certain sum of money on or before a future day appointed.

When issued by governments or corporations, they are made in denominations of convenient size, bearing interest usually payable semi-annually. They frequently have *coupons* or *interest-tickets* attached, bearing date, amount, signature, &c., which are due at the expiration of each successive half-year; these are cut off as they are paid, and held as receipts. For temporary loans, Treasury Notes have also been issued by the United States Government, payable with interest, some with and some without coupons. Exchequer Bills have been issued in England in the same manner.

326. A **Joint Stock Company** is an association of men having a capital that is divided into shares of equal value, which are transferable and may be bought and sold like any other property.

327. Certificates of Stock are issued to each stockholder, indicating the number of shares to which he is entitled. The first or original value of the shares is called their *nominal* or *par value.* When they sell for more than their par value, they are said to be *above par*, or at a *premium;* when for less, *below par*, or at a *discount.*

328. An **Instalment** is a certain portion of the capital paid at a particular time.

329. An **Assessment** is an amount for which the stockholders are called upon to make up deficiencies or losses.

330. The **Gross Earnings** consist of the entire receipts of a company.

331. The **Net Earnings** are what remains after the expenses are deducted.

332. The **Dividend** is the sum divided among the stockholders from the gains of the business.

333. Sometimes, in addition to the cash dividend, which is payable at a stated time, the company declare a *Scrip dividend*, for which certificates are issued payable on the contingency that the affairs of the company continue prosperous This Scrip bears interest, or not, as the company may determine. (See FORM OF CERTIFICATE OF SCRIP.)

334. A **Mortgage** is a conveyance of property as a pledge for the security of a debt, and becomes void when the debt is paid.

335. **Ground-Rents** is a term applied to leases of building lots, the rent of which is considered equivalent to the interest on the valuation of the land. The payment is generally secured by a claim on the building erected on the land occupied. By a recent law in Pennsylvania, no new ground-rent can be made irredeemable, but may be extinguished upon payment of a sum the interest of which is equal to the rent annually paid.

336. **Building Lots** are sometimes sold at so much per foot. The price is obtained by dividing the interest per annum on the valuation of the whole lot by the number of feet on the front; the quotient is the price per foot. Thus, a lot valued at $3000, with a front of 20 feet, is said to be worth $9 per foot; the interest on $3000, which is $180 per annum, being divided by 20, the number of feet on the front, gives $9 as the price.

337. The value of an investment depends upon its **security,** its **productiveness,** its **permanency,** its **facility of transfer,** and the **readiness** with which the income derived from it may be collected.

National Debt of the United States.

The following is a statement of the Public Debt of the United States on the 1st of March, 1866:—

Debt bearing Coin Interest.

6 per cent. Bonds, Dec. 31, 1867, and July 1, 1868 .	$18,323,591.80	
5 per cent. Bonds, Jan. 1, 1874	20,000,000.00	
5 per cent. Bonds, Jan. 1, 1871	7,022,000.00	
6 per cent. Bonds, Dec. 31, 1880, and June 30, 1881, called 6's of '81	282,693,100.00	
6 per cent. 5-20 Bonds, May 1, 1867, or May 1, 1882, int. May and Nov.	514,780,500.00	
6 per cent. 5-20 Bonds, Nov. 1, 1869, or Nov. 1, 1884, int. May and Nov.	100,000.000.00	
6 per cent. 5-20 Bonds, Nov. 1, 1870, or Nov. 1, 1885	61,263,000.00	
5 per cent. 10-40 Bonds, March 1, 1874, or March 1, 1904 . . . . - .	172,769,100.00	
6 per cent. Bonds, Oregon War., July 1, 1881 .	1,016,000.00	$1,177,867,291.80

Debt bearing Currency Interest.

6 per cent. Bonds, Union Pacific R.R. Co., Nov. 1, 1895	$1,632,000.00	
6 per cent. Bonds, Central Pacific R.R. Co., Jan. 16, 1895	2,362,000.00	
4, 5, 6 per cent. Temporary Loan, ten days' notice after thirty days	118,577,939.50	
Certificates of Indebtedness 1 year from date .	62,264,000.00	
1 and 2 year 5 per cent. notes, 1 and 2 years from date	8,536,900.00	
3-year Compound Interest Notes, 3 years from date,	174,012,141.00	
3-year 7-30 Treasury Notes, 3 years from date .	818,044,000.00	$1,185,428,980.50

Matured Debt not presented for Payment.

Texas Indemnity Bonds	$618,000.00	
3-year 7-30 Treasury Notes	167,350.00	
Bonds	81,268.00	
Treasury Notes	118,161.64	
Temporary Loan, coin	1,200.00	$985,979.64

Debt bearing no Interest.

United States Notes	$423,435,373.00	
Fractional Currency	27,523,734.52	
Gold Certificates of Deposit	12,627,600.00	$463,586,707.52
Total Debt		$2,827,868,959.46

The Public Debt of the United States on the 1st of March, 1867:—

Debt bearing Coin Interest.

5 per cent. Bonds	$198,091,350.00	
6 per cent. Bonds, '67 and '68	15,679,591.80	
6 per cent. Bonds, 1881	283,745,250.00	
6 per cent. 5-20 Bonds	954,839,000.00	
Navy Pension Fund	12,500,000.00	$1,464,855,191.80

Debt bearing Currency Interest.

6 per cent. Bonds	$12,922,000.00	
3 year Compound Interest Notes	141,308,830.00	
3 year 7-30 Notes	632,798,050.00	$787,028,880.00
Matured Debt not presented for payment		14,576,689.07
United States Notes	$376,235,626.00	
Fractional Currency	29,514,722.32	
Gold Certificates of Deposit	18,376,180.00	424,126,528.32
Total Debt		$2,690,587,289.19

Amount in the Treasury.

Coin	$107,271,031.12	
Currency	52,552,368.27	159,823,399.39
Amount of Debt, less cash, in Treasury		$2,530,763,889.80

The foregoing is a correct statement of the public debt, as appears from the books and Treasurer's returns in the Department on the 1st of March, 1867. (Signed) Hugh McCulloch,
Secretary of the Treasury.

Reduction of debt in one year $137,281,670.00

Amount in Treasury.

	March 1, 1866.	March 1, 1867.
Coin	$55,736,192	$107,271,031
Currency	60,282,767	52,552,368
Total	$116,018,959	$159,823,399
Debt, less amount in Treasury March 1, 1866		$2,711,850,000
Debt, less amount in Treasury March 1, 1867		2,530,763,890
Actual reduction of debt in one year		$181,086,110

At this rate of reduction, the entire debt could be paid in fifteen years.

Receipts and Expenditures of the United States for the year ending June 30th, 1866.

RECEIPTS.		EXPENDITURES.	
From Customs	$179,046,630.64	Civil, Foreign and Mis.	$41,049,965.96
From Public Lands	665,031.03	Pensions and Indians	16,253,300.44
From Direct Tax	1,974,754.12	War	284,449,701.82
From Internal Revenue	309,226,812.81	Navy	43,519,632.21
From Miscellaneous	65,125,966.46	Interest	133,074,737.27
Total	$556,039,195.06	Total	$518,347,337.70

Total receipts	$556,039,195.06
Total expenditures	518,347,337.70
Excess of receipts	$37,691,857.36

UNITED STATES BONDS.

338. The term **"Five-Twenties"** is applied to the 6% gold-bearing bonds of the United States, to which twenty years' half-yearly coupons are attached, but which may be paid off in gold by the Government, on due notice to the holders, at any time after *five years.*

339. The **5-20's** which were issued MAY 1, 1862, called "Old 5-20's," because they were the first issued, are redeemable after May 1, 1867, payable May 1, 1882. They bear interest at 6% payable on May 1st and November 1st.

340. The **5-20's of 1864** were issued November 1, 1864. Interest payable May 1st and November 1st.

341. The **5-20's of 1865,** NOVEMBER ISSUE, bear date November 1, 1865. Interest payable May 1st and November 1st.

342. The **5-20's of 1865,** JULY ISSUE, are issued in exchange for 7-30's, and bear date July 1, 1865. Interest on them is payable January 1st and July 1st.

343. The term **"Ten-Forties"** is applied to the 5% gold-bearing bonds of the United States, to which half-yearly coupons are attached for 40 years, but which may be paid off in gold, on notice to the holders, at any time after 10 years. Interest on them is payable, on the $500 and $1000 coupon bonds, and on all the registered bonds, March 1st and September 1st; and on the $100 and $50 coupon bonds yearly, on March 1st.

344. The **"Seven-Thirties"** represent a *Currency* Loan having 3 years to run, then convertible at the option of the holder into a gold-interest 6% stock having 20 years to run, but with the right reserved to the Government of paying off the loan in gold at any time after five years. The term "Seven-Thirties" is derived from the rate of interest which these three years' convertible notes bear, to wit: 2 cents per day on each $100, or for 365 days, seven dollars and thirty cents on each $100.

The **First Series 7-30 Treasury Notes** are dated August 15, 1864, and interest on them is payable in currency August 15th and February 15th.

Second Series 7-30 Notes, the same as first, except that they bear date June 15, 1865, and interest is payable June 15th and December 15th. They are convertible June 15, 1868, either into 5-20 bonds or money, at the option of the holder.

The **Third Series 7-30 Notes,** same as the first two, except that the Government reserves the right to pay the interest at any time at 6% in gold instead of $7\frac{3}{10}$ in currency, convertible 3 years from their date, viz., July 15, 1865, into 5-20's. Interest payable July 15th and January 15th.

345. The **6 per cents. of 1881,** sometimes called the long or unconditional 6% gold-bearing loan, cannot be redeemed by the Government at all, except by purchase, until after the year 1881, making this the most desirable of all the United States loans as a permanent investment. Interest on them is payable January 1st and July 1st.

346. The terms "Greenbacks" and "Legal-Tenders" are convertible. All the Greenbacks are legal tender.

All gold-bearing bonds are either coupon or registered.

All the coupon bonds are issued in denominations of $50, $100, $500, and $1000. Registered bonds the same, with $5000 and $10,000 additional.

The 7-30 Notes are issued in sums of $50, $100, $500, $1000, and $5000, all with coupons attached.

Any coupon bonds will be exchanged by the Government for registered of the same issue.

UNITED STATES TREASURY DEPARTMENT REGULATIONS.

347. Instructions to Correspondents.—"Letters relating to the redemption of public securities, the conversion of $7\frac{3}{10}$ Treasury Notes, or the exchange of coupon bonds for registered certificates, should be addressed to the Secretary of the Treasury. Letters relating to the transfer of registered stock, or payment of interest on the same, should be addressed to the Register of the Treasury. The transfer-books are closed for thirty days previous to the day for payment of dividends, and stockholders desiring the place of payment changed, must give notice to the Register one month at least before the day of payment. When bonds are sent for transfer, state where interest is to be made payable, and always inclose stock of different loans in separate letters. When specifying the different loans, or referring to the interest, name the amount of stock, and describe the loan by the date of the act of Congress authorizing it. Powers of attorney for the assignment of United States stock, and assignments, must be properly filled before transmission to the Register, as no blanks can be filled in his office. Powers of attorney to draw interest should be addressed to the First Auditor of the Treasury."

348. The **National Debt of Great Britain** is of two kinds, funded and unfunded. When a certain portion of the public revenue is appropriated for the payment of the interest on the debt, it is called funded, and it is called unfunded when no such division is made. *Exchequer Bills* (see Forms), which are somewhat similar to United States interest-bearing Treasury Notes, are a part of the unfunded debt. England has effected loans at different rates, 5, 4, $3\frac{1}{2}$, 3 per cent., &c.; and one of the conditions of such loans is, that while the stipulated interest is regularly paid, the Government cannot be called upon to return the principal.

349. Consols are a 3% English stock, which had its origin in the act of Parliament *consolidating* several separate Government stocks, called in the act *Consolidated Annuities*, and commonly quoted, for brevity, "Consols."

The stock, from its amount, and the immense number of its holders, is more sensitive to financial influence than any other. Its dividends are payable semi-annually,—January 5th and July 5th.

350. The other kinds of stock, bearing 3%, are the *Reduced Annuities*, which formerly bore a higher rate of interest, and the New Three per cent. Annuities.

NATIONAL DEBTS.

	Debt.	Population.	Average Amount per capita.
Great Britain,	$3,999,010,695	30,000,000	133.33
United States,	2,827,868,959	35,000,000	87.70
France,	2,000,000,000	36,500,000	54.79
Austria,	1,580,000,000	75,000,000	21.06
Russia,	1,395,000,000	68,932,000	20.23
Italy,	770,000,000	21,770,000	35.37
Spain,	745,000,000	16,000,000	46.56
Netherlands,	425,000,000	3,619,000	117.43
Turkey,	255,000,000	16,440,000	15.51
Prussia,	215,000,000	18,000,000	11.94
Portugal,	165,000,000	4,000,000	41.25
Hamburg,	23,000,000	222,000	103.60
Greece,	20,000,000	1,000,000	20.00

1. What is the annual interest on the debt of England, at the average rate of 3½ per cent., and what is the proportion for each inhabitant to pay?

2. What is the annual interest on the debt of the United States, as per Statement March 1st, 1867, and how much is each person's share? How much must be raised by the Government annually to pay the interest and cancel the debt in 30 years?

17

THE STOCK EXCHANGE.

351. The Stock Exchange is an association organized for the purpose of buying and selling stock. It is governed by stringent regulations, to prevent improper persons from being admitted, and to insure fidelity in the performance of engagements. The members are elected by ballot; if a certain number of black balls appear against a candidate, he is rejected. In Philadelphia, five are sufficient to prevent his becoming a member.

The admission fee varies: to the New York Stock Exchange it is $3000; to the Philadelphia and the Boston Stock Exchange it is $2000. In London the admission fee is 20 guineas, besides a yearly subscription of 10 guineas. The fee to become a member of the New York Open Board is $2000; to the Gold Board it is $2500. There are no dues to be paid in addition, but members are fined for non-attendance.

Rules are enacted by which the proceedings of the Exchange are governed, disputes settled, and by which the prices and terms in buying and selling stocks are regulated. The charges in our large cities for buying and selling United States bonds are ⅛ per cent., or 12½ cents for a bond of $100; for other bonds, ¼ per cent., or 25 cents per $100; for shares of companies, ¼ per cent., or 25 cents per share when the par value of the shares is $50 or more; when the par value is between $5 and $50, ⅛ per cent., or 12½ cents per share; when $5 or less, 6¼ cents per share. In London, the commission on the sale or purchase of stock in the English or foreign funds is ⅛, or 2*s.* 6*d.* per cent.; on exchequer bills, 1*s.* per cent.; on railway shares, when over £50 in value, ½ per cent. upon the value.

Stock is bought and sold during the sessions, or "boards," as they are termed, at which time a clerk calls the names of the different stocks in the market, and the members offer to sell or to buy at a price which they mention.

A charge against a member is instantly investigated, and, if he is found guilty of misconduct, or fails to fulfil his engagements, he is expelled.

The Stock Exchange has a language peculiar to itself. A stock "broker" is one who receives and executes orders for persons who are not members of the exchange. A stock "jobber" deals in stocks for his own account. A "stag," or "outsider," conducts his transactions outside the Exchange.

A "bull" is one who operates for a rise in prices,—so called from the nature of a bull to toss with his horns. He is usually one who has agreed to purchase stock, without any intention of holding or paying for it, but with a view to sell out again before "settling-day" arrives. A "bear" is one who endeavors to depress prices,—so called from the nature of a bear to tear down with his claws. He, generally, has agreed to deliver more stock than he possesses, and is consequently obliged to buy in order to settle his account. A "lame duck" is a member unable to fulfil his contracts, and is therefore expelled.

"Opening-day" is the first day the books of a corporation are opened after a dividend has been declared.

The term "selling short" is applied to sales of stock which the seller does not own, and over which he has no control. Securities sold in this manner are generally deliverable at a specified time, not exceeding 60 days. If the contract is for a longer period than three days, the seller receives interest.

"Seller's option" gives the person selling the privilege of making delivery at any time intervening before the expiration of that mentioned in the contract, by his giving one day's notice. "Buyer's option" gives the purchaser a claim for delivery at any time before the maturity of the contract, by a similar notice. The contract must be settled at least by maturity, unless extended by mutual agreement. The transactions are adjusted by delivery of property, or the payment in cash of the difference in prices. A postponement of settling-day is termed a "contango." By a law in Pennsylvania, contracts for the sale of stock to be executed or performed at any future period exceeding five judicial days next ensuing the date of such contracts, are prohibited under heavy penalties.

The "cornering" process, or "getting up a corner," is the act of a combination of operators, and is always the result of short sales. All the floating shares of a company are bought for future delivery, and when the stock has been rendered scarce in this manner, the shares thus bought are suddenly called for, to the loss of the short sellers, who are obliged to buy at an advanced rate, or pay the buyer the difference in price.

The following extract was taken from the *United States Gazette*:—

REPORTED BY JAY COOKE & CO., BANKERS.

SALES.		EXPLANATION.
26000 U. S. 5-20 bonds,	103⅝	5-20 bonds at $3.62½ premium.
100 Reading R.R., 2 ds.,	51⅜	Railroad stock sold at 2 days' credit.
100 " " 5 w.n.,		" " to be delivered before five days, without notice.
1000 Camden & Amboy 6's, 1889,	108½	6 per cent. bonds, due in 1889, at 8½ per cent. premium.
100 Reading R.R., b. 30,	67¾	To be delivered before 30 days.
100 N. Y. Central, b. 15 and int.,	103	" " before 15 days, with int.
15500 U. S. 6's, 1881, lots,	109½	U. S. 6 per cent. bonds, due in 1881, sold in lots, aggregating $15,500.
100 U. S. Treasury 7-30 F. & A.,	111¼	7-30 bonds, interest payable in February and August. A. & O. means Apr. & Oct.
100 Catawissa pref. s., w.n.,	26	Catawissa preferred stock, without notice.
2000 Penna. R.R., 2d M., 6's,	100¼	Second mortgage, bearing 6 per cent. int.
100 Penna. 6's, int. off,	104	Penna. 6 per cent. bonds, the interest last due having been paid.
100 " 5's,	99½	Penna. 6 per cent. bonds, bearing 5 per cent. interest.
400 " R.R. ex. div.,	75	Penna. R.R. shares without dividend.
500 Phila. & Erie R.R., b.o.,	32	500 shares at $32, at buyer's option when to take the stock.
300 " " " s.o.,	31	300 shares at $31, at seller's option when to deliver the stock.

The value of a given number of shares is found by multiplying the number of shares by the price per share.

NOTE.—In finding the cost of bonds, the rate of brokerage may be added to the price, as the brokerage and price are both calculated on the same amount.

EXAMPLE 1.—What must I pay for 100 shares of Chicago & Rock Island R.R. stock, purchased at $112.50 per share, brokerage at ¼% and revenue stamp included?

100 shares @ $112.50,	$11250.
¼% on $10000, par value of 100 shares,	25.
Revenue stamp, 1c. on every $100 of sales,	1.13
	$11276.13

Ex. 2.—What will I receive if I sell 300 shares Cleveland & Pittsburg R.R. stock, @ $72.00, after paying for revenue stamp and brokerage @ ¼% per share?

$72 × 300 = $21600

300 shares at ¼% per share (par value, $50) =	$75.00
Revenue stamp,	2.16
	$77.16

$21600 — 77.16 = $21522.84, Ans.

To find the dividend on any given number of shares of stock.

RULE.—*Multiply the par value of the stock by the rate of dividend, and divide the product by 100.*

EXAMPLES.

1. If I own 100 shares of Penna. Railroad stock, the par value of which is $50, how much will I receive when a dividend of 5% is declared?

50 × 5 = 2.50, dividend on 1 share.
100 × 2.50 = 250, " " 100 shares. Ans. $250.

2. How much will a stockholder of the New York Central Railroad Co. receive of a 4% dividend, who owns 500 shares, the par value being $100 per share?

352. To find the rate of dividend.

RULE.—*Multiply the dividend by 100, and divide by the par value of the stock.*

EXAMPLES.

1. The receipts of a mining company in one year are $170,000, clear of all expenses. The company has a capital of $500,000, divided into shares of $10 each. Reserving $50,000 as a contingent fund, what rate of dividend can it declare for the year? what per month? and how much can be paid on each share of stock?

$170000 - 50000 = 120000$, amount to be divided.
$120000 \times 100 = 12000000 \qquad 12000000 \div 500000 = 24$

Ans. 24% yearly, 2% monthly, 20c. per month on each share.

PROOF.—24% of 500000 = 120000, dividend to be declared.

2. A man subscribed for 300 shares of stock in a manufacturing company, the par value of which was placed at $50 per share; but, after paying three instalments, amounting to 75% per cent. of the par value, a dividend of 3% was declared. How much will he receive, and at what rate per cent. on the actual cost?

3% of 50 = 1.50, dividend on one share.
$1.50 \times 300 =$ $450, dividend on 300 shares.
75% of 50 = $37.50
$1.50 \times 100 = 150.00 \qquad 150.00 \div 37.50 = 4$
Ans. $450. Total dividend = 4% on actual cost.

353. To find what rate of income will be derived from a given investment.

RULE.—*Multiply the income by 100, and divide the product by the amount invested.*

EXAMPLES.

1. If I buy railroad stock at a premium of 6 per cent., and pay ¼ per cent. brokerage, what per cent. of income will I receive if its annual dividend is 7 per cent.?

$7 \times 100 = 700 \qquad 700 \div 106\frac{1}{4} = 6\frac{10}{17}$ Ans. $6\frac{10}{17}$%.

2. What per cent. will I receive if I buy stock, which pays 4% dividend, at a discount of 20%?

$100 - 20 = 80$, amount invested.
$4 \times 100 = 400 \qquad 400 \div 80 = 5$ Ans. 5%.

3. If I pay 106 for United States 6% bonds, having 15 years to run, what per cent. will I receive if I keep them until they mature, and then obtain the principal?

6% per year for 15 years =	$90 interest.
Principal,	100
Total amount received,	190
Cost of bond,	106
Total income,	84

To find what rate is required for 106 to gain 84 in 15 years, see Art. 79.

106 at 1% = 1.06 × 15 = 15.90, interest at 1% for 15 years.

```
15.90)8400(5.283+          Ans. 5 283/1000 %.
      7950
      ----
       4500
       3180
       ----
       13200
       12720
       -----
         4800
         4770
```

NOTE.—The interest on the semi-annual payments of interest is also to be considered.

4. What rate per cent. will be gained if I purchase United States 5-20 bonds, at a premium of 8%, if they are paid at the end of 6 years? Ans. $4\frac{26}{81}$.

354. To find the price to be paid for stock to obtain a given rate upon the investment.

RULE.—*Annex two ciphers to the rate per cent. which the stock produces, and divide by the required rate; the quotient will be the price to be paid.*

EXAMPLES.

1. At what price must railroad stock be purchased, which pays 6% on the par value of $100, in order to obtain 7% income on the investment?

$600 \div 7 = 85.71\frac{3}{7}$ Ans. $85.71.

2. At what price must I purchase railroad stock of the par value of $50 per share, which pays a dividend of 6%, that I may obtain an income of 8% on the investment? Ans. $37.50.

3. If I receive 9% on my investment in a company which pays a dividend of 6%, at what price did I purchase?

4. At what price must 5% stock be purchased in order to obtain 6% on the investment?

5. At what premium ought an 8% stock to sell, to equal 6% stock? Ans. $33\frac{1}{3}$.

6. At what rate must 6% stock be purchased to equal 8% stock? to equal 10% stock?

355. To find what rate must be obtained, that a given sum invested may bring a given income.

RULE.—*Multiply the given income by 100, and divide the product by the sum invested.*

EXAMPLE.

If I invest $5000, what rate per cent. must I receive to obtain an income of $325 per year?

$$32500 \div 5000 = 6\tfrac{1}{2}\%.$$

356. To find what sum must be invested, that a given income may be obtained.

RULE.—*Divide the required income by the rate of income per share, or per $100, for the number of shares or bonds required, and multiply the quotient by the given price.*

EXAMPLES.

1. What sum must be invested in United States 6% bonds, at 108, to realize an income of $1200 per annum?

$6 = income per $100,—$108 the price of $100 bonds.
1200 ÷ 6 = 200, the number of bonds of $100 each.
200 × 108 = 21600.

Ans. $21600.

2. What sum must be invested, at $65 per share, in railroad stock which pays a dividend of 10% on the par value of $50 per share, in order to obtain an income of $520?

10% of $50 = $5, income per share.
$520 ÷ $5 = 104, the number of shares.
104 × $65 = $6760. Ans. $6760.

3. If United States *Ten-Forties* are selling at 93, how much must I invest in them to obtain a yearly income of $1800, after paying 5% income tax?

357. To find the par value, when the premium or discount is given.

RULE.—*Divide the given value of the stock by 1 increased by the rate per cent. of premium, or diminished by the rate per cent. of discount.*

EXAMPLES.

1. Bought Mechanics' National Bank stock for 29, at which price I paid a premium of 16%. What is the par value? Ans. $25.

2. Sold Worcester & Nashua Railroad stock for $91.66⅔, and received 10% above the par value. What is the par value? Ans. $83.33⅓.

3. Bought Philadelphia & Erie Railroad stock for $47, which is 6% below par. What is the par value?

4. Bought Fulton Bank stock at 500% premium, for $180. What is the par value of the shares? Ans. $30.

358. To find at what price a bond, having several years to run, must be purchased, that the interest and final payment will be equivalent to a given rate per annum on the investment.

RULE.—I. *Find the Amount of the given bond.*

II. *Find the present worth of this amount at the proposed rate.*

NOTE.—No account is taken in this rule of interest on the annual payments of interest.

EXAMPLES.

1. What shall I pay for a bond of $100, having 5 years to run, with interest at 6%, in order to make it an 8% investment?

Amount of $100 for 5 years = $130.

By Art. 84, 130 ÷ 1.40 = 92.86. Ans. $92.86.

Interest on $92.86 at 8% for 5 yrs. = 37.14. 92.86 + 37.14 = 130.

2. At what price must I buy United States 5-20 Bonds, if they are paid in 4 years, in order to gain 7% on my investment?

3. Bought Kentucky State Bonds, bearing 5% interest, payable in 3 years, and received, when I obtained the principal, 6% on my investment. What did I pay?

MISCELLANEOUS.

1. What rate per cent. will the purchaser of Philadelphia Bank stock receive on his investment if the premium on the stock is 35% and the bank pays an annual dividend of 8%?

Ans. $5\frac{25}{27}$.

2. Which is the most profitable,—United States 10-40 Bonds purchased at 95, or the 5-20 Bonds purchased at 105?

3. Which is the better investment, a ground-rent bearing 6% interest, purchased at 98%, or railroad stock purchased at 10% premium, which pays an annual dividend of 7%? and how much?

4. What interest will a person receive who purchased United States 5-20 Bonds at 104, if he sells the gold received for interest at a premium of 30%?

STOCK TABLE,

Showing the rate of Interest received on Stocks purchased, from 25 per cent. discount to 25 per cent premium.

Purchase Price.	RATE RECEIVED ON STOCK BEARING INTEREST AT				
	5 per cent.	6 per cent.	7 per cent.	8 per cent.	10 per cent.
75.	6.666	8.00	9.333	10.666	13.333
80.	6.25	7.50	8.75	10.000	12.500
85.	5.882	7.143	8.235	9.411	11.764
90.	5.555	6.666	7.777	8.888	11.111
95.	5.263	6.316	7.263	8.421	10.526
97.50	5.128	6.156	7.179	8.205	10.256
100.	5.000	6.000	7.000	8.000	10.000
105.	4.761	5.714	6.666	7.619	9.523
110.	4.545	5.454	6.363	7.272	9.090
115.	4.347	5.130	6.086	6.956	8.695
120.	4.166	5.000	5.833	6.666	8.333
125.	4.000	4.800	5.600	6.400	8.000

UNITED STATES BONDS IN EUROPE.

The Five-Twenty Bonds issued in 1862, called the "Old" 5-20's, were the first known in Europe, and for that reason are in greatest demand, causing an advance over the issues of 1864 and 1865 of 1½ to 4½ per cent. The real value of the different issues is the same.

The quotations in London, Paris, Frankfort, Hamburg, and other places, are the prices of $100 bonds in American gold. Thus, "Frankfort, Feb. 9th, U. S. 5-20's 76¼," signifies that $76.25 in U. S. coin is the price of a bond for $100.

The interest which has accrued at the time of purchase forms a part of the value of the bond.

The principal causes of the difference in the quotations on the same day are the fluctuations in the rate of exchange and the difference in the basis of calculation.

It is necessary also to know whether the "old" or "new" issue is meant. The telegraphic report frequently omits the date of issue; in the Stock Exchange Circular, the prices of both are given.

To understand the subject fully requires a knowledge of exchange and stock calculations, and an acquaintance with the customs and manner of dealing among bankers.

Foreign Stock Quotations.

(PER ATLANTIC CABLE.)

LONDON, Mar. 1.	U. S. 5-20's,	73¼.
	Illinois Central R. R.,	76¼.
	Erie R. R.,	36½.
PARIS, "	U. S. 5-20's,	82⅞.
FRANKFORT, "	" "	76⅝.
LONDON, Mar. 23.	" "	74½.
FRANKFORT, "	" "	77½.

London Quotations.—The price quoted in London is at the nominal par of 4*s.* 6*d.* per dollar, or \$4.44$\frac{4}{9}$ per pound sterling. To this about 9½% must be added for the difference between the old par and the present value of our coins.

To obtain the currency value, the premium on gold must also be added.

EXAMPLES.

What is the value of \$1000 in U. S. 5-20 Bonds when quoted at 70 and the premium on gold is 35%?

```
   1000
     70
 ------
 700.00   Nominal par value.
     9½%
 ------
 630000
  35000
 ------
  66.5000 Exchange premium.
 700
 ------
 766.50   Value in American gold.
    35%
 ------
 383250
229950
 ------
268.2750  Premium on price in gold.
766.50
 ------
1034.7750 $103.48 in United States.
```

To a resident of the United States a purchase in London like this would require an addition of 1% commission, and interest equal to ½% more, which increases the price to \$105.03. The proceeds of a sale would be \$1.55 less than \$103.48 = \$101.93.

2. When gold is at a premium of 33%, what will be received from a sale of \$5000 U.S. 5-20's, at 72, allowing commission and interest at 1½%?

3. How much will a 5-20 Bond for \$5000, purchased in London, cost, in currency, when exchange is 109, and gold is at a premium of 30%, allowing commission at 1%?

Paris Quotations.—In Paris the price of exchange affects the quotations. On the Paris Bourse the bonds are estimated on the conventional basis of 5 francs to the dollar, while the actual value of a dollar in exchange transactions is 5.10 and 5.15, equal to a difference of \$2 to \$3 on \$100.

London quotations, being based on the old par, require the addition of about 9½% and the difference between the Paris Bourse rates and actual exchange rates, to give the comparative value of both places.

EXAMPLE.—February 23, 1867. London, U. S. 5-20's 73¾; Paris, 83¼.

Premium on \$73.75 @ 9½%,	=	\$7.00
Difference between Bourse and exch. rates	=	2.50
To be added to London rate,		9.50

73.75 + 9.50 = 83.25 Paris rate, as above.

NOTE.—The difference between the Bourse rate and the exchange rate should be taken from the Paris quotations to obtain the real price in Paris.

In Frankfort, when American gold is not paid, the value is computed at the rate of 2½ guilders per dollar.

1. On March 1, 1867, the quotations per Atlantic Cable were: London, U.S. 5-20's 73¼; Frankfort, 76⅝. In New York, exchange on London the same day was 109.

Value of \$73.25 in London, @ 9% prem.,	79.84
Price in Frankfort,	76.62
Difference between London and Frankfort,	3.22

With exchange on Frankfort at 41⅝, the difference is but a trifle.

2. On the same day, Illinois Central R. R. stock was quoted in London at 76¼, Erie Railroad at 36½. What are these prices equivalent to in U. S. currency, gold being at 140?

3. What is the value in United States currency of a bill of exchange on England, when quoted at 153, which includes the exchange premium and premium on gold?

COMPOUND INTEREST.

360. Compound Interest is interest on both principal and interest.

361. To compute compound interest.

RULE.—*Find the interest on the given principal to the time the interest becomes due, and add the principal. Then find the interest on this amount for the next period, and add as before, and so continue for each successive period to the time of settlement.*

Subtract the given principal from the last amount, and the remainder will be the compound interest.

When the time is for years, months, and days, find the amount for the years, and the interest on this for the remainder of the time.

When interest is payable oftener than once a year, find the amount for each interval in the same manner as when the interest is payable yearly.

EXAMPLES.

1. What is the compound interest of $500 for 3 years, at 5%?

$500	Given principal.
.05	
25.00	Interest for first year.
500	
525.00	Principal for second year.
.05	
26.25	Interest for second year.
525	
551.25	Principal for third year.
.05	
27.5625	Interest for third year.
551.25	
578.8125	Amount for three years.
500	Given principal.
$78.8125	Compound interest for 3 years.

2. What is the compound interest of $425 for 4 years, at 6%? of $275.50 for 3 years, 6 months, at 7%?

362. The labor of computing Compound Interest may be much abridged by the use of the following tables.

TABLE I.

Showing the AMOUNT *of One Dollar at Compound Interest, from ½ to 4½ per cent., for any number of years not exceeding twenty.*

	½ per cent.	1½ per cent.	2 per cent.	2½ per cent.	
1	1.005000	1.015000	1.020000	1.025000	1
2	1.010025	1.030220	1.040400	1.050625	2
3	1.015075	1.045670	1.061208	1.076891	3
4	1.020150	1.061350	1.082432	1.103813	4
5	1.025251	1.077270	1.104081	1.131408	5
6	1.030377	1.093429	1.126162	1.159693	6
7	1.035529	1.109830	1.148686	1.188686	7
8	1.041207	1.126479	1.171659	1.218403	8
9	1.046413	1.143375	1.195093	1.248863	9
10	1.051645	1.160526	1.218994	1.280085	10
11	1.056904	1.177934	1.243374	1.312087	11
12	1.062188	1.195603	1.268242	1.344889	12
13	1.067499	1.213537	1.293607	1.378511	13
14	1.072836	1.231740	1.319479	1.412974	14
15	1.078199	1.250216	1.345868	1.448298	15
16	1.083589	1.268969	1.372786	1.484506	16
17	1.089007	1.288003	1.400241	1.521618	17
18	1.094452	1.307323	1.428246	1.559659	18
19	1.099924	1.326932	1.456811	1.598650	19
20	1.105424	1.346835	1.485947	1.638616	20

	3 per cent.	3½ per cent.	4 per cent.	4½ per cent.	
1	1.030000	1.035000	1.040000	1.045000	1
2	1.060900	1.071225	1.081600	1.092025	2
3	1.092727	1.108718	1.124864	1.141166	3
4	1.125509	1.147523	1.169859	1.192519	4
5	1.159274	1.187686	1.216653	1.246182	5
6	1.194052	1.229255	1.265319	1.302260	6
7	1.229874	1.272279	1.315932	1.360862	7
8	1.266770	1.316809	1.368569	1.422101	8
9	1.304773	1.362897	1.423312	1.486095	9
10	1.343916	1.410599	1.480244	1.552969	10
11	1.384234	1.459970	1.539454	1.622853	11
12	1.425761	1.511069	1.601032	1.695881	12
13	1.468534	1.563956	1.665074	1.772196	13
14	1.512590	1.618695	1.731676	1.851945	14
15	1.557967	1.675349	1.800944	1.935282	15
16	1.604706	1.733986	1.872981	2.022370	16
17	1.652848	1.794676	1.947900	2.113377	17
18	1.702433	1.857489	2.025817	2.208479	18
19	1.753506	1.922501	2.106849	2.307860	19
20	1.806111	1.989789	2.191123	2.411714	20

TABLE II.

Showing the AMOUNT *of One Dollar at Compound Interest, from 5 to 12 per cent., for any number of years not exceeding twenty.*

	5 per cent.	6 per cent.	7 per cent.	8 per cent.	
1	1.050000	1.060000	1.070000	1.080000	1
2	1.102500	1.123600	1.144900	1.166400	2
3	1.157625	1.191016	1.225043	1.269712	3
4	1.215506	1.262477	1.310796	1.360489	4
5	1.276282	1.338226	1.402552	1.469328	5
6	1.340096	1.418519	1.500730	1.586874	6
7	1.407100	1.503630	1.605781	1.713824	7
8	1.477455	1.593848	1.718186	1.850930	8
9	1.551328	1.689479	1.838459	1.999005	9
10	1.628895	1.790848	1.967151	2.158925	10
11	1.710339	1.898299	2.104852	2.331639	11
12	1.795856	2.012196	2.252192	2.518170	12
13	1.885649	2.132928	2.409845	2.719624	13
14	1.979932	2.260904	2.578534	2.937194	14
15	2.078928	2.396558	2.759031	3.172169	15
16	2.182875	2.540352	2.952164	3.425943	16
17	2.292018	2.692773	3.158815	3.700018	17
18	2.406619	2.854339	3.379932	3.996019	18
19	2.526950	3.025599	3.616527	4.315701	19
20	2.653298	3.207135	3.869684	4.660957	20

	9 per cent.	10 per cent.	11 per cent.	12 per cent.	
1	1.090000	1.100000	1.110000	1.120000	1
2	1.188100	1.210000	1.232100	1.254400	2
3	1.295029	1.331000	1.367631	1.404908	3
4	1.411582	1.464100	1.518070	1.573519	4
5	1.538624	1.610510	1.685058	1.762342	5
6	1.677100	1.771561	1.870414	1.973822	6
7	1.828039	1.948717	2.076160	2.210681	7
8	1.992563	2.143589	2.304537	2.475963	8
9	2.171893	2.357948	2.558036	2.773078	9
10	2.367364	2.593742	2.839420	3.105848	10
11	2.580426	2.853117	3.151757	3.478549	11
12	2.812665	3.138428	3.498450	3.895975	12
13	3.065805	3.452271	3.883279	4.363492	13
14	3.341727	3.797498	4.310440	4.887111	14
15	3.642482	4.177248	4.784588	5.473565	15
16	3.970306	4.594973	5.310893	6.130392	16
17	4.327633	5.054470	5.895091	6.866040	17
18	4.717120	5.559917	6.543551	7.689964	18
19	5.141661	6.115909	7.263342	8.612760	19
20	5.604411	6.727500	8.062309	9.646291	20

363. To find the amount of any sum by the tables. *Multiply the amount of $1 for the given rate and time by the given principal.*

EXAMPLE.—What will be the amount of $500 for 10 years, at 6% compound interest?

Amount of $1 for 10 years at 6% = 1.790848
500

Amount of $500 = $895.424000

$895.42 — $500 = $395.42, the compound interest.

364. When the time extends beyond the limits of the table, find the amount for a convenient length of time, and use this amount for a new principal for the remainder of the time.

EXAMPLE.—$1.790848, amount for 10 years, at 6%, multiplied by 1.338226, amount for 5 years, equals $2.396558, amount for 15 years.

365. When the intervals are less than a year, find how many such intervals occur in 1 year, and divide the given rate by the number of intervals thus found; then under the rate shown by the quotient, and opposite the number showing the total number of intervals, will be found the amount.

EXAMPLES.—1. The amount of $800 for 3 years at 6 per cent. compound interest, payable semi-annually, is the same as the amount of $800 at 3 per cent. for 6 years, payable annually. If the interest was payable quarterly, it would be the same as the amount of $800 for 12 years at 1½ per cent.; if payable monthly, the same as for 36 years at ½ per cent.

2. What is the compound interest of $950 for 3 years, 6 months, at 12%, payable semi-annually?

3. What is the compound interest of $4600 for 2 years, interest payable quarterly, at 6% per annum?

366. *Compound Interest, and also the Compound Amount, vary in proportion to the principal.*

367. To find the principal or present worth at compound interest, the amount, time, and rate per cent. being given

RULE.—*Divide the given amount by the compound amount of $1 for the given time and rate.*

EXAMPLE.—What is the present worth of \$306.26, due 3 years hence, at 7 % compound interest?

Amount of \$1 for 3 years at 7 %, \$1.225043.

\$306.26 ÷ 1.225043 = \$250. Ans. \$250.

368. To find the principal or present worth, the compound interest, the time, and the rate per cent. being given.

RULE.—*Divide the given interest by the compound interest on \$1 for the given time and rate.*

EXAMPLE.—What principal at 7 % compound interest will produce \$351.81 in 15 years?

Compound interest of \$1 for 15 years at 7 % = \$1.759031.

\$351.81 ÷ 1.759031 = \$200. Ans. \$200.

369. To find the *time* or *rate*, when the other quantities are given.

RULE.—*Divide the amount by the principal, and look for the quotient in the Table, under the given rate, or opposite the given time.*

370. To compute compound interest by the use of logarithms.

RULE.—*Find the logarithm of the amount of \$100 for 1 year or the time specified, and reject 2 in the index.*

Then multiply it by the given number of years or time specified, and to the product add the logarithm of the principal; their sum will be the logarithm of the amount.

EXAMPLE.

What is the compound interest of \$340 for 7 years at 6 %?

Logarithm of \$106, rejecting 2 in the index,	0.02531
Number of years,	7
	.17717
Add logarithm of \$340,	2.53148
Logarithm of the amount,	2.70865
This logarithm gives,	\$511.23
Deducting the principal,	340.00
Compound interest of \$340 for 7 years,	\$171.23

ANNUITIES.

371. An **Annuity** is a yearly income or sum of money to be paid regularly at stated periods.

372. A **Perpetual Annuity** is one that is unlimited in duration, or which can be terminated by the grantor only on the payment of a sum whose interest will equal the annuity.

373. An **Annuity Certain,** or **Terminable Annuity,** begins and ends at a fixed time.

374. A **Contingent Annuity** depends upon some particular circumstance, as the life of one or more individuals. Life Insurance, Dowers, and Pensions are of this kind.

375. A **Deferred Annuity,** or **Annuity in Reversion,** is one that begins at some future time.

376. An **Annuity forborne** or **in Arrears** is one on which the payments remain unpaid after becoming due.

377. The **Amount** or **Final Value** of an annuity at compound interest is the sum to which all its payments at compound interest will amount at the end of the annuity.

378. The **Present Value** of an annuity is the sum which at interest would amount to its final value.

ANNUITIES AT SIMPLE INTEREST.

379. To find the final value of an annuity at Simple Interest.

RULE.—*Multiply the interest on the annuity for 1 year by the number of years less 1, and this product by one-half the number of years; then*

Add the product of the annuity multiplied by the number of years.

EXAMPLES.

1. What will be the amount or final value of an annuity of $150 for 8 years at 6 %?

Interest on $150 for 1 year = $9.
9 × 7 = 63. 63 × 4 = 252
150 × 8 = 1200

Ans. $1452

2. The rent of a house, which is $300 per year, has remained unpaid for 5 years. What amount is now due, allowing interest at 7 %? Ans. $1710.

380. To find the present value of an annuity at Simple Interest.

RULE.—*Find the final value of the annuity, and then find the present value of that amount.*

EXAMPLE.

1. What is the present value of the annuity mentioned in the first example under the preceding rule?

Final value, $1452. Present worth of $1452 for 8 years at 6 % = $981.81.

ANNUITIES AT COMPOUND INTEREST.

The amount of an annuity of $1, at 6 % Compound Interest, for
1 year = $1.060000.
2 yrs. = $1.123600.
3 " = $1.191016.

The final value of an annuity of $1 for

2 years.	3 years.	4 years.
$1.00	$1.0000	$1.000000
1.06	1.0600	1.060000
$2.06	1.1236	1.123600
	Final value for 3 years, $3.1836	1.191016
		Final value for 4 years, $4.374616

The final value of $300 for 4 years = $4.374616 × 300, = $1312.3848.

381. To find the final value of an annuity.

RULE.—*Multiply the amount of $1, as given in Table I., by the annuity: the product will be the final value.*

382. The final value may also be found by obtaining the principal required to produce an amount of interest equal to the annuity, and then multiplying this principal by the compound amount of $1 for the given rate and time.

383. To find the present value of an annuity.

RULE.—*Divide the amount or final value of the annuity by the amount of $1 at compound interest.* Or,

Multiply the present worth of $1, as given in Table II., by the given annuity.

EXAMPLE.—Find the present worth of an annuity of $1 for 3 years at 6%.

The final value of $1 for 3 years = $3.1836. Then, by Art. 368, Compound Interest, the present value of an annuity of $1 for 3 years = $3.1836 ÷ 1.191016 = $2.673012.

The present value of $500, at the same rate, for the same time, would be $2.673012 × 500 = $1336.506.

384. To find the present value of an annuity in reversion.

RULE.—*Find the present value of an annuity of $1 to the time the annuity commences, and also to the time it terminates; then multiply the difference between these present values by the given annuity.* Or,

Find the present worth of the final value of the annuity from the present time to the time it terminates.

EXAMPLE.—A father leaves an income of $500 per year to his son, to commence in 5 years and to continue for 10 years. What is the present worth of the legacy, at 6 per cent.?

By Table II., present worth of $1 for 15 years, $9.712249
" " " $1 " 5 " 4.212364

$5.499885

$5.499885 × 500 = $2749.94, *Ans.*

TABLE I.

Showing the FINAL VALUE *of an Annuity of One Dollar per annum, Compound Interest, from 1 year to 40, inclusive.*

Yrs.	3 per cent.	3½ per cent.	4 per cent.	5 per cent.	6 per cent.	7 per cent.
1	1.000 000	1.000 000	1.000 000	1.000 000	1.000 000	1.000 000
2	2.030 000	2.035 000	2.040 000	2.050 000	2.060 000	2.070 000
3	3.090 900	3.106 225	3.121 600	3.152 500	3.183 600	3.214 900
4	4.183 627	4.214 943	4.246 464	4.310 125	4.374 616	4.439 943
5	5.309 136	5.362 466	5.416 323	5.525 631	5.637 093	5.750 739
6	6.468 410	6.550 152	6.632 975	6.801 913	6.975 319	7.153 291
7	7.662 462	7.779 408	7.898 294	8.142 008	8.393 838	8.654 021
8	8.892 336	9.051 687	9.214 226	9.549 109	9.897 468	10.259 803
9	10.159 106	10.368 496	10.582 795	11.026 564	11.491 316	11.977 989
10	11.463 879	11.731 393	12.006 107	12.577 893	13.180 795	13.816 448
11	12.807 796	13.141 992	13.486 351	14.206 787	14.971 643	15.783 599
12	14.192 030	14.601 962	15.025 805	15.917 127	16.869 941	17.888 451
13	15.617 790	16.113 030	16.626 838	17.712 983	18.882 138	20.140 643
14	17.086 324	17.676 986	18.291 911	19.598 632	21.015 066	22.550 488
15	18.598 914	19.295 681	20.023 588	21.578 564	23.275 970	25.129 022
16	20.156 881	20.971 030	21.824 531	23.657 492	25.670 528	27.888 054
17	21.761 588	22.705 016	23.697 512	25.840 366	28.212 880	30.840 217
18	23.414 435	24.499 691	25.645 413	28.132 385	30.905 653	33.999 033
19	25.116 868	26.357 180	27.671 229	30.539 004	33.759 992	37.378 965
20	26.870 374	28.279 682	29.778 079	33.065 954	36.785 591	40.995 492
21	28.676 486	30.269 471	31.969 202	35.719 252	39.992 727	44.865 177
22	30.536 780	32.328 902	34.247 970	38.505 214	43.392 290	49.005 739
23	32.452 884	34.460 414	36.617 889	41.430 475	46.995 828	53.436 141
24	34.426 470	36.666 528	39.082 604	44.501 999	50.815 577	58.176 671
25	36.459 264	38.949 857	41.645 908	47.727 099	54.864 512	63.249 030
26	38.553 042	41.313 102	44.311 745	51.113 454	59.156 383	68.676 470
27	40.709 634	42.759 060	47.084 214	54.669 126	63.705 766	74.483 823
28	42.930 923	46.290 627	49.967 583	58.402 583	68.528 112	80.697 691
29	45.218 850	48.910 799	52.966 286	62.322 712	73.639 798	87.346 529
30	47.575 416	51.622 677	56.084 938	66.438 848	79.058 186	94.460 786
31	50.002 678	54.429 471	59.328 335	70.760 790	84.801 677	102.073 041
32	52.502 759	57.334 502	62.701 469	75.298 829	90.899 778	110.218 154
33	55.077 841	60.341 210	66.209 527	80.063 771	97.343 165	118.933 425
34	57.730 177	63.453 152	69.857 909	85.066 959	104.183 755	128.258 765
35	60.462 082	66.674 013	73.652 225	90.320 307	111.434 780	138.236 878
36	63.271 944	70.007 603	77.598 314	95.836 323	119.120 867	148.913 460
37	66.174 223	73.457 869	81.702 246	101.628 139	127.268 119	160.337 400
38	69.159 449	77.028 895	85.970 336	107.709 546	135.904 206	172.561 020
39	72.234 233	80.724 906	90.409 150	114.095 023	145.058 458	185.640 292
40	75.401 260	84.550 278	95.025 516	120.799 774	154.761 966	199.635 112

TABLE II.

Showing the PRESENT WORTH *of an Annuity of One Dollar per annum, at Compound Interest, from 1 year to 40, inclusive.*

YRS.	3 per cent.	3½ per cent.	4 per cent.	5 per cent.	6 per cent.	7 per cent.	YRS.
1	0.970 874	0.966 184	0.961 538	0.952 381	0.943 396	0.934 579	1
2	1.913 470	1.899 694	1.886 095	1.859 410	1.833 393	1.808 017	2
3	2.828 611	2.801 637	2.775 091	2.723 248	2.673 012	2.624 314	3
4	3.717 098	3.673 079	3.629 895	3.545 951	3.465 106	3.387 209	4
5	4.579 707	4.515 052	4.451 822	4.329 477	4.212 364	4.100 195	5
6	5.417 191	5.328 553	5.242 137	5.075 692	4.917 324	4.766 537	6
7	6.230 283	6.114 544	6.002 055	5.786 373	5.582 381	5.389 286	7
8	7.019 692	6.873 956	6.732 745	6.463 213	6.209 744	5.971 295	8
9	7.786 109	7.607 687	7.435 332	7.107 822	6.801 692	6.515 228	9
10	8.530 203	8.316 605	8.110 896	7.721 735	7.360 087	7.023 577	10
11	9.252 624	9.001 551	8.760 477	8.306 414	7.886 875	7.498 669	11
12	9.954 004	9.663 334	9.385 074	8.863 252	8.383 844	7.942 671	12
13	10.634 955	10.302 738	9.985 648	9.393 573	8.852 683	8.357 635	13
14	11.296 073	10.920 520	10.563 123	9.898 641	9.294 984	8.745 452	14
15	11.937 935	11.517 411	11.118 387	10.379 658	9.712 249	9.107 898	15
16	12.561 102	12.094 117	11.652 296	10.837 770	10.105 895	9.446 632	16
17	13.166 118	12.651 321	12.165 669	11.274 066	10.477 260	9.763 206	17
18	13.753 513	13.189 682	12.659 297	11.689 587	10.827 603	10.059 070	18
19	14.323 799	13.709 837	13.133 939	12.085 321	11.158 116	10.335 578	19
20	14.877 475	14.212 403	13.590 326	12.462 210	11.469 421	10.593 997	20
21	15.415 024	14.697 974	14.029 160	12.821 153	11.764 077	10.835 527	21
22	15.936 917	15.167 125	14.451 115	13.163 003	12.041 582	11.061 241	22
23	16.443 608	15.620 410	14.856 842	13.488 574	12.303 379	11.272 187	23
24	16.935 542	16.058 368	15.246 963	13.798 642	12.550 358	11.469 334	24
25	17.413 148	16.481 515	15.622 080	14.093 945	12.783 356	11.653 583	25
26	17.876 842	16.890 352	15.982 769	14.275 185	13.003 166	11.825 779	26
27	18.327 031	17.285 365	16.329 586	14.643 034	13.210 534	11.986 709	27
28	18.764 108	17.667 019	16.663 063	14.898 127	13.406 164	12.137 111	28
29	19.188 455	18.035 767	16.983 715	15.141 074	13.590 721	12.277 674	29
30	19.600 441	18.392 045	17.292 033	15.372 451	13.764 831	12.409 041	30
31	20.000 428	18.736 276	17.588 494	15.592 811	13.929 086	12.531 814	31
32	20.338 766	19.068 865	17.873 552	15.802 677	14.084 043	12.646 555	32
33	20.765 792	19.390 208	18.147 646	16.002 549	14.230 230	12.753 790	33
34	21.131 837	19.700 684	18.411 198	16.192 204	14.368 141	12.854 009	34
35	21.487 220	20.000 661	18.664 613	16.374 194	14.498 246	12.947 672	35
36	21.832 252	20.290 494	18.908 282	16.546 852	14.620 987	13.035 208	36
37	22.167 235	20.570 525	19.142 579	16.711 287	14.736 780	13.117 017	37
38	22.492 462	20.841 087	19.367 864	16.867 893	14.846 019	13.193 473	38
39	22.808 215	21.102 500	19.584 485	17.017 041	14.949 075	13.264 928	39
40	23.114 772	21.355 072	19.792 774	17.159 086	15.046 297	13.331 709	40

385. To find the present worth of an annuity in perpetuity.

This is equivalent to finding a principal the interest of which is equal to the given annuity.

RULE.—*Annex two ciphers to the annuity, and divide by the rate.*

EXAMPLE.—The annual income from an estate is $250. What is the present worth of the estate, allowing compound interest, at 6 per cent.? Ans.

386. To find an annuity from its present value.

RULE.—*Divide its present value by the present value of an annuity of $1 for the given rate and time.*

EXAMPLE.—The present value of an annuity for 10 years, at 5 per cent. compound interest, is $3000. What is the annuity? Ans. $388.513.

387. To find an annuity from its amount.

RULE.—*Divide the given amount by the amount of $1 for the given time and rate.*

EXAMPLE.—The final value of an annuity for 11 years, at 7 per cent. compound interest, amounts to $4735.08. What is the annuity? Ans. $300.

MISCELLANEOUS EXAMPLES.

1. What sum of money must a man invest annually at 6 per cent. compound interest, that he may have $5000 at the end of 10 years?
2. What is the present worth of $500 to be received annually for 6 years, allowing compound interest at 7 per cent.?
3. What sum invested at 6 per cent. compound interest will yield an income of $1800 per annum for 12 years?
4. The executors of an estate offer for sale an unoccupied lease that has 6 years to run, for a premium of $300. How much, added to the annual rent, will amount to the same sum?
5. What is an interest of $250 annually in an estate for 10 years worth, allowing money to be worth 7 per cent. compound interest?

BUILDING AND LOAN ASSOCIATIONS.

388. BUILDING AND LOAN ASSOCIATIONS have for their object the accumulation of a fund from which the members can obtain the means to build or buy houses, purchase lands, or for similar purposes.

The shares are usually estimated at $200 each, and are paid for in monthly instalments, generally $1 per month for each share. When the accumulated payments reach a certain sum, the funds are offered at auction, and given to the shareholder paying the largest bonus or discount. Interest on the loan thus made is paid monthly, or at the same time as the periodical dues. The loans are generally secured by mortgage on real estate. To prevent delinquency, fines are imposed of 5 or 10 per cent. per month on all sums not paid when due. When the total amount received by the association is sufficient to give each shareholder the amount originally agreed upon, the association closes.

As promotive of habits of economy, and as affording means of profitable investment, these associations have been highly successful. The chief benefit, however, is derived from the increase in the value of the property purchased, and in the convenient form in which the payments are made. Practically, these associations have given homes to hundreds who would otherwise never have owned them.

389. To find the cost of a share at simple interest, when the monthly dues, time, and rate of interest are given.

RULE.—*Multiply the interest on the monthly payment for one month by the number of months, less 1, that the association continues, and this product by one-half the number of months the association continues.* Then

Add the product of the monthly payment by the total number of months.

EXAMPLE.

What was the cost of a share for which $1 per month had been paid for 9 years, allowing 6 % simple interest?

Interest on $1 for 1 month, .005. 108 — 1 = 107
Number of months in 9 years = 108. 108 ÷ 2 = 54
107 × .005 = .535. .535 × 54 = 28.890
$1. × 108 = 108.000

Total cost, allowing 6 per cent. interest, $136.890

390. To find the cost of a share at compound interest.

RULE.—*Divide the monthly payment, after annexing two ciphers, by the given rate of interest, and find the compound interest of the quotient for the given rate and time.*

391. To find the cost of a loan at simple interest.

RULE.—*Add the present value of a share to the present value of the payment required for the loan.*

As it is impossible before the association closes, owing to the variations of discounts, number of borrowers, etc., to know the exact time the association will continue, an *approximate value* is all that can be found. From eight to ten years is the usual time.

EXAMPLES.

1. What is the cost of a loan of $200, the association requiring $1 interest in addition to $1 as regular payment to be paid monthly for 6 years, the present value of a share being $50?

Interest on $2 for 1 month = .01.
6 years = 72 months. .01 × 71 = 71¢.
71 × 36 = $25.56
$2 × 72 = 144.00

Value of payments to be made, $169.56

Present worth of payments for 6 years, $124 26
Value of share, 50

Cost of loan, $174.26 Ans.

A bonus of 10% on $200 would leave $180. A bonus of 20% would leave $160.

2. Which would be preferable, the above loan and payments, or to borrow $180 at 6 % compound interest?

392. To find the rate of interest paid for a loan.

RULE.—*From the cost of the loan subtract the amount received; then,*

Find the rate it will require for the loan to gain this difference in the given number of years.

393. To find the amount of fines on dues remaining unpaid.

NOTE.—The total amount of fines is equivalent to the sum of the compound interest of the dues for as many months as each payment remains unpaid; or to the final value of an annuity for the same time, with interest at the rate of the fine.

RULE.—*Multiply the compound interest of $1, at the rate of the given fine, by the dues for one month, commencing with the interest of one month, and continuing for the whole number of months. The sum of all the products will be the total amount of fines.* Or, by Annuity Tables,

From the final value of an annuity of $1 for one more year than the number of months that the dues remain unpaid, subtract one more dollar than there are such months; the remainder will be the fines on dues of $1 per month. This multiplied by the total dues per month, will give the total fines. Or,

Multiply the sum of the fines on $1, as given below, by the dues for 1 month.

EXAMPLE.

How much must a man, whose dues are $5 per month, pay for fines at 5% per month, on all sums remaining unpaid, after his dues remain unpaid 6 months?

BY COMPOUND INTEREST.

The interest on $1, at 5 per cent.,

For 1 month,	= .05000,	on $5, =	.25
" 2 "	= .102500,	" " =	.51
" 3 "	= .157625,	" " =	.79
" 4 "	= .215506,	" " =	1.08
" 5 "	= .276282,	" " =	1.38
" 6 "	= .340096,	" " =	1.70
	$1.142009		
Total fines for 6 mos., at 5 per ct., on unpaid dues of $5 per mo.,			$5.71

Fines on dues of $1 per month, remaining unpaid for 6 months, at 10 per cent. per month.

For 1 month, on $1,	=	.10
" 2 " " "	=	.21
" 3 " " "	=	.33
" 4 " " "	=	.46
" 5 " " "	=	.61
" 6 " " "	=	.77
Total fines for 6 months, at 10 per cent.,		$2.48

LIFE INSURANCE.

394. LIFE INSURANCE companies base their premiums upon the number of years each person is expected to live after insuring, and the use of money for that time.

395. The EXPECTATION OF LIFE is the *average* number of years remaining to a person at a given age, and is deduced from tables of mortality, which have been prepared from various observations made in different places and periods, showing, out of a given number of persons, how many complete each subsequent year, and how many die in it, till the whole are extinct.

The Carlisle tables, formed by Mr. Milne according to the mortality observed at Carlisle (Eng.), the Northampton tables, formed by Dr. Price (Eng.), the Wigglesworth tables, prepared by Dr. Wigglesworth from data founded upon the mortality of this country, and others, are employed. The Carlisle tables are in general use in England, and to a considerable extent here. The Wigglesworth tables have been adopted by the Supreme Court of Massachusetts in estimating life estates: they show a smaller expectation of life than the Carlisle tables.

396. The PROBABILITY that a person of any designated age will attain any greater age is expressed by dividing the number of survivors at the greater age by the number that attain the given age. Thus, by the Carlisle tables, of 10,000 persons born together, 5642 attain to 30, and 2894 to 66 years of age. The probability that a person now 30 years will reach the age of 66 years is, therefore, $\frac{2894}{5642}$,—about $\frac{1}{2}$, or 1 chance in 2. The value of a sum of money, the receipt of which depends upon the person being alive at that time, will be reduced by that contingency one-half; so that if the sum to be received is $1000, its value is reduced to only $500. The present worth of $1000, due 36 years hence, interest at 6 per cent., is $122.74; but, depending upon the same contingency, it is worth only $61.37.

TABLE

Of Mortality based upon observations at Carlisle (Eng.), showing the rate of extinction of 10,000 lives.

Age.	Number of Survivors.	Number of Deaths.	Age.	Number of Survivors.	Number of Deaths.	Age.	Number of Survivors.	Number of Deaths.
0	10000	1539	35	5362	55	70	2401	124
1	8461	682	36	5307	56	71	2277	134
2	7779	505	37	5251	57	72	2143	146
3	7274	276	38	5194	58	73	1997	156
4	6998	201	39	5136	62	74	1841	166
5	6797	121	40	5075	66	75	1675	160
6	6676	82	41	5009	69	76	1515	156
7	6594	58	42	4940	71	77	1359	146
8	6536	43	43	4869	71	78	1213	132
9	6493	33	44	4798	71	79	1081	128
10	6460	29	45	4727	70	80	953	116
11	6431	31	46	4657	69	81	837	112
12	6400	32	47	4588	67	82	725	102
13	6368	33	48	4521	63	83	623	94
14	6335	35	49	4458	61	84	529	84
15	6300	39	50	4397	59	85	445	78
16	6261	42	51	4338	62	86	367	71
17	6219	43	52	4276	65	87	296	64
18	6176	43	53	4211	68	88	232	51
19	6133	43	54	4143	70	89	181	39
20	6090	43	55	4073	73	90	142	37
21	6047	42	56	4000	76	91	105	30
22	6005	42	57	3924	82	92	75	21
23	5963	42	58	3842	93	93	54	14
24	5921	42	59	3749	106	94	40	10
25	5879	43	60	3643	122	95	30	7
26	5836	43	61	3521	126	96	23	5
27	5793	45	62	3395	127	97	18	4
28	5748	50	63	3268	125	98	14	3
29	5698	56	64	3143	125	99	11	2
30	5642	57	65	3018	124	100	9	2
31	5585	57	66	2894	123	101	7	2
32	5528	56	67	2771	123	102	5	2
33	5472	55	68	2648	123	103	3	2
34	5417	55	69	2525	124	104	1	1

397. The expectation of life may be obtained by finding the *sum of the probabilities* that the person will live to the extreme limit of life, plus $\frac{1}{2}$. The $\frac{1}{2}$ is added on the supposition that, on an average, the life will fail at the middle of the year. Thus, by the table, the probability that a person at 102 will live one year is $\frac{3}{5}$, that he will live 2 years is $\frac{1}{5}$: $\frac{3}{5}+\frac{1}{5}+\frac{1}{2}=\frac{13}{10}=1.30$ years. It may also be found by dividing the aggregate number of years which the persons who are alive at one time will live, by the number of persons. A short rule, which gives approximate results, is to take $\frac{2}{3}$ of the number of years between the person's present age and 80. Thus, a person at 20 has an expectation of 40 years; at 50, of 20 years.

The value of the probabilities and expectation of life under various circumstances is calculated by actuaries, and involves complications too extensive for an elementary work. From these calculations, tables are arranged, showing the rates at which companies will insure lives,—such rates including all probable losses, expenses, interest, and profits.

To all who have limited incomes, Life Insurance offers a provision against the accidents of life. By paying a small sum annually, a person at his death may leave his family—which would otherwise be dependent, either from lack of property, or from having heavily encumbered property—in comfortable circumstances.

By a *Joint Policy*, two persons may insure and the sum insured is paid to the other on the death of either. By the *Endowment Policy*, the amount can be made payable to the person insured at a stated time,—thus making provision against old age. A Life Insurance policy has enabled persons of unquestionable character and business ability, who have otherwise been unable to borrow on account of advanced age and the uncertainty of life, to obtain capital with which to conduct a profitable business.

VALUE OF LIFE INTERESTS, WIDOWS' DOWERS, ANNUITIES, &c.

Extract from Instructions issued by the Treasury Department, Washington, February 15, 1866.

"Where legacies are made payable at the expiration of a life or lives in being, the value of the legacy will be estimated by the Carlisle tables of life annuities, which are appended to these instructions.

"Where a legacy is made payable on a future contingency, the value of the legacy is to be estimated by a consideration of the time, certain or ascertainable by the annuity tables, when the legacy will become vested.

CARLISLE TABLES.

AGE.	Expectancy of life in years and hundredths.	Present value of annuity of $1.00 for the number of years and 100ths of years found in 2d column, at 6 per cent.	Present value of $1.00 to be received at the end of the number of years and 100ths of years as found in 2d column, interest at 6 per cent.	AGE.	Expectancy of life in years and 100ths.	Present value of annuity of $1.00 for the number of years and 100ths of years found in 2d column, at 6 per cent.	Present value of $1.00 to be received at the end of the number of years and 100ths of years as found in 2d column, interest at 6 per cent.
0	38.72	14.9202	.104788	41	26.97	13.2043	.207741
1	44.68	15.4325	.074065	42	26.34	13.0737	.215580
2	47.55	15.6225	.062645	43	25.71	12.9395	.223635
3	49.82	15.7521	.054874	44	25.09	12.8032	.231812
4	50.76	15.8008	.051953	45	24.46	12.6576	.240548
5	51.25	15.8252	.050490	46	23.82	12.5059	.249646
6	51.17	15.8213	.050722	47	23.17	12.3454	.259278
7	50.80	15.8029	.051830	48	22.51	12.1751	.269494
8	50.24	15.7742	.053551	49	21.81	11.9889	.280669
9	49.57	15.7385	.055689	50	21.11	11.7946	.292324
10	48.82	15.6972	.058168	51	20.39	11.5846	.304922
11	48.04	15.6523	.060860	52	19.68	11.3701	.317792
12	47.27	15.6055	.063670	53	18.97	11.1481	.331108
13	46.51	15.5573	.066559	54	18.28	10.9201	.344791
14	45.75	15.5072	.069566	55	17.58	10.6805	.359172
15	45.00	15.4558	.072650	56	16.89	10.4364	.373815
16	44.27	15.4028	.075832	57	16.21	10.1839	.388967
17	43.57	15.3501	.078996	58	15.55	9.9287	.404275
18	42.87	15.2956	.082267	59	14.92	9.6788	.419268
19	42.17	15.2384	.085695	60	14.34	9.4368	.433789
20	41.46	15.1778	.089331	61	13.82	9.2154	.447078
21	40.75	15.1151	.093095	62	13.31	8.9900	.460612
22	40.04	15.0500	.097002	63	12.81	8.7636	.474183
23	39.31	14.9972	.101248	64	12.30	8.5245	.488530
24	38.59	14.9068	.105592	65	11.79	8.2793	.503231
25	37.86	14.8307	.110157	66	11.27	8.0211	.518737
26	37.14	14.7521	.114876	67	10.75	7.7552	.534690
27	36.41	14.6685	.119892	68	10.23	7.4813	.551125
28	35.69	14.5829	.125024	69	9.70	7.1926	.568446
29	35.00	14.4982	.130105	70	9.18	6.9022	.585867
30	34.34	14.4123	.135258	71	8.65	6.5945	.604328
31	33.68	14.3240	.140560	72	8.16	6.3045	.621730
32	33.03	14.2343	.145938	73	7.72	6.0341	.637953
33	32.36	14.1366	.151789	74	7.33	5.7894	.652634
34	31.68	14.0344	.157932	75	7.01	5.5887	.664681
35	31.00	13.9291	.164255	76	6.69	5.3762	.677427
36	30.32	13.8174	.170957	77	6.40	5.1833	.688999
37	29.64	13.7021	.180796	78	6.12	4.9971	.700173
38	28.96	13.5833	.185000	79	5.80	4.7763	.713420
39	28.28	13.4579	.192530	80	5.51	4.5719	.725687
40	27.61	13.3289	.200208	81	5.21	4.3604	.738376

EXAMPLE.—If a person whose probability of life is 14.34 years inherits an estate having a rental value of $1000 per annum, the present worth of the annuity of $1000 for that term is 9.4368 × 1000 = $9436.80,—the valuation on which he is taxed.

THE CENTAL SYSTEM.

Efforts have been made by the Boards of Trade in most of our large cities, to introduce the Cental System in place of the bushel, in buying and selling all grains, seeds, and similar productions. The Cental is one hundred pounds. Several articles have been sold for years by the Cental; and its general introduction would be attended with many advantages. Dealings in grain especially—the quality of which is indicated by its weight—would be conducted with much less inconvenience than at present.

The weight of wheat, rye, barley, and oats, per bushel, as now estimated among shipping-merchants, may be found on page 228.

To find the price per cental when the price per bushel is given.

RULE.—*Multiply the price per bushel by 100, and divide by the number of pounds.*

EXAMPLE.—At $1.38 per bushel for wheat of the weight of 60 lbs. per bushel, what is the price per cental?

138 × 100 = 13800   13800 ÷ 60 = 230   Ans. $2.30.

To find the price per bushel when the price per cental is given.

RULE.—*Multiply the price per cental by the number of pounds in a bushel, and divide by 100.*

EXAMPLE.—At $2.50 per cental, what is the price of a bushel of wheat?

250 × 60 = 15000   15000 ÷ 100 = 150   Ans. $1.50.

398. SQUARE ROOT.

RULE.—I. *Point off the given number, commencing at units' place, into periods of two figures each.*

II. *Find the greatest square in the left-hand period, and place its root in the quotient; subtract the square number from the left-hand period, and to the remainder annex the next period of the dividend.*

III. *Double the root already found, for a divisor; find how many times the divisor is contained in the dividend exclusive of the right-hand figure; place the result in the quotient, and at the right hand of the divisor.*

IV. *Multiply the divisor by the last quotient-figure, and subtract the product from the dividend. Bring down the next period, and proceed as before.*

When a number is not a perfect square, annex ciphers, and continue the root to as many decimal places as are required.

NOTE.—Mixed decimals must be pointed off both ways from the decimal point.

To extract the square root of a fraction, extract the square root of both the numerator and denominator. When they are not perfect squares, reduce the fraction to a decimal, and extract the root.

EXAMPLES.

1. What is the square root of 50964?

```
         5̇09̇64̇(225.75+
         4
   42 | 109
         84
  445 | 2564
        2225
 4507 | 33900
        31549
45145 | 235100
        225725
```

2. What is the square root of 8796, and of 123562?

LUMBER MEASURE.

399. A standard board is one that is 12 feet long, 1 foot wide, and 1 inch thick, and therefore contains 12 square feet 1 inch thick. In timber for exportation, ¼ inch more is allowed for shrinkage, planing, &c. The length of boards, joists, beams, &c., is measured in even inches, odd inches not being counted.

400. To measure boards.

RULE.—*Multiply the length in feet by the width in inches, and divide the product by 12; the quotient will be the number of square feet. When the board is more or less than 1 inch thick, add or subtract in proportion. A plank 2 inches thick, 12 feet long, and 1 foot wide, would measure 24 feet, board measure.*

NOTE.—If the boards are tapering, take half the sum of the two ends for the mean width. Some inspectors measure only the narrow end.

401. To measure joists, beams, &c.

RULE.—*Multiply the width in inches by the thickness, and this product by the length in feet; divide by 12, and the quotient will be the contents in feet.*

402. To find the number of feet which a given log will contain when sawn square.

RULE.—*Square half the diameter in inches, and multiply by the length of the log in feet.*

Practically, it is customary to take two-thirds or $\frac{7}{10}$ of the diameter of the small end of the log, for the side of the square which can be sawn from a given log.

403. To find the number of boards which can be cut from a given thickness of log.

RULE.—*Divide the thickness of the log, minus ¼ inch, by 1 plus the saw-cut (¼ inch).*

GAUGING.

Gauging is the process of finding the contents or capacity of casks and other vessels.

Ullage is the difference between the actual contents of a vessel and its capacity, or that part which is empty.

The usual manner of gauging is by the diagonal rod, which gives only approximate results, but sufficiently accurate for ordinary purposes.

FOR SMALL CYLINDRICAL VESSELS.

RULE.—*Multiply the square of the diameter, in inches, by 34, and that by the height, in inches, and point off four figures; the result will be the capacity, in wine gallons and decimals of a gallon.*

If beer gallons are required, multiply by 28 instead of 34.

EXAMPLE.

A can measures 15 inches in diameter, and is 2 ft. 2 in. in height. How many gallons will it contain?

$15 \times 15 = 225 \times 26$ in. (height) $= 5850$
$5850 \times 34 = 19.8900$ Ans. $19\frac{89}{100}$ gals.

FOR CASKS.

RULE.—*Add $\frac{7}{10}$ of the difference between the head diameter and the bung diameter to the head diameter, for the mean diameter; then proceed as in the previous rule.* Or,

Add together the square of the bung and head diameters, and of twice the middle diameter between the bung and head. Multiply the sum by length of cask, and the product by .1309.

To find the contents of ullage casks.

RULE.—When the cask is standing—

Find one-third the sum of the head, mean, and bung diameters, and square the result; multiply by the height of the fluid in inches, and that product by .0034 for wine gallons, and by .0028 for beer gallons.

To test the accuracy of *dry measures* which are in the form of a cylinder.

Divide 2738 by the square of the diameter, in inches; the quotient will be the depth for a bushel; one-half the quotient will be the depth for a half-bushel; one-quarter of the quotient, for a peck, &c.

To test the accuracy of measures for *fluids* which are in the form of a cylinder.

Square the diameter, in inches, for a divisor.

Divide 294 for wine gallons.
" 359 " beer "
" 342 " dry "

GRAIN MEASURE.

To find the quantity of grain in a bin or wagon.

RULE.—*Multiply the height, length, and breadth together, in inches, and divide by 2150.42; the quotient will be the number of bushels.*

To find the quantity of grain when heaped on the floor in the form of a cone.

RULE.—*Square the depth and square the slant height, in inches; take their difference and multiply by the depth, and this product by .0005; the result will be the contents, in bushels.*

To find the quantity of grain when heaped against a straight wall.

RULE.—*Square one-half the depth, and proceed as in the previous rule.*

WEIGHT OF GRAIN PER BUSHEL, AS ESTIMATED AMONG SHIPPING MERCHANTS.

Wheat, ...	60 lbs.	Oats, ...	35 lbs.
Rye, ...	56 "	Corn, ...	56 "
Barley, ...	48 "		

CALCULATIONS IN NATURAL SCIENCE.

MECHANICAL POWERS.

Power, or Force, is a compound of weight and velocity. Machinery is employed to save either *time* or *force;* but no machine can save both: either force is gained at the expense of time, or time is gained at the expense of force.

Motion takes place only when the power is greater than the weight or resistance, including friction.

It is a principle in mechanics that the power is to the weight as the velocity of the weight is to the velocity of the power.

The mechanical powers, of which all machines, however complicated, are constructed, are three in number,—viz., LEVER, INCLINED PLANE, and PULLEY. The Wheel and Axle is a *revolving* lever; the Wedge is a *double* inclined plane; and the Screw is a *revolving* inclined plane.

The LEVER.—There are three kinds of levers:—

1. When the fulcrum is between the weight and the power.
2. When the weight is between the power and the fulcrum.
3. When the power is between the fulcrum and the weight.

The weight multiplied by its distance from the fulcrum is equal to the power multiplied by its distance from the fulcrum.

EXAMPLE.—The weight on the short arm of a lever is 120 lbs., at a distance of 1 foot from the fulcrum: what power applied to the long arm, at a distance of 8 feet, will balance it?

$$120 \times 1 = 120. \quad 120 \div 8 = 15 \text{ lbs. Ans.}$$

When the fulcrum or support is between the weight and power, the pressure upon the fulcrum equals the sum of the weight and power.

When the fulcrum is at one extremity and the power or weight at the other, the pressure upon the fulcrum equals the difference between the weight and the power.

The WHEEL and AXLE, or REVOLVING LEVER.—The power multiplied by the radius (half the diameter) of the wheel is equal to the weight multiplied by the radius of the axle.

EXAMPLE.—The diameter of a wheel is 80 inches, and that of the axle 6 inches: what power on the wheel will balance 600 lbs. on the axle?

Radius of wheel, 40 inches; radius of axle, 3 inches.
$600 \times 3 = 1800$. $1800 \div 40 = 45$ lbs. Ans.

PULLEYS.—Pulleys are of two kinds, fixed and movable pulleys. Fixed pulleys do not increase the power, but they are useful for applying it in the most convenient direction.

In the movable pulley all the parts of a cord are equally stretched, and therefore each cord from one pulley to another will bear an equal part. Hence the power is doubled for every movable pulley.

EXAMPLE.—What power is required to balance a weight of 1800 lbs., by means of 3 movable pulleys?

$3 \times 2 = 6$. $1800 \div 6 = 300$ lbs. Ans.

The INCLINED PLANE.—The power required to raise a body up an inclined plane, is equal to the product of the height and weight divided by the length of the plane.

The WEDGE, or Double Inclined Plane, derives its advantages from the fact that power can be applied to it by percussion or a stroke. As a theoretical rule, it may be said that when two movable bodies are forced apart, the power required is equal to the product of the resisting power multiplied by ½ the thickness of the back, divided by the length of one of the inclined sides.

When only one of the bodies is movable, the power required is equal to the product of the resisting power multiplied by the thickness of the back, divided by the length of the wedge.

The SCREW, or Revolving Inclined Plane, is an inclined

plane wound round a cylinder, and its length is found by adding the square of the circumference of the screw to the square of the distance between the threads, and extracting the square root of the sum. The height of the plane is the distance between any two contiguous threads; the base of the plane is the circumference of the screw. Having the length of the plane and its height, the power required is found as for the inclined plane.

If the power is applied at the end of a lever, the circumference of the thread may be taken as extending to the circle formed by the end of the lever.

Example.—If the distance of the centres of two threads be ¼ of an inch, and the radius of the lever attached to the screw be 12 inches, what is the power of the screw?

The circumference of the screw will be $12 \times 2 \times 3.14156 = 75\frac{1}{2}$ in., nearly. Therefore, to find the power of the screw, $75\frac{1}{2} \div \frac{1}{4} = 300\frac{1}{8}$, the power of the screw.

The power of a man, it is estimated, on an average, is able to raise 70 lbs. 1 foot high in a second for 10 hours per day.

Horse-Power, in machinery, is estimated at 33000 lbs. raised 1 foot every minute. A machine horse-power is considered equal to 4.4 horses. The strength of one horse is equivalent to that of 5 men. A draft horse can draw 1600 lbs. 23 miles per day, weight of carriage included.

Steam, under ordinary circumstances, is equal to the pressure of the atmosphere, or about 15 lbs. on the square inch. A cubic inch of water is converted into about 1 cubic foot of steam, producing a force equal to 2200 lbs. 1 foot high. Its weight is .488 that of the air; or 27.206 cubic feet of steam equal 1 lb. avoirdupois.

One cubic foot of boiler will heat 2000 feet of space to an average heat of about 70° or 80° Fahr.; and one square foot of steam-pipe is adequate to the warming of 200 cubic feet of space.

GRAVITY OF BODIES.

The gravity or weight of bodies above the surface of the earth decreases as the square of their distance from the earth's centre, in semi-diameters of the earth.

Example.—If a body weighs 1800 lbs. at the earth's surface, what will it weigh 2000 miles above the earth estimating the diameter of the earth at 8000 miles?

From the centre of the earth to the given height is $1\frac{1}{2}$ semi-diameter. $1\frac{1}{2} \times 1\frac{1}{2} = 2\frac{1}{4}$. $1800 \div 2\frac{1}{4} = 800$ lbs., Ans.

FALLING BODIES.

Gravitating bodies attract each other with forces varying inversely as the squares of their distances.

A body falling freely from rest will descend $16\frac{1}{12}$ feet the first second, and the space fallen through in any number of seconds equals the product of $16\frac{1}{12}$ by the square of the number of seconds. Thus, a body in 4 seconds will fall $4 \times 4 = 16 \times 16\frac{1}{12} = 257\frac{1}{3}$ feet; in 5 seconds it will fall $5^2 \times 16\frac{1}{12} = 402\frac{1}{12}$ feet.

To find the time required for a body to fall through a given space, divide the square root of the space by 4; the quotient will be the time, in seconds.

Example.—Required the time for a ball to fall from the spire of a church 256 feet high.

$$\sqrt{256} = 16. \quad 16 \div 4 = 4 \text{ seconds, Ans.}$$

The *Velocities* of falling bodies increase as the times. Thus, at the end of the first second the velocity will be $32\frac{1}{6}$; at the end of the second second, $64\frac{1}{3}$; at the end of the third second, $32\frac{1}{6} \times 3 = 96\frac{1}{2}$.

The *Mean Velocity* is found by taking the square root of the space in feet, multiplied by $64\frac{1}{3}$; or by dividing the space fallen through in feet by the number of seconds. The velocity acquired at any period is equal to twice the mean velocity during that period.

The *Momentum* with which a falling body will descend is equal to its weight multiplied by its velocity.

EXAMPLES.—1. What is the velocity of a weight falling $2\frac{1}{4}$ feet? $2\frac{1}{4} \times 64 = 144$. $\sqrt{144} = 12$ feet, Ans.

2. What is the force with which a weight of 200 lbs. will strike after falling $2\frac{1}{4}$ feet?

$$\text{Velocity} = 12 \times 200 = 2400 \text{ lbs., Ans.}$$

To find the number of feet fallen through, when the weight and momentum are given.

Divide the momentum by the weight for the velocity; then divide the square of the velocity by 64, for the height required.

EXAMPLE.—How high will it be necessary to raise a weight of 50 lbs. to produce a force at striking of 800 lbs.?

$$800 \div 50 = 16, \text{ the velocity.}$$
$$16^2 = 256 \div 64 = 4 \text{ feet, Ans.}$$

A fall of $\frac{1}{10}$ of an inch in a mile will produce a *current* in rivers.

SPECIFIC GRAVITY.

The SPECIFIC GRAVITY of any substance is its weight compared with that of an equal bulk of fresh water.

A cubic foot of rain-water, at a temperature of 60° Fahrenheit, weighs $62\frac{1}{2}$ lbs., or 1000 ounces avoirdupois. One cubic inch weighs $\frac{1000}{1728}$ ounces.

The specific gravity of a body may be found by dividing its weight by the weight of an equal quantity of fresh water. Bodies heavier than water, when immersed, lose the weight of an equal bulk of water. Floating bodies lose weight in proportion to the quantity of fluid they displace.

Tables have been constructed showing the specific gravities of most substances. Pure gold, cast, has a specific gravity of 19 258, or more than nineteen times as heavy as water; gold 22 carats fine, 17.486; pure silver, cast, 10.474; standard silver, 10.312; cast iron, 7.271; cast lead, 11.352; copper, cast, 8.788; common marble, 2.686; brick, 2.000; cork, .240; olive oil, .915; pure alcohol, .792; air at the earth's surface, $.001\frac{2}{7}$, or $\frac{1}{825}$; hydrogen, .070 that of air. Oxygen equals 1.106 of air.

Knowing the specific gravity and the size of a given body, we can ascertain its weight; or, having the weight and specific gravity, we are enabled to find its size.

EXAMPLES.—1. What is the weight of a cubic block of cast iron, each side being 2 feet?

$2 \times 2 \times 2 = 8$ cubic feet in the block.
Specific gravity of iron, $7.271 \times 8 = 58168$ ounces.
$58168 \div 16 = 3635\frac{1}{2}$ lbs., Ans.

2. What is the size of a cubic piece of marble weighing 1200 lbs.?

1200 lbs. = 19200 ounces. Specific gravity of marble, 2.686.
$19200 \div 2686 = 7\frac{398}{2686}$ cubic feet, Ans.

To determine the quantity of two ingredients in a compound which they form, or the quantity of adulteration, employ the following formula:—

As the product of the difference between the specific gravities of the heavier and the lighter body, multiplied by the specific gravity of the compound,	:	The weight of the compound,	::	The product of the difference between the specific gravity of the compound and that of the lighter body, multiplied by the specific gravity of the heavier body,	The weight of the heavier body.

To obtain the weight of the lighter body, substitute for the third term, "The product of the difference between the specific gravity of the heavier body and that of the compound, by the specific gravity of the lighter body."

HOW TO TRY SPIRITUOUS LIQUORS.—A cubic inch of good brandy, or other proof spirits, weighs 234 grains: therefore, if a true cubic inch of any metal weigh 234 grains less in spirits than in air, the spirits are proof. If the cube lose less, they are above proof; if it lose more, they are under proof: for spirits are lighter as they are better in quality.

PRESSURE OF THE ATMOSPHERE.

A cubic foot of air at the earth's surface weighs 1.222 ounces; 13.27 cubic feet weigh 1 lb. Water is about 825 times heavier than air. The air at the earth's surface, in consequence of the weight of the atmosphere above it, is in a state of compression. At a mean rate, the pressure is equal to the support of 29.5 inches of mercury, or 33.18 feet of fresh water, or 15 lbs. pressure upon the square inch.

The pressure of air on the surface of fluids causes them to rise in pipes or vessels when the air is removed above them, but not more than 33.18 feet.

A cubic inch of mercury weighs 7.866 ounces, or nearly half a pound avoirdupois: therefore 30 inches of mercury will weigh 15 lbs., and will balance the pressure of the atmosphere. The air presses equally on every side.

If the air was of the same uniform density upwards, we could easily tell its height; for if its weight is to water as 1.222 is to 1000, then 33.18 feet is in the same proportion to 5¼ miles, which would be the height. But the air becomes rarer as it ascends; and when the altitude is in arithmetical proportion the rarity will be in geometric proportion. Thus, if at 7 miles' height it is 4 times lighter than at the earth's surface, at 14 miles' it will be 16 times, and at 21 miles' 64 times lighter; and, by similar calculation, the atmosphere has been found to reach the height of about 50 miles A column a foot square, reaching to the height of the atmosphere, is equal to 2116.8 lbs.

The heights of mountains have been calculated by the use of the barometer, which rises or falls according to the pressure or density of the atmosphere. The following short method is sufficiently correct for all ordinary purposes.

Take the height of the mercury at the top and at the bottom of the mountain, and then employ the following formula:—

$$\left\{\begin{matrix}\text{Sum of the}\\ \text{heights}\end{matrix}\right\} : \left\{\begin{matrix}\text{Difference of}\\ \text{the heights}\end{matrix}\right\} :: \left\{ 52000 \right\} : \left\{\begin{matrix}\text{Height of mountain,}\\ \text{in feet.}\end{matrix}\right.$$

EXAMPLE.—If the barometer stands 29.8 at the bottom of a mountain, and 27.2 at the top, what is the height of the mountain?

$$\begin{array}{llll} 27.2 & 29.8 & & \\ \underline{29.8} & \underline{27.2} & & \\ 57 : & 2.6 :: 52000 : 2372 \text{ feet, Ans.} \end{array}$$

The pressure of condensed air is in proportion to its condensation. Thus, air compressed into $\frac{1}{4}$ its usual space will press with a force equal to $15 \times 4 = 60$ lbs. per square inch; but, as the pressure outside is 15 lbs. per square inch, the real pressure is $60 - 15 = 45$ lbs. per square inch

VELOCITY AND FORCE OF THE WIND.—At a velocity of 5 miles an hour, wind presses $\frac{1}{8}$ lb. on a square foot; at 15 miles an hour, $1\frac{1}{8}$ lbs. per square foot; at 30 miles an hour, or 22 feet a second, $4\frac{1}{2}$ lbs. per square foot, and is what is called a brisk blow; at 50 miles an hour, the pressure is $12\frac{1}{2}$ lbs. per square foot, and produces a storm; at 100 miles an hour, the pressure is 50 lbs. per square foot, and is sufficient to tear up trees.

VELOCITY OF SOUND.

Sound travels 1142 feet, or $\frac{3}{14}$ of a mile, per second, or a mile in about $4\frac{2}{3}$ seconds. Sound of all kind travels at the same rate, the whisper as fast as the cannon's roar. Sound passes in water at the rate of 4708 feet per second.

EXAMPLES.—1. A flash of lightning was observed 5 seconds before the thunder was heard. What was the distance of the cloud?

$$\tfrac{3}{14} \times 5 = \tfrac{15}{14} = 1\tfrac{1}{14} \text{ miles, Ans.}$$

2. The report of a minute-gun at sea was heard 4 seconds after the flash was seen. How far distant was the gun?

LIGHT.

LIGHT travels from the sun to the earth, 95,000,000 miles, in 8½ minutes. The intensity of light at any distance from a luminous body is in an inverse proportion to the square of the distance. Thus, at a certain point, a board 1 foot square will cast a shadow 2 feet square at double the distance, 3 feet square at 3 times the distance, 4 feet square at 4 times the distance. The areas being increased as the squares of the distances, the light, consequently, is decreased in the same proportion.

Solids shine in the dark when heated from 600° to 700°.

Light from gas, as usually obtained, is not in proportion to the gas consumed. It is more economical to have one good large gas-light than several small ones. An argand burner, consuming five feet per hour, giving the light of 12 candles, 6 in a pound, when reduced so that only three-fourths of that quantity is burned, instead of giving the light of 9 candles, the proportional quantity, produces the light of 6 candles only, a positive loss of 36 per cent. of light. A burner consuming two feet per hour gives the light of two and a quarter candles only, while a burner consuming 7½ feet per hour gives the light of twenty-two candles, the pressure being uniformly $\frac{4}{10}$ of an inch.

A clear glass globe obstructs about 12 per cent. of the light; a clear globe engraved with flowers, about 24 per cent.; a globe ground all over with flowers, about forty per cent.; an opal globe with flowers, about 60 per cent.

HEAT AND COLD.

HEAT expands all bodies, with few exceptions, but in different degrees. It expands liquids more than solids, and gases more than liquids. The thermometer, by its scale of equal divisions marked upon the tube, indicates the degree of heat in a given case. The mercury in the thermometer expands as heat is applied, and the scale enables us to determine the amount. The temperature of melting ice is called the freezing point, and is marked 32°. The temperature of boiling water is marked 212°. When the temperature is 68°, it is called summer heat; 98° is called blood heat; 108°, fever heat. This is the scale commonly used in this country, England, and Holland, and it is known by the name of the inventor, Fahrenheit. Above the boiling point, heat is measured by an instrument called a pyrometer. For very low temperatures, spirit-of-wine thermometers are employed. Mercury, in freezing, contracts, and therefore does not burst the thermometer.

The Celsius, or Centigrade, thermometer, universally used in France and Northern Europe, and the Reaumer thermometer, used in Spain, commence with zero as the freezing point. 1° Fahrenheit $= \frac{5}{9}$° Centigrade $= \frac{4}{9}$° Reaumer: so that in making comparisons 32° is to be taken from Fahrenheit, and then that part of the remaining degrees which is expressed by the fractions just given.

Common fire is estimated to be at a temperature of 790°.

Lead expands at 212° Fahrenheit from 1,000,000 parts to 1,002,848; it melts at 594°, and does not, when cold, return to its original dimensions. Lead pipes which convey hot water or steam become permanently elongated, and leaden linings, where hot water is used, become gathered into ridges. Tin at 212° expands from 1,000,000 parts to 1,001,937, and melts at 421°. At the same degree silver expands to 1,001,909, and melts at 1850°. Gold expands to 1,001,466, and melts at 1983°; copper, to 1,001,718, and melts at 2160°.

Iron expands to 1,001,182, becomes red-hot in the dark at 752°, in daylight at 1077°, and melts at 2754°.

The effects of heat may be seen in the iron rails on the railroads throughout the country. There is a variation of 80° in the temperature between the cold of winter and the heat of summer. This is sufficient to elongate a bar of iron ten inches long, five one-thousandths of an inch, or $\frac{1}{2000}$ part, which would require, to produce the same effect, a force of fifty tons upon the square inch. The tubes of Menai Bridge vary in length with the changes of the air, from half an inch to three inches every twenty-four hours. Iron bars, when much heated, frequently injure masonry, instead of supporting it, from the same cause.

Mercury expands between 32° and 212° from 1,000,000 to 1,018,155, and boils at 662°. Ether boils at 95°. Vinous fermentation begins at 60° to 77°; acetous fermentation begins at 78°.

Most metals occupy less space when solid than when melted, and therefore produce imperfect casts. For this reason coins, medals, and ornamental wares are stamped instead of cast, to secure the requisite size, sharpness, and beauty.

Alcohol expands $\frac{1}{9}$ between 32° and 212°, and, under ordinary changes of atmosphere, would increase from 20 gallons in January to 21 gallons in July. It boils at 173°.

Water in a vacuum boils at 124° less of heat than when under the ordinary pressure of the atmosphere, or when the barometer is 30 inches. On Mt. Blanc water boils at 187°. The boiling point of water, with a pressure indicated by the barometer of between 27 and 31 inches, varies 1.65° for every inch.

Water converted into steam occupies about 1700 times as much space as before. In freezing it expands $\frac{1}{7}$ of its bulk, and $\frac{1}{395}$ for every degree from 40° to 212°: hence ice floats on the surface of water, and close vessels are burst when the water they contain is frozen. Melted snow produces about $\frac{1}{8}$ of its bulk in water.

Sea-water freezes at 27°, strong wine at 20°, brandy at 7°

At the depth of 45 feet the temperature of the earth is uniform during the entire year.

FREEZING MIXTURES are frequently required; and the one most convenient for common use, such as freezing ices and creams, is composed of 2 parts ice or snow and 1 part common salt. With this a temperature of 5° below zero, or 37° below the freezing point, can be obtained. Another compound, of 3 parts snow or ice and 4 parts chloride of calcium, will produce a temperature of 14° below zero.

Heat is absorbed most rapidly and longest retained by dark and dull surfaces, and is generally conducted least by substances in condition of least density. Heat and light are both reflected best by bright surfaces. Compared with a rough, blackened surface as 1, the reflective power of tin is 80, of brass, polished, 93, of gold and silver, polished, 97.

THE STRENGTH OF MATERIALS.

The strength of a beam increases as the square of one of its homologous sides, while the weight of the beam increases as the cube; and therefore long beams are weak from their own weight.

A beam twice as broad as another is *twice* as strong, one twice as deep is *four* times as strong, and one twice as long has only *half* the strength.

A triangular beam is twice as strong when resting on its broad base as when resting on its edge.

If the beam is supported in the middle and loaded at each end, it will bear the same weight; that is, each end will bear half the weight.

A beam fixed at both ends and loaded in the middle will bear one-half more weight than it will when the ends are loose.

When the weight is distributed uniformly over the whole length of the beam, it will bear double what it will when the entire weight is in the middle. A beam fixed at one end and loaded at the end projecting, will bear only one-fourth the weight it will when loaded in the middle and supported at the ends.

From various experiments, it appears that the ultimate strength of various bodies, an inch square and an inch round bar of each, 1 foot long, loaded in the middle and lying loose at both ends, is as follows :—

	Square bar.	Round bar.
Oak	800 lbs.	628 lbs.
Ash	1137	893
Elm	569	447
Pitch Pine	916	719
Deal	566	444
Cast Iron	2580	2026
Wrought Iron	4013	3152

One-third of the above weights is considered sufficient in most cases for a permanent load.

To find the strength of any rectangular beam supported at both ends and loaded in the middle, or supported in the middle and loaded at both ends.

RULE.—*Multiply the number in the table by the breadth and square of the depth in inches, and divide the product by the length in feet: the quotient will be the weight, in pounds.*

EXAMPLE.—What weight will break a pitch pine plank 16 feet long, 10 inches broad, and 2 inches thick, when supported at both ends and loaded in the middle?

$$\frac{916 \times 10 \times 2^2}{16} = 2290 \text{ lbs., Ans.}$$

A plank of the same length and thickness, 20 inches broad, would require twice the weight, or 4580 lbs., to break it, and one of the same length and breadth, twice as thick, would require 4 times the weight. A plank twice as long, of the same breadth and thickness, would break with 1145 lbs., or $\frac{1}{2}$ the above weight.

PROPERTIES OF NUMBERS.

Any number may be divided by $1\frac{1}{4}$, 2, $2\frac{1}{2}$, or 5, without a remainder, when its right-hand figure may be thus divided.

The square root of a number is greater than any of its prime factors.

Any number may be divided by an aliquot part of a hundred when its *two right-hand figures* may be thus divided.

Any number may be divided by an aliquot part of a thousand when its three right-hand figures may be thus divided.

Any number divided by 3 or 9 will leave the same remainder as the sum of its digits divided by 3 or 9.

The difference between any number and the sum of its digits is a multiple of 9.

The difference between a number and the digits of the same number arranged in another order is always divisible by 9.

MISCELLANEOUS RULES.

To find two numbers when their *sum* and *difference* are given.

Rule.—*Add one-half their sum to one-half their difference, for the larger number, and take one-half their difference from one-half their sum, for the smaller.*

To find two numbers when their sum and product are given.

Rule.—*Take the square root of the difference between the square of the sum and four times their product; the result will be the difference between the numbers.*

To find two numbers when their difference and product are given.

Rule.—*To the square of their difference add four times the product, and the square root of the sum will be the sum of the numbers.*

To find two numbers when their sum and quotient are given.

Rule.—*Divide the sum by the quotient increased by 1; the result will be the smaller number.*

To find two numbers when their difference and quotient are given.

Rule.—*Divide the difference by the quotient less 1, for the smaller number.*

To find two numbers when their sum and the sum of their squares are given.

RULE.—*From the square of their sum take the sum of their squares, and half the remainder will be the product; then proceed by Rule above.*

To find two numbers when their sum and the difference of their squares are given.

RULE.—*Divide the difference of their squares by their sum; the quotient will be their difference.*

To find two numbers when their product and quotient are given.

RULE.—*Divide the product by the quotient, and the square root of the result will be the smaller number.*

To find two numbers when the square of their sum and the sum of their squares are given.

RULE.—*From the square of the sum take the sum of the squares; the remainder will be twice the product of the numbers. Subtract four times the product from the square of the sum, and the remainder will be the square of their difference. Extract the roots, and proceed as in Rule above.*

RULES IN MENSURATION.

To find the contents of an irregular body.

Immerse the body in a vessel full of water, and measure the quantity of water displaced.

To find the area of a rectangle.

Multiply the length by the breadth.

To find the area of a triangle.

Multiply the base by one-half the altitude. Or,

From half the sum of the three sides subtract each side separately; multiply together the half sum and the three remainders, and extract the square root of the product.

To find the circumference of a circle.

Multiply the diameter by 3.14156, or $3\frac{1}{7}$.

To find the diameter of a circle.

Divide the circumference by 3.14156; or multiply it by .318309.

To find the area of a circle.

Multiply half the diameter by half the circumference. Or,

Multiply the square of the diameter by .785398.

To find the side of a square equal to a given circle.

Multiply the diameter by .886227, or $\frac{1}{2}$ of $\sqrt{3.14156}$.

To find the diameter of a circle equal to a given square.

Multiply the side of the square by 1.12838.

To find the side of an inscribed square.

Multiply the diameter by .707106, or $\sqrt{5}$*; or the circumference by .225079.*

To find the side of the largest inscribed equilateral triangle.

Multiply the diameter by .866025.

To find the circumference from an inscribed square.

Divide the side of the square by .225079.

To find the diameter of the three largest equal circles that can be inscribed in a given circle.

Divide the diameter of the given circle by 2.155.

To find the contents of a cube.

Multiply three sides together.

To find the surface of a cube.

Multiply the square of the length of one of its sides by 6.

To find the surface of a sphere.

Multiply the diameter by the circumference.

To find the solidity of a sphere.

Multiply the square of the diameter by 3.1416. Or, *Multiply the cube of the diameter by .5236.*

To find the solidity of a cylinder.

Multiply the area of one end by the length.

A CUBIC FOOT OF

		Pounds.			Pounds.
Loose earth or sand	weighs	95	Clay and stones	weigh	160
Common soil	"	124	Cork	weighs	15
Strong "	"	127	Tallow	"	59
Clay	"	135	Bricks	"	125
Lead	"	708¾	Marble	"	171
Brass	"	534¾	Granite	"	165
Copper	"	555	Sea-water	"	64 3/10
Wrought iron	"	486¾	Oak wood	"	55
Anthracite coal	"	50 to 55	Red pine	"	42
Bituminous "	"	45 to 55	White pine	"	30
Charcoal (hard wood)	"	18½	Charcoal (pine wood)	weighs	18

BUSINESS FORMS

AND

INFORMATION.

BUSINESS MAXIMS.

Endeavor to be perfect in the calling in which you are engaged.

Think nothing insignificant which has a bearing upon your success.

There is more in the *use* of advantages than in the measure of them.

Make no investments without a full acquaintance with their nature and condition; and select such investments as have intrinsic value.

Of two investments, choose that which will best promote your regular business.

Become known,—and favorably known.

Never refuse a choice when you can get it.

Goods well bought are half sold.

Goods in store are better than bad debts.

Nothing valuable is lost by civility.

By prosecuting a useful business energetically, humanity is benefited.

Keep accurate accounts, and know the exact condition of your affairs.

Be economical: a gain usually requires expense; what is saved is clear.

Reality makes no allowances for wishes or bad plans.

PAYMENTS AND LEGAL TENDER.

The law gives the debtor who owes several debts to the same creditor, the right to apply a voluntary payment, *at the time of making it*, to whichever debt he prefers. If the debtor does not exercise the right, it passes to the creditor; and if neither party makes an application of it, the law will apply it according to its own view of the intrinsic justice and equity of the case.

Payment of debts cannot be enforced after the lapse of a certain number of years, which are specified in the several States in what are called the statutes of limitations.

STATUTE LIMITATIONS IN THE UNITED STATES.

NAMES OF STATES.	Open Acc't.	Notes.	Judgments.	NAMES OF STATES.	Open Acc'ts.	Notes.	Judgments.
	Yrs.	Yrs.	Yrs		Yrs.	Yrs.	Yrs.
Alabama,	3	6	20	Minnesota,	...	6	10
Arkansas,	3	5	10	Mississippi,	3	6	7
California,	1	4	5	Missouri,	5	10	20
Connecticut,	6	6	17	New Hampshire,	6	...	20
Delaware,	3	6	...	New Jersey,	6	16	16
Florida,	5	5	...	New York,	6	6	20
Georgia,	4	6	20	North Carolina,	3	3	...
Illinois,	5	5	20	Ohio,	6	15	...
Indiana,	6	20	20	Pennsylvania,	6	6	20
Iowa,	...	10	20	Rhode Island,	6	6	20
Kentucky,	1	5	15	South Carolina,	4	4	....
Louisiana,	3	5	...	Tennessee,	3	6	16
Maine,	6	6	20	Texas,	2	4	...
Maryland,	3	3	12	Vermont,	6	14	8
Massachusetts,	6	6	...	Virginia (store % 2y)	5	5	20
Michigan,	6	6	...	Wisconsin,	6	6	...

In some States, to renew the obligation and take the case out of the operation of the statute of limitations, it is necessary that a promise to pay, or acknowledgment of the debt, be made in writing; in others, a payment made, or an acknowledgment and promise to pay to the creditor, in the presence of witnesses, is sufficient.

The tender of payment of a debt, duly made, operates in bar of any claim for damages and interest, and also in bar of the costs of an action brought to recover the debt. A creditor who refuses a tender, sufficient in amount and duly made, cannot afterwards, for the purpose of oppression or extortion, avail himself of his refusal. The debtor, however, remains liable to pay whenever called upon.

A man to whom payment is made is not bound, under ordinary circumstances, to give a receipt or to make change.

A payment made to the proper person, in "*lawful money of the United States*," is indisputably good.

By an act of Congress, the payment of debts *with coin* is regulated as follows :—

All gold coins, at their respective values, for *any amount*.

The *half-dollar*, *quarter-dollar*, *dime*, and *half-dime*, at their respective values, for debts *under five dollars*.

Three-cent pieces, for debts of any amount *under thirty cents*.

The *one-cent pieces*, for debts of any amount *under ten cents*.

The Treasury notes, called "greenbacks," are also a legal tender.

Bank notes are a good tender, *unless expressly objected to*, if the bank is in good credit.

A payment made in *counterfeit coin or notes* is no payment, if the receiver gives notice to the payer within a reasonable time that the coin or notes are counterfeit.

The taking of a promissory note for a pre-existing debt, or a contemporaneous consideration, is treated *prima facie* as a conditional payment only; that is, as payment only if it is duly paid at maturity.

When the creditor voluntarily, having free choice, and not from necessity, accepts the promissory note or bill of a *third person* for a pre-existing debt, the debt is extinguished, though the security may prove to be worthless.

When money is *remitted by mail* to the creditor, the debt is discharged if the debtor can show that the letter containing the money was properly mailed, and that it was done in accordance with the express direction of the creditor, or a custom from which such authority might be implied. If this can be shown, and a loss occurs, it is the loss of the creditor; if otherwise, it is the loss of the debtor.

The receiver of a check, if he receives it in the town or city where it is payable, should present it for payment to the bank or bankers, at the *farthest, on the next succeeding day after it is received.* If payment is not thus demanded, and the bank or bankers should fail before the check is presented, the loss will be the loss of the holder.

A creditor is not bound to accept a check remitted to him, and he may commence a suit for debt even while the check remains in his hands.

Money paid voluntarily in a transaction, with full knowledge of the facts, cannot be recovered.

Interest is not due on a note except from maturity, unless it is so mentioned in the note.

One claim may be set off against another, when it exists at the commencement of a suit and in the claimant's own right.

When part of a claim is admitted, the debtor should tender the amount admitted; this will relieve him from costs, if the disputed portion is decided in his favor.

RECEIPTS.

A RECEIPT is an acknowledgment in writing that a sum of money, or other consideration of value, has been received. A receipt is evidence of a payment against the person whc signs it, and is a voucher used by agents to prove the correctness of their accounts. It is also evidence in proving facts quite distinct from the payment stated in it.

A Simple Receipt is merely written evidence: it does not exclude verbal evidence of payment; and upon satisfactory proof that it was obtained by fraud, or given under error or a mistake as to facts, it may be inquired into and corrected at law or equity.

A man is not bound by law to give a receipt; although, by universal custom and courtesy of business, receipts are generally given when desired. When refused, the facts may be proved by witnesses.

A full and complete receipt states,—

That a payment has been received.

The date of the payment.

The amount or article received.

From whom; and if for another, on whose behalf payment is made.

To what debt or purpose it is to be applied.

By whom received; and if for another, on whose behalf it was received.

When the receipt is signed by the very person to whom the payment is ultimately to go, his signature is sufficient. Where the receipt is made out and signed by an agent, he may either write the receipt as if the principal himself were to sign it, then write his principal's name underneath, and his own name below his principal's, using the prefix "per" or "by," to signify the agency, in the following manner:—

Received, &c.

Edward M. Sawyer,
per John T. Warren.

Or, he may draw up the receipt for himself, and sign it in his own name, mentioning in the body of it, however, that he received the money "for" or "on account of" his principal.

The first form is more suitable for an agent who acts as a mere messenger to take the money and is not authorized to assume any responsibility or exercise any discretion in respect to the case. Clerks in stores are of this class.

The last form is suitable for an agent of more extended powers: of this class are lawyers, to whom collections are intrusted.

The most important of all the special clauses in the receipt is that which defines the debt or purpose to which the payment is to be applied.

Payments upon Account.—When, for want of time, or other circumstances, a payment is made in part, or with the intention to leave the application of it to future adjustment, it is common to state that the money was "received on account."

Payments upon a Specified Debt.—When a payment is made, and the debt intended to be paid is clearly distinguished, the receipt, as evidence of application, can only be set aside by proof of fraud or serious mistake.

Payments in full.—A receipt for a sum "in full" of a debt mentioned is evidence of something more than the mere payment of that sum. The law infers from it the adjustment of the amount due, after consideration of the rights of both parties, and payment of the sum specified as final satisfaction of those rights. Receipts "*in full of all ac-*

counts" do not affect claims which are not properly matters of account. Receipts "*in full of all demands*" prevent any further claim for any demand whatever, existing and known, or which ought to have been known, to the parties at the time, unless some serious or excusable mistake can be shown.

Payments to be accounted for.—As the law presumes that when money is paid it is paid in satisfaction of a debt, it is desirable, when money is received as a loan or deposit, or to be used or paid out for the benefit of the party paying it, to embody in the receipt an admission of the purpose for which it is received, somewhat as follows:—

Received, &c., One Hundred Dollars, to be repaid with interest; Received, &c., One Hundred Dollars, to be accounted for, or returned; Received, &c., One Hundred Dollars, to be expended in purchasing, &c.

Care should be taken in drawing a receipt when the transaction involves an agreement, because, in case of legal controversy, no explanation inconsistent with its language can be given.

If a person to whom a note is offered in payment consents to receive the note only upon the understanding that if it be not paid when due he shall return it to the debtor and renew his original claim, it is advisable to state the medium of payment. and that "*when paid*" it will be in full satisfaction for the debt.

A check made payable to the creditor's order is equivalent to a receipt for the amount, as the money cannot be obtained until the check has been properly indorsed.

It is not usual to take a receipt on paying a note, draft, or other instrument indorsed by the payee, because the instrument *itself*, with the indorsement, is returned, and thus becomes a receipt.

Partial payments indorsed on the instrument are concise admissions of payment, and need no other receipt. Partial payments of a bond should be indorsed on the bond.

A receipt for money paid to an estate is good when signed by but one executor; although it is well to have the signature of both.

It is advisable, when payments of importance are made, or disputes are apprehended, to take receipts. They should be kept where they are easy of access, and in a place of safety. When not in a receipt-book, they should be appropriately folded, labelled, and filed.

One of the advantages of the statutes of limitations is, that debtors are not obliged to take care forever of documents or vouchers which prove that a demand has been satisfied, and a limit is fixed beyond which there is no necessity for producing them.

When a bill which is receipted is retained by the person to whom it is presented, and payment is not made, the signature at the foot of the bill should be torn off or defaced. If payment is refused after a receipt has been delivered, evidence may be given to that effect.

Sealed or Special Receipts.—The Sealed or Special Receipt is, in general, conclusive and absolutely binding. Deeds signed and sealed, which include "the receipt of which is hereby acknowledged," are of this character. (See page 310.)

FORMS OF RECEIPTS.

RECEIPT FOR PAYMENT ON ACCOUNT.

Received, Philadelphia, July 5, 1865, from S. H. Crittenden & Co., Two Hundred and Fifty Dollars on account.

$250. ———————— *Ringwalt & Brown.*

RECEIPT IN SETTLEMENT OF ACCOUNT.

Philadelphia, Nov. 11, 1866.

Received from William H. Brown One Hundred and Twenty-Five $\frac{50}{100}$ Dollars, in settlement of account to date.

$125 $\frac{50}{100}$. *James, Kent, Santee & Co.*

RECEIPT IN FULL OF ALL DEMANDS.

St. Louis, Jan. 10th, 1867. Received of Henry D. Holmes One Thousand Dollars, in full of all demands.

$1000. *John Andrews.*

RECEIPT FOR A PARTICULAR BILL.

Rec'd, New York, July 2d, 1866, from James G. Atwater, One Hundred and Thirty-Five $\frac{62}{100}$ Dollars, in payment for a bill of Broadcloth of this date.

$135\frac{62}{100}$. *A. T. Stewart & Co.,*
per B. J. Yates.

RECEIPT FOR A NOTE.

Baltimore, May 7th, 1867.

Rec'd from Messrs. Watson, Gray & Co. their Note of this date, at three months, our favor, for Twelve Hundred and Twenty-Five $\frac{75}{100}$ Dollars, which, when paid, will be in full for account rendered to 1st instant.

$1225\frac{75}{100}$. *James H. Johnson.*

RECEIPT FOR RENT.

Rec'd, Rochester, March 6th, 1867, from Porter K. Smith, One Hundred and Twenty-Five Dollars, in full for one quarter's rent of House No. 10 St. Joseph St.; due on 1st inst.

$125. *George H. Matthews, Trustee.*

RECEIPT FOR INTEREST DUE ON A BOND.

Received, Boston, September 18th, 1866, of Gilbert Lawrence, One Hundred and Eighty Dollars, in full for six months' interest due this day, on his Bond to me, bearing date Sept. 18th, 1864, for Six Thousand Dollars.

$180. *John W. Thornton.*

RECEIPT FOR SERVICES.

Rec'd, Lowell, June 13th, 1866, from Joseph T. Chester & Co., Ninety-Six Dollars, in full for services to date.

$96. *Henry T. Chase.*

INDORSEMENT OF A PARTIAL PAYMENT ON A NOTE.

Rec'd, Phila., March 6th, 1867, on account of the within Note, Six Hundred Dollars.

Walter H. DeHaven.

$600.

RECEIPT FOR PAYMENT BY THE HAND OF A THIRD PARTY.

Rec'd, Memphis, Dec. 30th, 1864, from Leonard W. Bailey & Co., by the hand of Samuel Trumpler, Four Hundred Dollars, in full for proceeds of sales of Iron, Invoice bearing date of Nov. 10th, 1864.

George S. Powell.

$400.

RECEIPT FOR BORROWED MONEY.

(Or Borrowed-Money Due Bill.)

$300. *Syracuse, Mar. 17th, 1865.*

Borrowed and received, from William S. Balch, Three Hundred Dollars, which I promise to pay on demand, with interest.

Daniel S. Browning.

SHIPPING RECEIPT.

Albany, Sept. 10th, 1864.	*Albany, Sept. 10th, 1864.*
Shipped on board	*Received from Charles Sansom & Co., in good order, on board the "Isaac Newton," bound for New York, the packages marked and entered as below :—*
bound for	
packages	Marks. M. T. *10 sacks Garden Seeds.*
Marks	C. H. *100 bbls. Oswego Flour.*
	Robert L. Brown, Ag't.

When a large number of hands are employed, or when payments to a large number of persons are to be made, it is usual to have forms of receipts printed, leaving the date and amount to be filled according to circumstances; or a large book ruled in the manner shown below. Some take a receipt at every payment; while others take receipts only quarterly, yearly, or at other stated intervals, or when business relations are dissolved, and then in full to date of receipt.

The following is a convenient form when a large number of persons are paid :—

We, the undersigned, do hereby severally acknowledge that we have received from Matthew Baldwin & Co. the sums set opposite our respective names, in full for services to date.

No.	Date.		Amount.			Stamp.	Signatures.
	1865.						
1	July	20	Forty-Five Dollars.	45	00	☐	*Joseph L. Barrett.*
2	"	"	Thirty-Seven $\frac{50}{100}$ Dolls.	37	50	☐	*Thomas P. Jones.*
3	"	"	Twelve "	12	00		*Samuel G. Brown.*
				$94	50		

FORM FOR DIVIDEND LIST OF JOINT STOCK COMPANIES.

We, the subscribers, severally acknowledge that we have received from the Treasurer of the Saratoga Fire Insurance Co., of New York, the sums set opposite our respective names, in full for Dividend on all Stock of said Company held by us.

NAMES.	No. of Shares.	Dividend.	Arrears of Dividend.	Date of Receipt.		SIGNATURES.
				1865.		
Chas L. Somers,	100	$40		June	15	*Chas. L. Somers.*
Thos. C. Smith,	50	20	$20	"	16	*Thos. C Smith.*
Jos. T. King,	200	80				
Philip S. Hall,	150	60				

BOOK ACCOUNTS.

Entries of transactions should be made at or near the time of their occurrence.

The time to make a charge against a purchaser is when the goods are ready for delivery.

Entries, to be admissible as evidence, should be made by a proper person, and be without erasure, alteration, or interlineation.

Mistakes should be corrected by marking the erroneous entry *void*, and then making a correct entry; or, if the entry has been transferred to other books, by making another entry in explanation.

Items and particulars should be specified, as a general charge cannot be supported by this kind of evidence. The entry must be made for the purpose of charging the debtor; a mere memorandum for any other purpose is insufficient.

As a general rule, copies of all important papers, such as letters, orders, accounts current, and account sales, should be kept, as they may be required for proof or reference; but, usually, a copy is not a voucher, and nothing but the original paper will answer.

To collect a debt on the evidence of a book account, from a person in a distant place, a copy of the account should be made out, and accompanied with an affidavit in the usual form, setting forth:—1st, that the above copy of account is correctly taken from the book of original entries; 2d, that the charges were made at or about the times of their respective dates; 3d, that the goods were sold and delivered at or about the time the charges were made; 4th, that the charges are correct and the account just; and, 5th, that the person named is not entitled to any credits. This affidavit should be sworn to before a magistrate or commissioner, and will save the trouble of producing the books. (See AFFIDAVIT, page 315.)

BILLS, INVOICES, AND STATEMENTS.

A Bill is a written description of particulars or items.

A Bill of Goods, or Bill of Parcels, is a description of the quantity and price of goods sold, with the time of the transaction and the names of the purchaser and seller.

An Invoice is a full account of goods or merchandise, in which the marks, numbers, contents, and value of each package are described, together with the charges for commission, insurance, packing, &c.

A Statement is a synopsis of an account, or a brief enumeration of bills which have been purchased within a certain time. Some mercantile houses send statements monthly, or at other regular periods, to their customers who purchase on credit, that a comparison of account may be made, and, that if any error exists, it may be remedied in time.

FORMS OF BILLS.

1. *Bill ——, unreceipted.*

Rochester, *March 18, 1867.*

Mr. Henry L. Stone,

Bought of George S. Thompson.

10 lbs. Java Coffee,	@	.40	4	00
5 " Green Tea,	"	1 20	6	00
12 " Brown Sugar,	"	.14	1	68
25 yds. Muslin (Wamsutta),	"	.23	5	75
17 " Flannel,	"	.45	7	65
1 doz. Linen Hdkfs.,			3	00
12 yds. Mous. de laine,	"	.20	2	40
			$30	48

2. *Bill receipted by Firm.*

NEW ORLEANS, *December 26, 1866.*

MR. J. J. BIBB,

To B. H. FENTON & Co., *Dr.*

To 48 yds. Muslin,	@	.22		
" 12 " Drilling,	"	.18		
" 10 " Gingham,	"	.35		
" 20 " French Chintz,	"	.40		
" 7 " Broadcloth,	"	3.25		
" 2 doz. Spools Thread,	"	.75		
" 1 " Linen Napkins,	"	2.00		
" 3½ yds. French Cassimere,	"	1.90		
			$	
Rec'd payment,				
B. H. FENTON & Co.				

3. *Bill receipted by Clerk.*

{ Shipped at buyer's risk. }

CHICAGO, *Feb. 19, 1867.*

MESSRS. H. H. APPLEGATE,

TERMS, *Note at 60 days.* *To* JAMES HARRIS SON & Co. *Dr.*

820 25 boxes Cheese, 82 738,	@	.12	$88	56
10 bags Flaxseed, 1206 — 11 = 1195 lbs. 21$\frac{19}{56}$ bus.,	"	3.00	64	02
2 bbls. Eggs, 141 — 6 = 135 doz.,	"	.25	33	75
3 kegs Butter, 295 — 31 — 6 = 258 lbs.,	"	.35	90	30
5 tierces Leaf Lard, 1620 — 271 = 1349 lbs.,	"	.21	283	29
			$359	92
Rec'd payment, STAMP JAMES HARRIS, SON & Co., per L. M. WILSON.				

4. *Bill receipted by Clerk.*

PHILADELPHIA, *11mo., 7, 1867.*

MR. SETH W. OSBORN,

O. B. 55, page 150.
TERMS, *4 months.*

Bought of J. M. & T. H. SAUNDERS.

Packages	Nos.					
365	20	2 doz. Men's Blk. Cassr. Hats,	@	$24.00	$48	00
"	16	6 " " " Wool "	"	18.00	108	00
"	12	3 " Boys' Drab " "	"	15.00	45	00
"	21	3 " Child's Fancy Wool Hats,	"	15.00	45	00
"	17	3 " Men's White Canton Hats,	"	13.50	40	50
1320		60 prs. Women's Calf Pegged Boots,	"	2.25	135	00
1350		96 " Misses' " " Balmorals,	"	1.15	110	40
1216		36 " Women's Morocco Welt "	"	2.10	75	60
1301		36 " Child's Kid Pump Boots,	"	60	21	60
		2 Cases,			1	50
					$630	60

STAMP

Received payment,
J. M. & T. H. SAUNDERS,
per J. L. GURNEY.

5. *Bill paid by Note.*

PLEASE EXAMINE PACKAGES CAREFULLY FOR MISSING ARTICLES.

NEW YORK, *January 13, 1867.*

MESSRS. GEO. W. MCWILLIAMS & CO.,

O. B. 4, page 75.

Bought of FISHER & COLLINS.

7	Doz. Edg'd Muffins, $\frac{2}{1.00}$, $\frac{4}{1.20}$, $\frac{1}{1.35}$,	8	15
2	Sets W. Gran. Tea Sets, 46 ps., @ $8.50,	17	00
2	Doz. Mocco. Pitchers, $\frac{1}{4.50}$, $\frac{1}{7.00}$,	11	50
6	" Table Tumblers, @ 1.25,	7	50
50	" W. Gran. Dishes, $\frac{10}{50}$, $\frac{15}{1.00}$, $\frac{10}{1.50}$, $\frac{10}{2.00}$, $\frac{5}{3.00}$,	70	00
20	Sets " Teas, @ 1.10,	22	00
1¼	Doz. Edg'd Bakers, $\frac{\frac{1}{2}}{2.00}$, $\frac{\frac{1}{2}}{4.50}$, $\frac{\frac{1}{4}}{6.00}$,	4	75
	Crate, 2.00 Box, 25 and Porterage, 50	2	75
		$143	65

STAMP

Rec'd payment by Note at 4 mos.,
FISHER & COLLINS.

Bills for Services, &c.

6. WORCESTER, *July 7, 1867.*

MR. JAMES L. RUSHTON,

To FREDERICK T. STONE, *Dr.*

1867.				
Jan.	7	For Professional Services in Family,	$10	00
"	20	" 5 visits to son, Charles Rushton,	5	00
May	10	" 3 " " " Henry L. Rushton,	3	00
			$18	00

7. BUFFALO, *August 19, 1866.*

MR. JOHN H. WAGNER,

To WM. H. TURNER, *Dr.*

1867.				
May	11	For Repairing House, as per Contract,	$25	00
"	"	" 800 feet Pine Boards, @ $8,	6	40
"	"	" Lock and Key for door,	2	25
"	"	" Nails, Hooks, &c.,	1	00
			$34	65
		Received payment, W. H. TURNER.		

8. CHICAGO, *July 3, 1866.*

MR. OWEN T. JONES,

To HENRY G. LANGDON, *Dr.*

		For Instruction of son, William T. Jones,			
		in English branches, 3 mos.,	$15.00		
		in Latin, "	20.00	$35	00
		" Instruction of daughter, Louisa J. Jones,			
		in English branches, 3 mos.,	$15.00		
		in Music, "	15.00		
		" Use of Piano,	10.00	40	00
		" Books and Stationery furnished during the Term,		3	50
				$78	50
		Received payment, HENRY G. LANGDON, per S. Y LANGDON.			

9. *Items of an Account.*

MECHANICSVILLE, *Jan. 1, 1867.*

MR. S. B. MOREHOUSE,

To O. TOMPKINS & Co. *Dr.*

1866.					
Apr.	5	To 5 bbls. Genesee Flour, extra,	@ $15.00	$75	00
May	9	" 10 lbs. Pearl Starch,	" .18	1	80
June	16	" 20 " English Breakfast Tea,	" 2.25	45	00
Sept.	14	" 2 bbls. Prime Pork,	" 17.50	35	00
				$156	80
		CR.			
May	5	By 17 yds. English Broadcloth, @ $3.00,	$51.00		
"	10	" 25 " French Chintz, " .40,	10.00		
July	11	" 12 " English Beaver Cloth, " 3.00,	36.00	97	00
		Balance due,		$59	80
		Settled by due-bill,			
		O. TOMPKINS & Co.			

INVOICES—DRY GOODS.

CINCINNATI, *Jan. 17, 1867.*

MESSRS. LEONARD & CURTIS,

Bo't of JOSEPH CUSHING & Co.

Terms, 3 mos. Note to your own order.

L. & C.	301	2 cases Merrimac Prints, 80 ps., 2804 yds.,	@ .17		
"	312	1 case Satinets, 450 yds.,	" .78		
	540	5 ps. Extra Black Cassimere, 120 yds.,	" $2.75		
	17	10 " Satin Stripe Muslin, 200 "	" 1.30		
	137	40 Check Square Shawls,	" 2.13		
	15	6 Imperial Long "	" 11.00		
	801	3 ps. Solferino Opera Cloth, 90 yds.,	" .85		
	4267	12 Ladies' Mourning Long Shawls, 60 × 120,	" 9.00		
	No. 1	2 ps. Taffeta Ribbons,	" 1.50		
		5 " Buff Chambrays, 155 yds.,	" .42		
	142	2 " Printed Plaid Flannel, 90 yds.,	" .52		
E. C.	46	15 " Plain Mousseline de Laines, metres 674.1 = 730½ yds.,	" .28½		
		Rec'd payment,			
		JOS. CUSHING & Co.,			
		per L. R TAYLOR			

Invoice of TWO *packages of Merchandise purchased by* W. B. LONGWORTH & Co., *and forwarded to* B. G. BABCOCK, *Liverpool, for shipment per "Kangaroo" S. S., bound for* NEW YORK, *for account and risk of* MESSRS. HOMER, COLLADAY & Co., *Philadelphia, and to them consigned.*

					£	s.	d.			
Ⓐ H										
※ 30	7743	$\frac{16}{4}$ Fancy Wool Long Shawls,	70	24/-	84					
		" " " "	18	17/-	15	6				
		" " Square "	12	9/-	5	8				
	$\frac{100}{1244}$	$\frac{100}{734}$ Broche Borders, yds.	200	1/-	10					
	2301	" "	200	10½*d*	8	15				
	2302	" "	200	8*d.*	6	13	4			
		Cases, Packing, Oil-Cloth, &c.				19	10	131	2	2
※ 31		$\frac{16}{4}$ Fancy Wool Long Shawls,	72	23/-	82	16				
		" " " "	48	12/-	28	16				
		Case, Packing, &c.				19	6	112	11	6
								243	13	8
		Discount on £241 14*s.* 4*d.*, @ 2½,						6		10
								237	12	10
		Charges, Cartage, 1/6, Commission 1½ per cent., £3 11*s.* 4*d.*,						3	12	10
		Cash, 1st Sept. 1866,						£241	5	8
		E. E.								
		GLASGOW, 11th August, 1866.								
		W. B. LONGWORTH & Co.								

Other invoices may be found under PROFIT AND LOSS.

MONTHLY STATEMENT.

Monthly Statement.

BOSTON, *Jan. 31, 1867.*

MESSRS. B. H. BRADFORD & Co.,

To A. A. LAWRENCE & Co. *Dr.*

1867.				
Jan.	4	To Mdse., as per Bill rendered, @ 3 months,	$75	00
"	17	" " " " " 3 "	132	00
"	26	" " " " " 60 days,	318	00
"	29	" " " " " 3 months,	123	75
			$648	75

BILLS OF LADING.

A **Bill of Lading** is a formal receipt subscribed by the master of a ship, or other common carrier, acknowledging the receipt of goods intrusted to him for transportation, and binding himself, under certain exceptions, to deliver them, in like good condition as received, at the place and to the person named in the bill, or his assigns, for a remuneration or freightage. The bill of lading is the evidence of shipment and the title to the goods shipped, and may be indorsed or transferred to other parties.

Three sets are usually made out: one to be sent to the person to whom the goods are consigned, one for the person shipping the goods, and a third to be retained by the carrier, or master of the vessel. The bills of lading contain a description of the packages shipped, including their number, marks, weights, &c.

Common Carriers are those who hold themselves out to carry all goods intrusted to them, or all goods of a particular kind. They are of two kinds,—inland carriers by land or water, and carriers by sea. They are answerable for all losses which do not fall within the excepted cases of inevitable accident and the acts of the public enemies of the country. The carrier may limit his responsibility by agreement with his customer; but he cannot exempt himself by notice or agreement from responsibility for *actual negligence*. He has a lien on the goods carried, and may retain them until he has been paid his freight.

Primage is an allowance made for loading the goods. The term "Average" refers to general or marine average, in which, if loss arise during the voyage, the cargo is required to bear a proportionate share.

A **Manifest** is a list containing the marks, description, and number of packages of the ship's cargo, together with the names of the shippers and consignees, and must be certified by the master of the vessel before the collector of customs, or the consul.

A **Consul** is an officer appointed by Government to reside in a foreign country, for the purpose of protecting the commercial interests of the subjects of his own nation. Documents of any kind attested by the consul, under his hand and seal of office, are admitted as evidence in courts of justice.

BILL OF LADING, SIGNED BY MASTER OF VESSEL.

Shipped,

In good order and well-conditioned, by **B. Gallaway, Jr.**, as Agent, in and upon the good ship called the Kathleen, whereof is Master for this present voyage, **U. E. Roberts**, and now riding at anchor in the river Thames, and bound for **Philadelphia**, via Falmouth, **Eighteen Bales Merchandise**, being marked and numbered as in the margin, and to be delivered in the like good order and well-conditioned, at the aforesaid Port of **Philadelphia** (*the act of God, the Queen's enemies, fire, and all and every other dangers and accidents of the seas, rivers, and navigation, of whatever nature and kind soever, excepted*), unto **Mr. Porter Morgan, Philadelphia**, or to his assigns, he or they paying freight for the said goods, £5 11*s.*, in full. Primage and Average accustomed.

P.M.
P.

18 Bales.

※ 1/18.

Rate 20/–.

	£	s.	d.
Freight,	5	5	9
Primage,		5	3
	£5	11*s*.	

In Witness whereof, the Master or Purser of the said Ship hath affirmed to **three** Bills of Lading, all of this tenor and date, the one of which Bills being accomplished, the others to stand void.

Weight and contents unknown; and not accountable for leakage, breakage, or rust. Freight payable at the current rate of exchange on the day the ship enters at the Custom-House.

Dated in LONDON, this 23d day of Dec., 1865.

Contents unknown.

U. E. ROBERTS,
Master.

BILL OF LADING SIGNED BY CLERK OF R. R. CO.

Camden & Amboy Railroad and Transportation Company.

Philadelphia, Feb. 24, 1866.

Received, of Messrs. Barclay & Barclay,
30 casks Linseed Oil,

MARKED:—H. L. T.—※ 1 to 30.

To be transported to NEW YORK, and delivered to Mr. H. L. Turner, or order, upon the following

TERMS:

[Here the conditions are inserted.]

W. P. MURPHY,
For the Company.

STEAMBOAT BILL OF LADING.

Received by the **Wilmington Steamboat Line**, in apparently good order, from H. Y. HEALD, marked and entered as below (contents unknown), which we promise to deliver at Wilmington (breakage and leakage excepted), and not being responsible, if lost, stolen, or damaged, beyond the value of Fifty Dollars per package.

1 Case Merchandise.

MARKED :—GEORGE DANBY,
Wilmington, Del.

PHILADELPHIA, Jan. 19, 1867. P. T. SIMPSON, *Agent.*

FREIGHT BILL.

FORM No. 69.—SERIES B.

No. 12118. *Philadelphia, Nov. 8, 1866.*

Mr. Robert B. Stewart,

To PENNSYLVANIA R. R. CO. DR.

For Freight from .... *Mill Creek* :................................ *on*

	Weight.	Rate.	Freight.		Expenses.		Total.	
3 boxes Apples,	1935	56	10	83		57	11	40
4 " Mdse.,	1450	60	8	70		50	9	20
							$20	60

Rec'd payment for the Company,
THOS. Y. MURRAY.

WAREHOUSE RECEIPT.

Syracuse, June 18, 1867.

Delivered to **John Cottrell & Co.**, in good order, for which they have paid the charges thereon.

Marks.	Articles.	Quantity.	Charges.	
J. C. & Co. X. L.				
※ 1 to 20	Oswego Flour, extra,	20 bbls.		
※ 20 " 30	Corn Starch,	10 "		
	Freight from Oswego,		1	50
	Drayage, Storage, &c.,		3	00
	T. & L. MOSIER.		$4	50

ACCOUNT SALES.

An **Account of Sales** is a detailed statement of goods sold and the charges incurred thereon, and is made for the purpose of showing the net proceeds of sales. When goods have been sold on commission, the agent or commission merchant makes out an account sales, to be sent to the consignor, or person for whom the goods were sold.

Account Sales are made out in various forms; that form being used which is most convenient for the branch of business in which it is used. Sometimes they are made out in the form of a ledger account; the quantity of goods sold, with their marks, prices, &c., being entered on the credit side, and the various charges on the debit side. The difference between the two sides exhibits the net proceeds, and is entered on the smaller side, to produce a balance.

Another form, and the one which is generally adopted, is to enter the sales, with all the particulars, first, and the charges underneath.

When the goods are not all sold, a minute of those still on hand should accompany the account sales.

To make out an account sales, turn to the consignment account in the ledger, and from thence to the original entries, to obtain all the items affecting the account. When the goods are sold for cash, or when the consignor guaranties the sale, it is not necessary to give the names of the purchasers; although this is frequently done.

A *del-credere* commission, or guaranty, is a commission charged for becoming responsible for the debts of those who purchase the goods on credit.

Account Sales are averaged to find the date when the proceeds may be paid without loss of interest to either party. (See AVERAGE OF ACCOUNTS.)

Sales of {200 bus. Wheat, 150 bbls. Flour,} *received per Barque* AURORA, *for Account of* JAMES T. HOYT, *Berlin, Md.*

		To whom sold.		Description.	Price.		
1866.							
Dec.	19	Jefferson Andrews,	25 bus.	Ohio Wheat,	1.15	$28	75
1867.							
Jan.	5	R. J. Long,	50 bbls.	Elm Grove Fam. Flour,	9.50	47	50
"	8	Chas. S. Brown,	100 bus.	Kentucky Wheat,	1.20	120	00
"	13	L. S. Harris & Co.,	20 "	Ohio "	1.18	23	60
"	"	"	75 bbls.	Oregon Fam. Flour, Ex.,	8.50	637	50
"	25	Henry G. Stone & Co.	55 bus.	Ohio Wheat,	1.10	55	00
"	"	"	25 bbls.	Flour, Grant's Mills,	11.00	275	00
						$1187	35
		——— CHARGES. ———					
		Freight and Drayage,			$45.00		
		Insurance on $1000, @ 1¼ per cent.,			12.50		
		Storage and Labor,			7.25		
		Commission and Guaranty, 5 per cent. on 1187.35,			59.37	124	12
		Net Proceeds due per average, ———, 1867,				$1063	23
				LEONARD B. HUDSON.			
		NEW YORK, Jan. 28, 1867.					

Account Sales of 75 Bales of Wool received per Pennsylvania Railroad, and sold for Account of MESSRS. SMITH & WILLIAMS, *Salem, Columbiana Co., Ohio.*

1866.					
Nov.	10	Three-quarter blood Merino Fleece, Net 9238 lbs., @ 60c.,	30 days,	5542	80
Dec.	15	Half-blood Merino Fleece, Net 2638 lbs., @ 55c.,	"	1450	90
"	"	Unwashed Merino Fleece, Net, 240; ⅓ discount, 80; 160 lbs., @ 55c.,	30 days,	88	00
1867.					
Jan.	5	Common and quarter-blood Fleece, Net 985 lbs., @ 50c.,	30 days,	492	50
				$7574	20
		——— CHARGES. ———			
		Freight and Drayage,	$192.33		
		Commission, including Insurance, Storage, and Labor, 2 cents per lb. on 13,101 lbs.,	262.02	454	35
		Net Proceeds due Dec. 22, 1866,		$7119	85
		E. E. THAW & WALKER.			
		PHILADELPHIA, Jan. 10, 1867.			

ACCOUNTS CURRENT.

Accounts Current are statements in detail of accounts which have been open or running from one time to another. They are usually made out twice a year, or whenever circumstances require, by the parties desiring settlement.

The object of an Account Current is to furnish the person to whom it is sent a statement, that he may know the extent of his dealings, and what balance may be due from him to settle his account.

Accounts Current are drawn from the accounts in the Ledger, with which they must agree, and should contain a description of every transaction, with date, items, and amounts, as expressed in the books of original entry, allowing for the difference of style. When particulars are not supplied, reference should be made to the entries or papers in which they may be found. Interest is allowed, or not, according to custom or the understanding between the parties. The time for which interest is calculated is counted from the date when the amount is due, or equivalent to cash, to the date of settlement. For the different methods of calculating the interest, see INTEREST ACCOUNTS. Accounts Current are sometimes averaged as in Average of Accounts.

If there are errors in an Account Current received, it should be objected to within a reasonable time, or it becomes an Account Stated, which does not require a proof of items.

The letters E. E. and E. O. E., appended to invoices and accounts, are for the purpose of intimating the right of correcting errors or of supplying omissions.

For additional Accounts Current, see pages 91 and 94; and for finding interest on English Accounts, see INTEREST IN ENGLAND.

FORM OF ACCOUNT CURRENT.

MESSRS. H. S. MOREHOUSE & Co. *in Account Current and Interest Account with* S. D. DOUGLASS & Co. *to January 1, 1867.*

Date.		Amt.		When due.	Days.	Int.		Date.		Amt.		When due.	Days.	Int.	
1866. July 7	To Mdse., as per bill rendered, at 3 mos. . .	1250	00	Oct. 7	86	17	92	1866. Aug. 15	By Inv. of Sugar @ 60 days,	950	00	Oct. 14	79	12	51
" 15	" Mdse., as per bill rendered	1540	00	" 15	78	20	02	Sept. 5	" Your Draft on Gray & Bro. at 30 days . . .	250	00	" 12	81	3	38
Aug. 10	" Mdse. (Net), as per bill rendered	1300	00	Aug. 10	144	31	20	Oct. 17	" R. Hunter & Co.'s Draft on Commercial Bank at sight	1500	00	" 17	76	19	00
" 15	" Net Proceeds of Wheat, as per your Account Sales	3800	00	Sept. 10	113	71	57	" 15	" Your ½ Net Proceeds of 1500 bbls. Flour, as per Acct. Sales rendered	3800	00	Nov. 3	59	37	37
" 20	" Our Drft. on L. T. Adams at 30 days	425	00	" 19	104	7	36	1867. *Jan. 1*	" *Balance of Interest* . .					*75*	*81*
		8315	00			148	07			6500	00			148	07
	Add Bal. of Interest, .	75	81					" "	" *Balance*	*1890*	*81*				
		8390	81							8390	81				
1867. Jan. 1	To Bal. due us	1890	81												

E. E.

S. D. DOUGLASS & Co.

PITTSBURGH, Jan. 1, 1866.

ORDERS.

An Order is a written request to deliver money or goods to some person mentioned, or to his order, or to the bearer, on account of the person signing the request. It is used by the person receiving it as a voucher that the person signing it is responsible, and that the thing or things mentioned have been delivered. Orders may be made negotiable; but the persons on whom they are drawn are not under obligation to pay them unless they have been accepted.

ORDERS FOR MONEY.

Lancaster, Aug. 16, 1867.

Mr. James T. Fordley,

Please pay to M. B. Brown, or order, One Hundred Dollars, and charge to our account.

$100. *Jas. W. Andrews & Co.*

Messrs. Alfred Slade & Co.

Gentlemen:—Please pay to Thomas Brown, or order, Thirty Dollars, due on my account, and oblige

Yours, respectfully,

Philada., Aug. 12, 1866. *Robert H. Jenkins.*

ORDERS FOR GOODS.

Baltimore, Feb. 19, 1867.

Mr. William B. Linden,

Please pay to Andrew B. Jones, or bearer, Sixty Dollars in Goods from your store, and place to account of

Henry W. Wilkins.

Albany, Mar. 25, 1867.

Mr. Charles Riqua,

Please send me, per bearer, Ten Barrels Flour, Genesee Extra, and oblige

Yours truly, *Henry Burnham.*

Dayton, O., August 16, 1866.

Messrs. L. A. Tiers & Son,

New York.

Dear Sirs:

Please send immediately Five (5) Half-Chests Imperial Tea, Hugo & Otto, ※7, as per sample sent us, and oblige

Yours, truly,

Corbin & Walworth.

St. Louis, Jan. 3, 1867.

Messrs. E. C. & J. Biddle,

Philadelphia, Pa.

Gentlemen:—Please send us, per Adams Express,

60 Crittenden's Book-Keeping, C. H. Edition.
25 do. do. H. S. do.
30 Lynd's Class-Book of Etymology.
12 Cleveland's American Literature.
16 Alsop's Algebra.

Upon receipt of your Bill, with Goods, we will remit by Draft or Express, as you may direct.

Respectfully, yours,

A. B. M. Thompson & Co.

CHECKS.

A Check is a written order or request, addressed to a bank or banker, by a person having money deposited, requesting the payment, on presentment, of a certain sum of money to a person therein named, or to his order, or to the bearer.

When drawn payable to a person *or bearer*, it is transferable without indorsement, and the holder is entitled to payment; when drawn payable to a person *or his order*, it must be indorsed by the person to whom the check is made payable; when made payable to a person without the words "or order," or "bearer," or to a particular person "only," it is not negotiable.

As checks made payable to a person's order compel the payee to indorse them, they are, when drawn in this form, often used in lieu of receipts.

The drawer of a check may countermand its payment at any time previous to its payment or acceptance by the bank.

A check received from others should be presented without unnecessary delay, as the drawer will not otherwise be responsible for its payment in case of the failure of the bank.

Every holder of a check is liable to every subsequent holder only for the time for which he would be held if originally liable.

A post-dated check is payable on the day of its date; but, as circumstances may arise that will render void a check which is payable in the future, some prefer dating the check with the day on which it is drawn, and stating in the body of the check the day when it is to be paid.

When made payable on a future day mentioned, different from that of the date, they have been treated as bills of exchange, and as such are entitled to days of grace, and require revenue stamps, the same as bills of exchange.

The amount of a check should always be written out in words. The amount in figures is placed in the corner, that the sum for which the check is drawn may be seen at a glance, and also as a precaution against any alteration which might be made.

CHECK PAYABLE TO BEARER.

STAMP. No. 7. *Cincinnati, Aug. 16, 1867.*

First National Bank,

Pay to .... *Samuel Wallace,* .... *or Bearer,*

Three Hundred $\frac{50}{100}$ *Dollars.*

\$300$\frac{50}{100}$. *Hugh Graham.*

STAMP. No. 127. Baltimore, Nov. 22, 1865.

The National Bank of Baltimore,

Pay to .... James S. Brown, ... or Order,

........One Hundred and Seventy........ $\frac{38}{100}$ Dollars.

$\$170\frac{38}{100}$. Wm. F. Grant.

CHECK PAYABLE AT A FUTURE TIME.

STAMP. No. 173. New York, Mar. 13, 1867.

National Park Bank,

Pay to.............. John F. Hope, ...or Order,

Eight Hundred Dollars,

on the 27th inst., without grace. Acceptance waived.

$800. Robert R. Andrews.

CERTIFIED CHECKS.

A certified check is one for the payment of which the bank becomes responsible, upon being certified, or marked "good" by the paying teller, with his signature attached. Certified checks are used to prevent the inconvenience and risk of withdrawing and counting sums of money that are to be immediately paid to others. They are also used instead of drafts for making remittances to distant places.

STAMP. No. 122. Philadelphia, April 6, 1867.

Philadelphia National Bank,

Pay to .... Hugh Graham,......... or Order,

One Thousand......... Dollars.

$1000. M. E. Bradford & Co.

Good when properly indorsed.
W. H. Wells, Teller.

CERTIFICATES OF DEPOSIT.

Certificates of Deposit are used when money is temporarily deposited, and no regular bank account is kept. When made payable to another person's order, they are frequently employed for making remittances, in the same manner as certified checks.

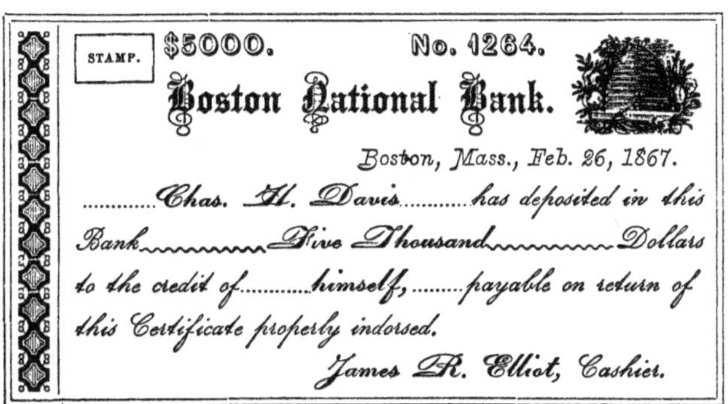

STAMP. $5000. No. 1264.

Boston National Bank.

Boston, Mass., Feb. 26, 1867.

............Chas. H. Davis..........has deposited in this Bank Five Thousand Dollars to the credit of..........himself,.........payable on return of this Certificate properly indorsed.

James R. Elliot, Cashier.

TRANSACTIONS WITH BANKS.

Banks are organized institutions for the employment of capital. Banks of "circulation and deposit" have the use, under certain restrictions, of the capital paid in by the stockholders, the money belonging to depositors, and the notes of their own circulation. The National Banks are required to deposit with the Treasurer of the United States interest-bearing bonds of the United States, in proportion to the capital stock paid in. All bonds so deposited are held exclusively as security for the circulating notes delivered to the banks depositing the bonds. The following suggestions may be found useful to those who have dealings with banks:—

Make your deposits in the bank as *early in the day as you conveniently can*, and never without your bank-book.

For your own security, it is well to have ONE PARTICULAR

PERSON to do your business at the bank, who shall be competent to take charge of the money and papers you intrust to his care, and sufficiently intelligent to understand and properly deliver the messages and explanations you may have occasion to make; also, that you write or stamp OVER YOUR INDORSEMENT, upon all checks which you send to be deposited to your credit in the bank, the words "FOR DEPOSIT TO OUR CREDIT," which will prevent their being used for any other purpose.

Always use the deposit tickets furnished by the bank, and examine the date and indorsement of every check. When checks are deposited, the banks require them to be indorsed by the depositor, whether drawn to his order or not.

Keep your check-book, when not in use, under your own lock and key. Make it a rule to give checks only out of YOUR OWN CHECK-BOOK.

Draw as few checks as possible. When you have several sums to pay, draw ONE CHECK for the whole, and take notes of such denominations as will enable you to distribute the amount among those you intend it for.

Do not allow your bank-book to run too long without being balanced, and when returned by the bank compare it with your own account, and examine your cancelled checks without delay. If you wish to preserve your cancelled checks, deface or destroy the signature as soon as returned, in a manner that will prevent their being copied, and place the checks out of the reach of others.

In filling up checks, do not leave space in which the amount may be increased. It has been decided that when a check is so carelessly drawn that an alteration may be easily made, the loss arising from the alteration, if any, must be borne by the drawer.

Write your signature with your usual freedom, and never vary the style of it.

Offer notes for discount or collection in good season. Do

not put off the offering of notes for discount until the last day of your need. When notes are discounted or collected for you, hand your bank-book to the clerk, that they may be entered in it to your credit.

COUNTERFEIT BANK-NOTES.

A *counterfeit* note is a *fac-simile* of the genuine, or as nearly like it as it can be made. A *spurious* note is made up of designs different from the genuine, and calculated to pass where the genuine is not known. An *altered* note is one altered from a lower to a higher denomination; or one on a broken or bogus bank, on which the name or locality is changed for that of a bank in good standing.

RULES FOR DETECTING COUNTERFEIT NOTES.

Examine the vignette or picture at the top of the note: see if the faces have a lifelike expression; if the eyes are well defined, showing the pupil distinctly, the white clearly; see if the drapery or dress fits well, looks natural and easy, and shows the folds distinctly—if the whole figure harmonizes. See if the sky is clear, or transparent, or soft and even, and not scratchy, and if the different objects have a finished appearance. In the genuine, small figures in the background are always exceedingly well executed.

Examine the medallion rulings and circular ornaments around the figures, &c.; see if they are regular, smooth, and uniform. When there are two medallions on a bill designed to be alike, they are exactly alike, being from the same original die. This work is done by a geometrical lathe, a machine of immense cost, and which produces fine and ornamental circles of such uniformity and exquisite perfection that it is almost an impossibility for the counterfeiter to produce a good imitation.

Examine the letters and figures; see if they are perfect in every respect,—all perfectly true and uniform and regular. In counterfeits the round handwriting is seldom well executed. Carefully study the hair-lines and curves, the shade or parallel ruling on the face or outside of the letters; see if they are without breaks or flaws, and have a finished, graceful appearance. Examine the engraver's signature or imprint; see if it is clearly and beautifully engraved; if the letters are all of one size and one slant; if the distances apart and the thickness of stroke are equal.

Examine the President's and Cashier's signatures. In some counterfeits the signatures are lithographed *fac-similes*, inked over with a pen, which gives them a stamped appearance, the stroke a dead color and a rough edge, and sometimes the pen does not follow the hair-stroke curve correctly; while the genuine signatures, which are written with a pen, have rather a glossy appearance, and the stroke a smooth edge.

Bank-notes altered by what is termed the "pasting process" may be detected by holding them to the light, when the parts pasted on will be discovered. When the alteration has been made by substituting figures or letters for others which have been extracted, the denomination in the centre of the note, when examined letter by letter, will be found to be poorly formed and blurred, and the parallel lines irregular and imperfect. The texture of the paper between the letters is very often destroyed,—a defect which may be discovered by comparing the paper between the letters with that immediately above and below; the ink of the altered part is also sometimes different from the rest of the note.

Avoid all hurry and confusion when taking money, as much of the bad money passed is passed under such circumstances.

DESCRIPTION OF NATIONAL CURRENCY.

NATIONAL BANK-NOTES.

UNITED STATES and title of bank on each of the different denominations.

1s.—Two females standing in front of an altar, one of them pointing upward. A large 1 on the left end, on which is, "Secured by Bonds," &c.

Reverse Side.—Landing of Pilgrims, in large oval; ONE, eagle in shield; ONE, on right; ONE, arms of the State; ONE, on left end.

2s.—Large 2, extending almost across length of note; United States, &c., on upper part, and 2 on lower part, on left end; female seated holding American flag, on which is a wreath.

Reverse Side.—Sir Walter Raleigh erect, smoking pipe; six men and a boy grouped around him at a table. 2, eagle and shield, on right; 2, arms of the State, on left end.

5s.—Columbus introducing America to Europe, Asia, and Africa, —the countries represented by female figures. Columbus discovering America; four men. 5 on right end, FIVE on left end.

Reverse Side.—Landing of Columbus and men. Spread eagle on right; arms of the State on left; FIVE and 5 on each end.

10s.—Female seated on spread eagle in clouds. Franklin drawing lightning from clouds with a kite; boy seated; 10 on right, TEN on left end.

Reverse Side.—De Soto on horseback, with his army, discovering the Mississippi. Spread eagle; arms of the State; 10, 10, on each side.

20s.—On right, allegorical representation of Loyalty; figure of Liberty in foreground, bearing national flag; farmers, artisans, &c., rallying around the flag. On left, battle of Lexington. 20 on each end.

Reverse Side.—Baptism of Pocahontas. Eagle and shield; arms of the State; 20 on the right, XX on left end.

50s.—Allegorical representation of Victory: three figures in a cloud; soldier kneeling. Washington and men in a boat crossing the Delaware. 50 on each end.

Reverse Side.—Embarkation of the Pilgrims. Eagle and shield; arms of the State; 50 and L on each side.

100s.—Female with wings, seated—allegorical representation—maintenance of Liberty and Nationality. Men in a row-boat in foreground, two vessels in background. 100, C, on right end; C, 100, on left end.

Reverse Side.—Signing Declaration of Independence. Eagle in an oval; arms of the State; 100 on right, C on left side.

TREASURY NOTES, OR GREENBACKS.

1s.—UNITED STATES. A long oval portrait of Hon. S. P. Chase on left end. A strip of lathe-work between signatures. 1 in green and 1 in fancy die. Oval in the lower centre, in which the rays converge to the number showing the denomination of the note, which is on a white ground.

2s.—A side view of Alexander Hamilton in lower left centre. Two strips of lathe-work. II in green die; 2 on each end in fancy die. Oval in lower centre, with rays similar to the "ones."

5s.—FIVE DOLLARS. 5 on a strip of lathe-work; right end, male portrait; 5 above; left end, female erect, with sword and shield.

10s.—Upper centre, eagle on a shield. 10 in green die each side. Right end, female erect by pedestal, holding tablet, &c.; left end, portrait of President Lincoln.

20s.—Centre, female erect, with sword and shield; figure 20 and green die each side. TWENTY DOLLARS across each end in green die-work.

50s.—Side view of Alexander Hamilton in oval die. Treasury die in pink on right of vignette. 50 on die on each end of note.

100s.—Large spread eagle on a rock. 100 in green die on right; 100 in black die in right upper corner; 100 in black die in lower left corner.

500s.—In centre, portrait of Albert Gallatin in round green die. 500 on each end. FIVE HUNDRED DOLLARS on a strip of lathe-work below.

1000s.—In centre, portrait of Robert Morris in green round die. M, with 1000 across it, on each end. ONE THOUSAND DOLLARS on a green strip of lathe-work below.

DUE-BILLS.

A **Due-Bill** is a simple acknowledgment of a debt, in writing. It is not payable to order, nor is it assignable by mere indorsement. *Bouv. L. D.* It is subject to all the offsets and equitable rights between the original parties, and action must be brought in the name of the original obligee. Due-bills do not draw interest unless specified.

DUE-BILL FOR MONEY.

$125. *Philadelphia, July 10, 1866.*

Due Henry W. Chase, for value received, One Hundred and Twenty-Five Dollars, with interest.

DUE-BILL FOR GOODS.

Due, New York, August 9th, 1866, to H. Y. Bennett, for value received, Sixty-Five $\frac{50}{100}$ Dollars, in goods from my store.

65\frac{50}{100}$. *Geo. W. Hanson.*

PRODUCE NOTES.

A **Produce Note** is a written engagement to deliver specific articles to a specified amount. Like due-bills, produce notes are not assignable by mere indorsement. The maker of the note must be able to prove that he was ready at the proper *time and place*, and continued ready, to deliver the articles, or he may be compelled to pay their value in money

PRODUCE NOTE.

$37 $\frac{25}{100}$. *Lebanon, July 2, 1866.*

For value received, we promise to pay to Thos. J. Stewart, on demand, Thirty-Seven $\frac{25}{100}$ Dollars, in goods at our store.

R. B. Painter & Co.

FORM OF ASSIGNMENT OF A PRODUCE NOTE.

(*To be indorsed on the back of the Note.*)

For value received, I assign the within Note to A. J. Gordon, without (or with) recourse, this 17th day of July, 1866.

Thos. J. Stewart.

PROMISSORY NOTES.

A **Promissory Note** is a written promise to pay, unconditionally and at all events, a specified sum of money. Promissory notes are either *negotiable* or *non-negotiable*.

A note is negotiable when the promise is made not only to the person named in it, but to his *order* or *bearer*, and may be collected by whomsoever may be the holder of the note at the time of its maturity.

If a note be made payable to Jas. Graham, or *bearer*, it may be collected by Jas. Graham, or by any one who may hold or bear it, and is negotiable by mere *delivery*.

FORM OF NOTE PAYABLE TO BEARER.

$500. *Portland, July 3, 1866.*

Three months after date, I promise to pay to James Graham, or bearer, Five Hundred Dollars. Value received.

Chas. J. Raymond.

A note made payable to James Graham, or *order*, may be collected by any one to whom James Graham may order it to be paid. The order is commonly written upon the back of the note, and is called an indorsement. If James Graham simply wrote his name on the back of the note, it would be an indorsement in blank, and is equivalent to "Pay to bearer," and would then be negotiable by delivery. (See INDORSEMENTS.)

NOTE PAYABLE TO A PERSON, OR ORDER.

$1000. *Troy, June 29, 1866.*

Thirty days after date, for value received, we promise to pay to James Graham, or order, One Thousand Dollars.

J. R. Flannigan & Co.

A note made payable to James Graham, or James Graham only, is not negotiable, and is payable only to the party named.

NON-NEGOTIABLE NOTE.

$300. *Worcester, June 10, 1866.*

Sixty days after date, I promise to pay to James Graham Three Hundred Dollars. Value received.

Henry J. Gordon.

A custom prevails in the mercantile community of drawing notes payable to the maker's own *order*, with his indorsement, for the purpose of facilitating their transfer without requiring the holder to indorse them.

NOTE TO ONE'S OWN ORDER.

$1800. *Pittsburgh, September 20, 1866.*

Four months after date, I promise to pay to the order of myself Eighteen Hundred Dollars, without defalcation. Value received. *Philip T. Wharton.*

In Pennsylvania, the words "*without defalcation*" must be inserted in the note in order to render it negotiable. In New Jersey, "*without defalcation or discount;*" in Missouri, "*negotiable and payable without defalcation or discount;*"* in Indiana, the words "*without any relief whatever from valuation or appraisement laws*" are inserted.

The words "value received" imply a consideration, which is necessary to make a promise binding on the maker of it.

The person who promises to pay is called the *promisor*, *maker*, or *drawer;* the person to whom the note is made payable is called the *payee;* the person who writes his name upon the back of the note is called the *indorser;* and the person to whom it is transferred by indorsement is called the *indorsee.*

All the parties who have written their names on a note are liable for the amount due, but only one satisfaction can be recovered.

A note given on Sunday is void; so is a note founded upon fraud, or when the consideration is illegal. Any material alteration in a note—as, for instance, in the date, or amount, or time of payment—discharges all parties who have not consented to such alteration.

If a person at the time of taking a note has notice that it is void through fraud or upon any legal grounds, he places himself in the position of the payee. A note as a gift is void from want of consideration.

Notes made payable at a fixed time are allowed three days after the expiration of the time expressed for payment. These three days are called "days of grace."

* By a recent law, these words are no longer necessary.

Demand for payment must be made upon the last day of grace; or, if that falls on Sunday, or on a leading holiday, such as the Fourth of July, Thanksgiving, Christmas, New Year, and, in Pennsylvania, Washington's Birthday, demand must be made on the day previous.

If a note is given by a person who cannot write, it is important to have a witness who can testify to the genuineness of his mark.

Promissory notes do not bear interest until after maturity, unless so specified.

If a note is paid before due, and afterwards comes into the hands of a *bona fide* holder for value, he can still claim full payment from the maker at maturity.

A note after it is dishonored or over-due is not negotiable, but subject to all the equities which the maker may have against the original payee; and no more can be collected than the original payee could have recovered.

A note given by a minor is voidable at the election of the minor; and, until ratified by him after his arrival at full age, it is of no effect.

If no time is fixed for payment in the note, it is payable upon demand; if payable to a fictitious person, it is payable to bearer.

If a promissory note, or bill of exchange, has been lost or destroyed, payment must be demanded and notice given as if the note was still in possession.

The amount of a negotiable or non-negotiable bill or note which has been destroyed by fire or other accident, may be recovered upon sufficient proof.

Payment of a non-negotiable note which has been lost may be enforced; but if a note or bill negotiable and transferable is lost, it is held in some States that a suit at law may be maintained against the maker; in others, that it cannot; and, again, in others, that the holder may recover upon sufficient security and indemnity being given.

The amount of a note should always be written out in words; it is usually written in both words and figures. When the sum in figures differs from that expressed in words, the latter is taken as the amount of the note.

PRESENTMENT FOR PAYMENT.—The presentment of a bill of exchange or promissory note should be made on the day of its maturity,—that is, on the last day of grace,—and *not before*, and must be made personally, either by the holder or his authorized agent, and cannot be made by a written demand sent to him through the post-office.

In order to charge an *indorser*, if the bill or note is payable at a particular place, a bank for instance, it must be presented there for payment on the very day it becomes due; if no place is mentioned, the demand must be made at the maker's place of business during business hours, or at his dwelling-house within reasonable hours. If the note is given by joint makers, it must be presented to them all. In case of the death of the maker, it should be made to the executor or administrator, if they have been appointed; if not, at the dwelling-house of the deceased. When the maker has absconded, no presentation is necessary.

A **Notary**, or **Notary Public**, is an officer authorized by law, whose business it is to attest documents or writings of any kind to give them the evidence of authenticity.

A **Protest** of a promissory note or bill of exchange is a formal declaration made by a Notary Public under hand and seal, at the request of the holder of a bill or note, for non-acceptance or non-payment. This declaration is a protest to the drawer and all other parties to the bill against any loss which may be sustained by the payee or holder. (See BILLS OF EXCHANGE.)

It is not necessary, to fix the liability of the *maker* of a note, that there should be demand, protest, or notice; but *notice of non-payment*, either verbal or written, but well authenticated, *to the indorser, is necessary to hold him liable.*

The notice should be given on the same day on which the note falls due, or the next day thereafter; otherwise the indorser will be discharged.

The notice should state that the bill or note was duly presented, and that payment was refused, and should contain a correct description of the note, so that there can be no mistake in regard to its identity; it should also contain a declaration that the person to whom the notice is sent will be looked to for payment and indemnity. (See Notice, page 292.)

It is advisable, when a note is not paid by three o'clock on the day of its maturity, to place it in the hands of a notary for protest, as the protest is evidence that the note was properly presented for payment and that payment was refused. The notary will send the notices required.

An **Accommodation Note** is one for which the maker receives no consideration, but which he makes for the purpose of lending his credit to the payee to enable him to raise money. The party for whom such an accommodation was made, cannot recover from the maker; but if it is indorsed for value to a third person, although he may have notice that it is an accommodation note, and no consideration was given for it, that third person can nevertheless recover from the original maker. An accommodation note is drawn in the ordinary negotiable form, and is either made payable to the party accommodated, or passed by the payee to the credit of the drawer.

A **Collateral Note** is one given with stocks or other property as security, empowering the payee to sell if the note should not be paid when it becomes due.

A **Joint Note** is one which is written thus, "we promise to pay," &c., signed by two or more persons, or written "we promise to pay," and signed "A. B., principal, H. T., security." The words *principal* and *security* only show the relation of the makers to each other; they do not affect other parties.

When a note is written "we jointly and severally promise," or "I promise," &c., and signed by two or more persons, it is a **Joint and Several Note.**

The promisors of a joint note must be sued jointly, while either promisor of a joint and several note may be sued alone.

A release of the maker, or of one joint maker, by the holder, is a discharge of all the indorsers.

If a seal is added to a promissory note, it is not debarred or cut off by the Statute of Limitations, but it then becomes non-negotiable, and can be transferred only by assignment.

A **Judgment Note** differs from a common promissory note in having a seal appended, with a power of attorney to confess judgment.

The maker, by this power of attorney, authorizes the payee to have judgment entered, which is a lien against his lands or estate, and authorizes the issuing of an execution without resort to a suit by the ordinary course of law.

An agent is personally liable on the contract he makes, if he makes himself so expressly, or transcends his authority. (See AGENCY.)

If an agent exceeds his authority in signing the name of his principal to a note, the note will be void as to the principal, even in the hands of a *bona fide* holder. A general authority to transact business, even if it is expressed in words of very wide meaning, will not be held to include the power of making the principal a party to negotiable paper.

If an agent having authority gives a note beginning "I promise," &c., and signed "A. for B.," it has been decided that this is the note of the principal, and not of the agent.

If an agent of an incorporated company makes a note beginning "I promise," &c., and signs it "A. B., agent for —— Company," the company, and not the agent, is liable on the note.

FORMS OF NEGOTIABLE NOTES.

$600. *New York, July 17, 1866.*

Three months after date, I promise to pay to George H. Morehead, or order, at the Metropolitan National Bank, Six Hundred Dollars. Value received. *Samuel H. Stewart.*

$675. *Philadelphia, August 8, 1866.*

Sixty days after date, we promise to pay to Edmund A. Souder, or order, Six Hundred and Seventy-Five Dollars, without defalcation. Value received. *L. H. Burton & Co.*

$3500. *Trenton, N. J., August 9, 1866.*

Thirty days after date, for value received, I promise to pay to Geo. L. Bower, or bearer, Three Thousand and Five Hundred Dollars, without defalcation or discount.

Robert H. Turner.

NOTE WITHOUT DAYS OF GRACE.

250\frac{75}{100}$. *New Orleans, April 4, 1867.*

Ten days after date, without grace, I promise to pay to Samuel G. Milburn, or order, Two Hundred and Fifty $\frac{75}{100}$ Dollars. Value received. *Philip S. Chester.*

ONE FORM OF ACCOMMODATION NOTE.

$500. *Lancaster, March 13, 1867.*

Sixty days after date, I promise to pay to the order of John D. Laverty Five Hundred Dollars, at the Lancaster National Bank, without defalcat[illegible] Value received.

Credit the drawer,
John D. Laverty. *S. F. Powell.*

NOTE BEARING INTEREST.

$290. *Albany, August 16, 1866.*

Six months after date, I promise to pay Charles Riqua & Co., or order, Two Hundred and Ninety Dollars, with interest. Value received. *John L. Brown.*

A JOINT NOTE.

Montgomery, August 11, 1866.

Three months after date, we jointly promise to pay to Walter L. Vaughan, or order, Three Hundred and Fifty Dollars. Value received.

$350. *William H. Tracy,*
Darwin L. Hunter.

A JOINT AND SEVERAL NOTE.

Montpelier, October 11, 1866.

Sixty days after date, we jointly and severally promise to pay to the order of John B. Felshaw Seven Hundred and Thirty $\frac{50}{100}$ Dollars, without defalcation. Value received.

$730 $\frac{50}{100}$. *Henry A. Tyson,*
James C. English.

NON-NEGOTIABLE NOTE.

Harvard, Ill., April 9, 1867.

Thirty days after date, I promise to pay to A. D. Groesbeck One Thousand Dollars. Value received.

$1000. *Charles J. Fisher.*

JUDGMENT NOTE.

SIXTY DAYS *after date, I promise to pay to* AUGUSTUS H. ROBINSON, *of Buffalo, or order, One Thousand Dollars, with interest, for value received.*

AND FURTHER, *I do hereby authorize any attorney of any Court of Record in Pennsylvania, or elsewhere, to appear for me, at any time after the above note becomes due and remains unpaid, and after declaration filed thereupon, to confess judgment against me for the above sum, with costs of suit, release of errors, &c.*

WITNESS *my hand and seal, at Cincinnati, this 17th day of August, in the year one thousand eight hundred and sixty-six.*

Signed, sealed, and delivered
in the presence of
ORLANDO BARNES,
HENRY F. FOSTER.

JOEL F. HARRISON. [Seal.]

A NOTE PAYABLE BY INSTALMENTS.

$1200. *Baltimore, September 10, 1866.*

For value received, I promise to pay to Charles M. Williamson, or order, Twelve Hundred Dollars, with interest, in the manner following, viz., Two Hundred Dollars two months after date, and the balance in instalments of Two Hundred Dollars each, payable every two months thereafter, until the whole amount shall be paid.

James L. Bennett.

FORM OF NOTE USED BY MANY WHOLESALE HOUSES.

$150. *Philadelphia, May 19, 1867.*

Four months after date, I, the subscriber, residing in Massillon, Stark Co., State of Ohio, promise to pay to the order of Young, Moore & Co. **One Hundred and Fifty Dollars,** *for value received, negotiable and payable without defalcation or discount, and without relief from any valuation or appraisement law, with current rate of exchange on Philadelphia, Pa.*

No. 89. Due Sept. 19/22. *Jas. A. Jackson.*

INDIANA PARTNERSHIP NOTE.

JAS. J. HUMES, CHAS. J. LINN.

$100 $\frac{75}{100}$. *Indianapolis, June 16, 1864.*

Four months after date, we, the subscribers, of Blue River, county of Johnson, State of Indiana, promise to pay to the order of Hunter, Simons & Co.

(without any relief whatever from appraisement or valuation laws, with the current rate of exchange)

One Hundred $\frac{75}{100}$ Dollars, without defalcation, for value rec'd, payable and negotiable at the State Bank of Indiana.

Samuel Hunter, *Humes & Linn.*
Alfred Simons,
William Smith.

COLLATERAL NOTE.

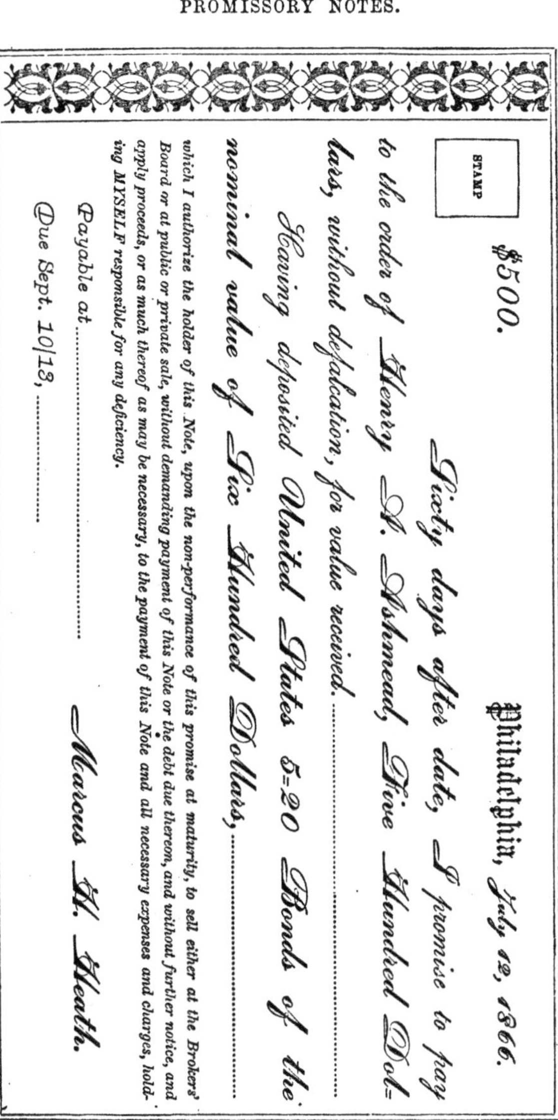

STAMP

$500. Philadelphia, July 12, 1866.

Sixty days after date, I promise to pay to the order of Henry A. Ashmead, Five Hundred Dollars, without defalcation, for value received.

Having deposited United States 5-20 Bonds of the nominal value of Six Hundred Dollars,

which I authorize the holder of this Note, upon the non-performance of this promise at maturity, to sell either at the Brokers' Board or at public or private sale, without demanding payment of this Note or the debt due thereon, and without further notice, and apply proceeds, or as much thereof as may be necessary, to the payment of this Note and all necessary expenses and charges, holding MYSELF responsible for any deficiency.

Payable at

Due Sept. 10/13,

Marcus H. Heath.

FORM OF PROTEST AND NOTICE.

United States of America.

Be it Known, That on the day of the date hereof, at the request of HENRY L. DAWSON, of Philadelphia, the holder of the original note of which a true copy is hereunto annexed, I, the undersigned, Notary Public for the Commonwealth of Pennsylvania, by lawful authority duly commissioned and sworn, residing in the city of Philadelphia, presented the same, during the usual hours of business for such purposes, at the place of business of the maker, to a proper person there duly acting and attending, and competent to give answers, and demanded payment thereof, which was refused, and answer was made that the maker of the note was not within, and that there were no funds provided there for its payment.

Whereupon I, the said Notary, at the request aforesaid, have Protested, and do hereby solemnly Protest, against all persons and every party concerned therein, whether as Maker, Drawer, Drawee, Acceptor, Payer, Indorser, Guarantee, Surety, or otherwise howsoever against whom it is proper to protest, for all Exchange, Re-exchange, Costs, Damages, and Interest, suffered and to be suffered for want of payment thereof:—Of which demand and refusal I duly notified WOODWARD & WARNER, the indorsers thereof.

[SEAL.] STAMP

Thus done and Protested, at Philadelphia aforesaid, the nineteenth day of Jan., 1868.

HARRISON M. BOYD, *Notary Public.*

NOTICE TO INDORSER.

PHILADELPHIA, Jan. 19th, 1868.

Payment of a Promissory Note drawn by RICHARD S. WILTON in favor of yourselves, and by you indorsed, dated Nov. 16th, 1867, for Five Hundred Dollars, delivered to me for Protest by HENRY L. DAWSON, the holder, being this day due, demanded, and refused, you will be looked to for payment, of which you hereby have Notice.

HARRISON M. BOYD, *Notary Public.*

To Messrs. WOODWARD & WARNER.

DRAFTS AND BILLS OF EXCHANGE.

A **Draft** or **Bill of Exchange** is an order, or open letter of request, for a sum of money, addressed to a person in a distant place.

A Bill of Exchange must be for the payment of *money*, and also payable absolutely at all events, and must not depend upon any uncertainty or contingency.

When the order is addressed to a person residing in a foreign state or country, it is called a *Foreign Bill of Exchange.*

When addressed to a person residing in the same State or country as the drawer, it is called a *Draft*, or an *Inland* or *Domestic Bill of Exchange.*

The different States of the United States, in law, are foreign to each other: so that a bill drawn in Pennsylvania upon a person in Illinois is considered a foreign bill.

There are, however, no essential differences between foreign and inland bills, except that the rights of proceeding and remedies thereon are governed by different rules and regulations in different countries; and in the case of foreign bills, when acceptance or payment is refused, *a protest is indispensably necessary.* This instrument is admitted in foreign countries as a legal proof of the refusal.

A protest is not absolutely required to entitle the holder of an *inland bill* to recover from the drawer or indorser when acceptance or payment has been refused. *Due notice*, however, must be given of the non-acceptance or non-payment.

Drafts, or bills of exchange, are used for safety in making remittances. They are drawn payable to the order of the person to whom sent, and are, therefore, not to be paid until indorsed by him.

Their use avoids the expense and trouble of sending coin

or currency, and as they are left in the hands of the person making the payments, they thus become vouchers to prove that the money has been properly paid.

Bills of Exchange may be made payable at sight, that is, on presentation; or a certain time after sight, or on demand, or a certain time after date.

They are sometimes drawn at *usance*, which is the usual time allowed by custom or law in the place where they are made payable, and varies from *fourteen days* to *three months*. The *usance* of England is *sixty days after sight*, with three days of grace; of France, *thirty days*.

If made payable in so many days *after sight, or demand*, they should be presented for acceptance, in order to fix the period of payment; but if the bill is payable *on demand* or at *sight*, or a certain number of days *after date*, it need not be presented merely for acceptance, but only for payment. It is usual, however, and advisable, to present all bills except those drawn payable at sight, or on demand, for acceptance.

If the bill contains the words "*as per advice*," the drawee may wait for further directions or advice; and if he accepts or pays without doing so, he does it at his own peril.

Bills of Exchange are usually collected through the medium of banks or bankers, and, when desired for the purpose of making remittances, may be purchased from them, generally, at a small premium or discount on the amount of the bill.

The person who writes or draws the bill is called the *drawer*. The person to whom it is addressed is called the *drawee*. The person to whom payment is made is called the *payee*. If the *drawee* agrees to pay the money signified in the bill, he does it by writing his name across the *face* of the bill, and is then said to *accept* it, and is called the *acceptor*. If the person to whom the bill is made payable assigns it to another person, he does it by writing his name upon the *back* of the bill, and is then called the *indorser*.

Accepting a bill binds the acceptor the same as signing a

note of the same tenor. Every indorser, as well as the acceptor, is security for the bill, and if protested for non-acceptance or non-payment, they and the drawer are liable to the holder for the principal sum, the interest, and the expense incurred by the dishonor,—such as cost of protest, broker's commission, and rate of exchange. Most of the States of the Union have provided by statute a certain fixed sum or percentage in lieu of damages and re-exchange. The parties to a bill are liable to the holder according to the law of the place where they entered into their respective contracts; the drawer, according to the law of the place where the bill is drawn; the acceptor, according to the law of the place of acceptance; and the indorsers, of the place where the indorsements were made.

When a person draws a bill of exchange, he subjects himself to the payment of it should the person on whom it is drawn refuse either to accept or pay, if the holder of the bill gives him due notice.

If acceptance is refused, or if payment is not made on the day when the bill becomes due, notice should be given, *without delay*, to each party liable, that they may be held.

The holder should give notice to the other parties to the bill, if the acceptance is in part, or qualified, or not in full, if he intends having recourse to them in case of non-payment when due.

The acceptor, who is the party originally held bound, may be allowed whatever indulgence or delay the holder pleases, short of the time allowed by the statute of limitations.

A DRAFT OR INLAND BILL OF EXCHANGE.

No. 37. $1000. Rochester, Nov. 24th, 1865.

STAMP

..........At Ten Days' Sight, Pay to the Order of ....CHARLES McCLINTOCK.......... ....ONE THOUSAND DOLLARS,.......... Value received, and charge to Account of

To Duncan & Sherman,
New York.

Thomas Perrins.

ACCEPTED DRAFT.

STAMP

$250 75/100 Dover, Dec. 8th, 1865.

Ten Days after Sight, Pay to the Order of ....THOMAS W. MOORE.......... ....Two Hundred and Fifty..........75/100 Dollars, Value received, which place to Account of

To R. R. Robinson & Co.
Wilmington, Del.

James Merrell.

Accepted Dec. 12, 1865.
R. R. Robinson & Co.

Drafts are sometimes accepted in the following form:—"Accepted Apr. 4th, 1867, payable at the City National Bank, Charles Ennis."

FOREIGN BILLS OF EXCHANGE.

Foreign Bills of Exchange are usually drawn in Sets, called the First, Second, and Third, etc. of Exchange, all of the same tenor and date, and so worded that when one is paid the others are rendered void. They are sent by different mails or conveyances, as a precaution against loss or inconvenience arising from accident or miscarriage. *Sola* is the name given to a single bill.

FIRST OF A SET OF EXCHANGE ON LIVERPOOL.

Exchange for £1000. Boston, Apr. 30, 1867.

At Sixty Days' Sight of this FIRST *of Exchange (Second & Third of same tenor and date unpaid) Pay to the Order of* ....PETER WALKER............

One Thousand Pounds Sterling

for Value received, and place the same to account of

To Brown, Shipley & Co.,
Liverpool, Eng.

1

George Peabody.

SECOND OF A SET OF EXCHANGE ON PARIS.

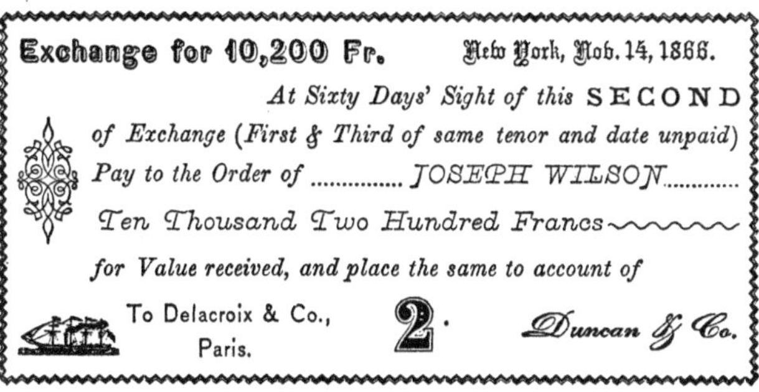

Exchange for 10,200 Fr. New York, Nov. 14, 1866.

At Sixty Days' Sight of this SECOND *of Exchange (First & Third of same tenor and date unpaid) Pay to the Order of* ....JOSEPH WILSON............

Ten Thousand Two Hundred Francs

for Value received, and place the same to account of

To Delacroix & Co.,
Paris.

2.

Duncan & Co.

THIRD OF A SET OF EXCHANGE ON FRANKFORT.

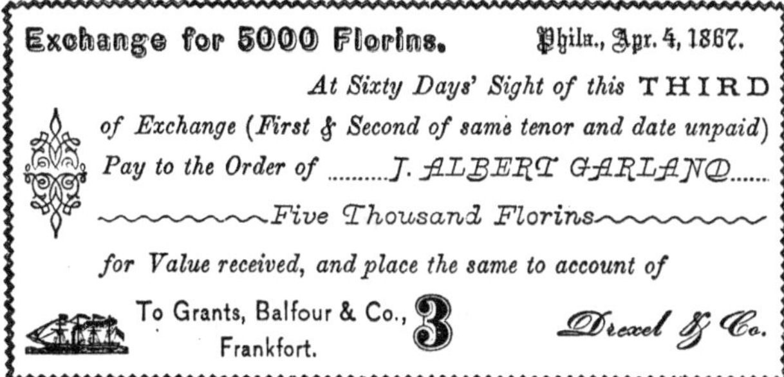

Exchange for 5000 Florins. Phila., Apr. 4, 1867.

At Sixty Days' Sight of this THIRD *of Exchange (First & Second of same tenor and date unpaid) Pay to the Order of* ....J. ALBERT GARLAND......

Five Thousand Florins

for Value received, and place the same to account of

To Grants, Balfour & Co.,
Frankfort.

3

Drexel & Co.

INDORSEMENTS, ACCEPTANCES, &c.

INDORSEMENTS.

The word indorsement signifies a writing on the back of a bill or written instrument; but it is well settled that this is not essential in order to charge a person as an indorser. The indorsement may be on any part of the note, or on a paper annexed to it, and in ink or pencil; but it is better that the signature should be in ink, to prevent erasure.

When a note or bill is drawn payable to a person or his order, it is properly transferable only by indorsement; nothing else, in law, will hold the parties to a note directly liable to the holder.

FORMS OF INDORSEMENTS.

1. INDORSEMENT IN BLANK.

John S. Barton.

2. INDORSEMENT IN FULL.

Pay to Jas. Jones, or order.
John S. Barton.

3. QUALIFIED INDORSEMENT.

Without recourse.
John S. Barton.

4. RESTRICTIVE INDORSEMENTS.

Pay Robert Hunter, for my use.
John S. Barton

Pay to Chas. Harrison only.
John S. Barton.

5. CONDITIONAL INDORSEMENT.

Pay George Gray, or order, the within, unless before due he receives the amount from my agent.
John S. Barton.

6. INDORSEMENT BY AN AGENT.

John S. Barton,
Agent for Howard Chester.

7. A GUARANTY ON A NOTE.

For value received in cash, I hereby guaranty the payment of the within Note.
John S. Barton.

1. A blank indorsement makes a note transferable by mere delivery only, and by it the indorser is made liable for the payment of the note. If the note or bill is lost after such

blank indorsement, any person who should become the holder of it, in good faith, for a valuable consideration, without notice, would be entitled to receive the amount thereof.

2. Indorsements in full prevent a subsequent *holder* from recovering against the antecedent parties, unless he can deduce a regular title to the bill from the person whose name stands as first indorser.

If all the subsequent indorsers are in blank, the holder may make himself the immediate indorsee of any one of them, or he may deduce his title through them all in succession.

If some of the subsequent indorsements are in full and some in blank, then he must make a regular deduction of title through them all, or make himself the immediate indorsee, under some prior blank indorsement.

Persons taking a bill or note subsequently to a blank indorsement may transfer it, either by delivery or by indorsement.

3. A qualified indorsement is one which affects the liability of the indorser, but not the negotiability of the note. If the holder of a note wishes to transfer it without being held liable for its payment, he can do so by writing his signature and adding "*without recourse*," or other words to that effect.

4. The holder who has absolute property in a bill or note has the power of limiting payment to whom he pleases. A restrictive indorsement will not, however, be presumed from equivocal language, as restrictive indorsements tend to impair the negotiability of bills and notes.

5. If the payee or indorsee of a bill or note annexes a condition to his indorsement, *before acceptance*, the drawee who afterwards accepts it is bound by the condition. If the terms of the condition are not complied with, the property in the bill reverts to the payee, and he may recover the sum payable in an action against the acceptor.

6. An agent should expressly indorse as agent, or write the name of his principal; otherwise the indorsement would

be inoperative. When an agent is compelled to indorse notes or bills over to his principal, to avoid responsibility, he should use a restrictive form of indorsement.

In Pennsylvania, a factor who remits a bill to his principal, in payment of goods sold on his account, and indorses the bill, does not thereby become *personally responsible to his principal*, if he receives no consideration for guaranteeing and does not expressly undertake to do so. 4 *Rawle*, 384–389; 5 *Whart.* 288.

An indorsement in the form of *A. B., Treasurer of —— Company*, has been held not to render the agent liable as an indorser, but considered as intended only to pass the paper, and as equivalent to an indorsement "without recourse."

7. An indorsement implies a contract to pay the note if dishonored, if due notice is given of dishonor, and not otherwise; whereas a *guaranty* implies a contract, if due notice is given of dishonor *within a reasonable time.*

The guaranty should contain words importing consideration, and, *unless made expressly negotiable*, is good only to him who first takes the note and advances money upon it. If the guaranty is upon a separate paper, it should describe the note with sufficient distinctness.

If, upon proper presentation, payment of a note or bill is refused, the holder must give prompt notice of such refusal to each indorser whom he wishes to hold for payment, and inform him that he will be held for the payment of the same; otherwise the indorser will be discharged. If the holder could delay, he might injuriously affect the indorser, and his remedy against other persons.

The holder of a note or bill may commence suit against any of the indorsers, or against all of them at once.

When there are several indorsers, each is liable to those after him, and should give notice to all parties indorsing prior to himself.

Each indorser may require any one whose name precedes

his own to make good to him the loss he may sustain, provided he gives notice of his intention to do so on the day he receives his own notice, or the day after.

This notice may be given by any person competent to serve it; but a notary public is usually employed for the purpose.

ACCEPTANCES.

An Acceptance is an engagement to comply in whole or in part with the terms of a bill. When the drawee engages to pay according to its terms, it is called a *general acceptance;* when he agrees to pay with some qualification or condition different from the bill, it is called a *conditional* or *qualified acceptance.*

When a bill is presented for acceptance, the drawee is entitled to twenty-four hours, if he desires it, to decide whether he will accept it or not. In New York and Missouri, if the bill is not returned within twenty-four hours, it is deemed by law to be accepted.

Acceptances are usually written across the face of the bill, and, for distinctness, in red ink.

Any words not refusing its request, or the signature of the acceptor in blank, is *prima facie* evidence of acceptance; and when not otherwise provided for by law, the acceptance may be either verbal or in writing,—a written acceptance, of course, being more easily susceptible of proof.

In New York it is held that no person shall be charged as an acceptor of a bill of exchange unless the acceptance be in writing, and every holder may, on presentation of the bill, require that the acceptance be written on the bill, and if such acceptance is refused, the bill may be protested for non-acceptance.

The holder may assent to a qualified acceptance, and it will be good as far as it extends; but he takes it at his own risk, and he must give notice to the antecedent parties, or they will not otherwise be held bound by it. The condition of the acceptance should appear upon the face of the acceptance in writing, as any subsequent holder for value, without notice, would not be bound by verbal conditions.

The holder is not bound to take any but an unqualified or unconditional acceptance; and when refused, if he wishes to maintain a claim against the other parties, he should treat the bill as dishonored, unless they assent to the proposed conditional acceptance. If the holder declines the conditional acceptance, it will be a waiver of all right to hold the drawee.

Form of Conditional Acceptance written across the face of a Draft.

"Accepted if in funds from consignment shipped us on 3d instant. ROGER B. GRAY.

"NEW YORK, Oct. 17/66."

AGENCY.

An **Agent** is a person having power to act for another, who is called a principal.

A man may do by his agent whatever he can lawfully do himself, and his agent can do for him.

A *General Agent* is one appointed to transact all the business of his principal, or all his business of a particular kind.

A *Special Agent* is appointed for a specific and particular purpose.

A **Broker** is an agent employed to negotiate between other parties, and is presumed to act in the name of his principal.

A **Factor** or Commission Merchant is an agent to sell goods for his principal, but who acts for several persons in that capacity. He differs from the broker in having actual possession of the goods. A Factor may buy and sell in his own name as well as in the name of his principal.

An Attorney is an agent acting in behalf of his client.

The authority of an agent may be constituted in three ways: by deed under seal, by a writing without seal, or by mere words.

The authority of an agent may be revocable or irrevocable. It is irrevocable when an interest in the subject-matter is conveyed to the agent, or the authority is given for a valuable consideration; it is revocable when no interest is conveyed, in which case the principal can revoke the authority at his pleasure, subject in some cases to a claim for damages.

An agency may be revoked by the operation of law, by expiration of time, by changes producing incapacity to act, by the extinction of the subject-matter or its complete fulfilment, or by the death of the principal. A power of attorney to sell goods or stocks ceases with the life of the principal, and upon his death may become valueless.

Where the conveyance or any act is required to be under seal, the authority to execute it must be under seal also.

Verbal authority, ordinarily, is sufficient; but an agent ought, for his own security, to act under written authority, and to disclose his character whenever he executes a contract. In signing his name, the mere use of the word "agent" is not sufficient; the name of the principal must also appear. Instead of writing "Henry Grant, Agent," it should be "R. Brown, per Henry Grant;" or, "R. Brown, by his attorney, Henry Grant."

If an agent does an act or makes a contract unauthorized by his principal, though in the name of the principal, he is personally liable; but if the principal, with the knowledge of all the facts, adopts or acquiesces in the acts done under an assumed agency, he cannot afterwards impeach them under the pretence that they were done without authority, or even contrary to instructions. If the principal does not dissent and give notice of it within a reasonable time after being informed of what has been done, his assent and satisfaction will be presumed.

"An agent is personally liable if he makes himself so expressly, or if he transcends his authority or departs from its terms and directions, or if he conceals his character as agent, or if he purposely conceals the name of his principal, or, perhaps, if he does not actually state the name of his principal."

It is the duty of the agent to follow implicitly his instructions, and to keep his principal fully and promptly informed in regard to the business intrusted to him.

An agent is liable for interest if he has made it on the money in his hands, but not if it has lain idle.

As a general rule, an agent cannot appoint a substitute, or delegate his authority to another. But a power of substitution may be expressly given, or it may be inferred from the nature of the act to be performed, or where there is a known and established custom of substitution.

POWER OF ATTORNEY.

A Power of Attorney, or Letter of Attorney, is a written instrument, usually under seal, by which authority is given to one person to perform some lawful act for another.

Authority to execute a deed must be given under seal, and be acknowledged by both husband and wife, and must be done in the name of the principal.

Upon the death of the principal, the authority delegated by power of attorney ceases, and all subsequent acts under it are void.

The authority intended to be conferred should be expressed in clear and intelligible terms, and be properly executed, attested, and acknowledged.

FORM OF POWER OF ATTORNEY.

Know all Men by these Presents, That I, of , County of , and State of , have made, constituted, and appointed, and by these presents do make, constitute, and appoint , of . , County of , and State of , my true and lawful attorney, for me, and in my name, place, and stead, and in my behalf, to (here insert the things which the attorney is to do); giving and granting unto my said attorney full power and authority generally to do and perform all and every act and thing whatsoever requisite or proper to effectuate all or any of the premises, with the same powers, and to all intents and purposes with the same validity, as I, if personally present, could (giving and granting, also, unto my said attorney full power to substitute one or more attorney or attorneys under him my said attorney in or concerning the premises, or any part thereof, and the same at his pleasure to revoke; and) hereby ratifying and confirming whatsoever my said attorney (or his substitute or substitutes) shall and may do by virtue hereof in the premises.

In Witness whereof, I have hereunto set my hand and affixed my seal, this eighteenth day of September, in the year of our Lord 18

Signed, sealed, and delivered [Seal.]
in the presence of
Henry R. Linden,
Wm. H. Moult.

N.B.—By omitting the words in brackets, no power to appoint a substitute is given.

SHORT FORM.

Know all Men by these Presents, That

do make, constitute, and appoint
true and lawful Attorney for and in name

with power, also, an attorney or attorneys under for that purpose to make and substitute, and to do all lawful acts requisite for affecting the premises; hereby ratifying and confirming all that the said attorney or substitute or substitutes shall do therein by virtue of these presents.

In Witness whereof, have hereunto set hand and seal the day of , in the year of our Lord one thousand eight hundred and [L.S.]

Signed, sealed, and delivered
in the presence of

POWER TO TRANSFER STOCK.

Know all Men by these Presents, That I, K. W. Y., of Oswego, County of Oswego, and State of New York, do make, constitute, and appoint Leonard D. Gray, of the same place, my true and lawful attorney, for me, and in my name and behalf, to sell, transfer, and assign unto Hosea W. Hunter, of said Oswego (or, any other person or persons), One Hundred Shares in the capital stock of the Syracuse National Bank, in Syracuse, State of New York, standing in my name on the books of said corporation; and to do all necessary acts and to make the necessary acquittances and discharges to effect the premises (add, if desired, and I do further empower him to substitute any person or persons under him, with like power); hereby ratifying and confirming all my said attorney (or his substitute or substitutes) shall lawfully do by virtue hereof.

In Witness whereof, &c.

POWER TO RECEIVE DIVIDEND.

Know all Men by these Presents, That I, H. Y. Bell, of Oswego. County of Oswego, State of New York, do constitute and appoint Hiram Howell, of Meridian, Cayuga county, to receive from the Cashier of the Oswego National Bank the dividend or dividends now due me on all stock standing to my name on the books of the said bank, and to receipt for the same; hereby ratifying and confirming all that by him may lawfully be done by virtue hereof in the premises.

Witness my hand, etc.

Signed and delivered in presence of, &c.

SEALED INSTRUMENTS.

A contract which is under seal is called in law a *specialty*. Bonds are of this class. All other contracts, whether oral or in writing, are called *parole* contracts. A *specialty* is distinguished from a simple contract by its *seal*. An impression upon wax, wafer, or, as in most of our States, a scrawl of ink, attached to the signature, is regarded as a sufficient seal. A seal implies consideration, and is in general absolute; but in New York a seal is only *prima facie* evidence of consideration, which may be rebutted as if the instrument were not sealed.

A specialty is not negotiable like a promissory note: it may be assigned, however (see Form of Assignment), the assignee taking it at his own peril, and having only the rights of the original obligee: if the obligor has any set-off or claim against the obligee at the time of the assignment, the assignee will be compelled to allow it.

If the assignee, previous to taking the assignment, obtains from the obligor an admission in writing, or in the presence of witnesses, that he has no defence or set-off, the obligor is liable to the assignee for the whole amount.

In Pennsylvania, and in some other States, bonds are made legally assignable; and the assignees can sue in their own name when they are for payment of money, and drawn "to order" or "to assigns," and the assignment is "under hand and seal" and in the presence of two or more witnesses; the intent of the act being to enable the assignee to sue in his own name and prevent the obligee from releasing after assignment.

If they are not drawn in the above form, bonds may be assigned for a valuable consideration, with permission to sue in the assignor's name.

The indorsement in blank of a specialty does not make the indorser liable as in the case of a negotiable note.

An instrument under seal is not barred by the statute of limitations, and, if originally good, is so for twenty years.

BONDS.

A bond is an obligation for the payment of money, or for the performance or non-performance of certain acts, with a penalty annexed in case of failure to comply with the conditions of the bond. It requires no technical words: any sealed writing which distinctly acknowledges a debt is a bond; but generally there is a condition added, that if the obligor does some particular act, the obligation shall be void, or else shall remain in full force.

The penalty in a bond is usually double the amount of the real debt, for the purpose of covering the full debt, together with interest and costs. All that can be recovered of a *penalty* in a bond, in addition to the amount of the debt, is the interest and costs; but when a specified amount is agreed upon for liquidating damages, it must be distinctly so expressed, and then such specified sum is the amount to be paid.

Where it is the intention to bind the heirs of the obligor, the term *heirs* must be named. Executors and administrators are bound though not named.

If the obligation of a bond becomes impossible by the act of God, *after* making it, the penalty is saved; if it be impossible at the time of making it, it is said the condition alone is void, and the bond shall stand, single and unconditional.

Where several payments are due at different times on a bond, if one payment is delayed and the bond is so drawn, judgment may be recovered for the whole of the real debt, with stay of execution on the several payments till such specified times as those payments become due.

COMMON FORM OF BOND.

Know all Men by these Presents, that I, , in the county of and State of , am held and firmly bound unto , of , in the county of and State aforesaid, in the sum of One Thousand Dollars, lawful money of the United States, to be paid to the said , or his certain attorney, executors, and administrators or assigns; to which payment, well and truly to be made and done, I do bind myself, my heirs, executors, and administrators, and every of them, firmly by these presents. Sealed with my seal, and dated the day of , Anno Domini one thousand eight hundred and

The condition of this obligation is such, that if the above bounden , his heirs, executors, administrators, or any of them, shall and do well and truly pay, or cause to be paid, unto the above-named , his executors, administrators, or assigns, the just and full sum of Five Hundred Dollars, lawful money, aforesaid, with legal interest for the same, on or before the day of next, without fraud or further delay, then the above obligation to be void and of none effect, or else to be and remain in full force and virtue.

Signed, sealed, and delivered in [SEAL.]
the presence of

CLAUSE FOR JUDGMENT BOND.

And I do hereby authorize and empower any attorney of any court of record in the State of , or elsewhere, to enter judgment against me, my heirs, executors, and administrators, and in the favor of the above-named , his executors, administrators, or assigns, for the above sum, as of the past, present, or any future term of said court, with release of errors, costs of suit, &c.

INTEREST CLAUSE.

And it is hereby expressly agreed, that should any default be made in the payment of the said interest, or of any part thereof, on any day whereon the same is made payable, as above expressed, and should the same remain unpaid and in arrear for the space of thirty days, then and from thenceforth, that is to say, after the lapse of the said thirty days, the aforesaid principal sum of Five Hundred Dollars, together with all arrearage of interest thereon, shall, at the option of the said , his executors, administrators, and assigns, become and be due and payable immediately thereafter, although the period above limited for the payment thereof may not then have expired, any thing hereinbefore contained to the contrary notwithstanding.

SEALED RECEIPT OR RELEASE.

GENERAL RELEASE OF ALL DEMANDS.

Know all Men by these Presents, that I, Howard C. Burton, of New York, for and in consideration of the sum of Three Hundred and Seventy-Five Dollars to me paid by George C. Taylor, of Philadelphia, the receipt of which I do hereby acknowledge, have remised, released, and forever discharged, and I do for myself, my heirs, executors, and administrators, remise, release, and forever discharge, the said George C. Taylor, his heirs, executors, and administrators, of and from all debts, demands, actions, and causes of action, in law or equity, of every kind, character, and nature soever, against him, from the beginning of the world to this day.

In Testimony whereof, I have hereto set my hand and seal, this thirteenth day of July, A.D. 1865.

Signed, sealed, and delivered in presence of
ETHAN YOUNG,
ALEX'R R. RUNDLE.

HOWARD C. BURTON. [Seal.]

A **Deed** is a writing or instrument sealed and delivered. As generally used, it is a writing for the conveyance of property.

In Pennsylvania, a scroll enclosing the word "seal," or "L. S.," is a good and valid seal; but not in all the States.

A **Fee-Simple** interest is the absolute ownership in an estate.

A **Warranty Deed** is so called because the grantor covenants to insure and defend the lands mentioned against the persons and to the extent specified.

A **General Warranty** covenants and warrants against all persons whatsoever; a **Special Warranty,** only against himself, his heirs, and those claiming under him. Deeds by executors, administrators, or guardians generally contain no warranty; and every requisition of the law should be complied with, to obtain a good title.

A **Quit-Claim Deed** is one which conveys all the interest which the grantor may possess, whatever it may be, in the land specified.

A **Deed Poll,** or **Single Deed,** like a quit-claim deed, is made by one party only (for example, a sheriff's deed).

A **Trust Deed** is given to persons to hold for the use of some other person who is entitled to the proceeds, profits, or use of the property.

A **Ground-Rent Deed** conveys land, with a reservation of a certain sum of money in the nature of rent, to be paid at specified times, and may be for life, for a term of years, or in fee.

A **Mortgage** is a conditional conveyance of property as a pledge for the security of a debt.

All kinds of property, real and personal, which may be sold absolutely may be mortgaged. As a general thing, *chattel mortgages*, or mortgages on personal property, are not good against third parties or creditors unless the property is actually delivered, or the mortgage acknowledged and recorded.

When a mortgage is paid by instalments, each payment should be receipted upon the record of the mortgage as it is made.

When the debt is paid, the mortgagee is bound under a penalty to enter satisfaction on the records within a limited time; and care should be taken by the mortgagor that it be done. If the death or removal of the mortgagee occur before satisfaction is entered, petition should be made to the Court of Common Pleas that it may be so ordered.

CONTRACTS.

A contract is an agreement, upon sufficient consideration, to do, or not to do, some specified thing.

A consideration may be *any benefit to the party promising, or some trouble or injury to the party receiving the promise.*

In general, an offer or proposal becomes a contract as soon as it is accepted, and acceptance may be made before the expiration of the time limited, or at any reasonable time before knowledge of a retraction of the offer.

In the majority of the United States, no action can be brought against a person upon an agreement not to be performed within one year from the making of it, unless some note or memorandum of the agreement be signed by the party to be charged, or his lawfully appointed agent.

Persons under twenty-one years of age, married women, and insane persons, are incompetent to make a contract. A minor, however, may contract for necessaries; so, also, may a married woman when her husband, without good reason, refuses to make suitable provision for her.

The subject-matter of the contract must be possible; it must also be lawful. A contract founded upon fraud, or to do an illegal or immoral act, is void. A contract in total restraint of the exercise of a man's trade or profession would not be enforced by the courts, because it is against public policy; but a contract restraining him in any particular city or place is valid.

Care bestowed in clearly expressing the contract in plain and unambiguous language, may be the means of preventing lawsuits and the loss of friendship as well as the loss of money. "Three things should be attended to in writing a contract. 1st. Weigh well your words, and ascertain their exact import or value. 2. Use enough of them to express all that you mean or intend by the contract. 3d. Arrange them in such a manner that they have but one meaning, and that the meaning you intend."—HON. JOEL JONES.

Verbal evidence may be admitted to explain, but not to change, the original contract.

Contracts of Sale.—A sale is a contract for the transfer of property for a valuable consideration. The subject-matter and the price must be certain, or capable of being made so, to constitute a sale. The subject-matter should be perfectly identified, ascertained, and designated, so as to be distinguished from every thing else. After the sale is completed, the goods are at the risk of the purchaser.

If in a contract for the sale of goods no time be mentioned for payment, the law implies a contract to pay for them on delivery, and the buyer is entitled to the goods only on payment or tender of the price. The buyer acquires a right of property by the contract, but until he pays or tenders the price he does not acquire a right of possession. If the sale be made upon credit and nothing be said as to the time of delivery, the buyer is entitled to possession immediately; although the seller can reclaim the goods if the buyer is insolvent and they are in the hands of a common carrier or have not yet come into the actual possession of the buyer.

In the several States, excepting Louisiana, no contract for the sale of any goods is binding, when the price is above a certain sum, unless the buyer shall accept part of the goods so sold and actually receive the same or give something in part payment, or unless some writing of such bargain be made and signed by the party to be charged. The sum required in Massachusetts and New York is $50; in Vermont, $40; in Connecticut, $35; in New Hampshire, $33.33; and in New Jersey, $30.

In dissolving a contract, the law requires that it shall be done by the same means that render it binding: if the contract was under seal, the release or discharge must be under seal also; if the contract was required by law to be in writing, it cannot be dissolved by a verbal agreement.

GENERAL FORM OF AGREEMENT.

This Agreement, made the sixteenth day of February, A.D. 1868, between JOHN T. EVANS, of Sandusky, County of Erie and State of Ohio, of the first part, and HENRY W. WARD, of Houston, County of Shelby and State aforesaid, of the second part,

Witnesseth, That the said JOHN T. EVANS, for the consideration hereinafter mentioned, doth covenant and agree to and with the said HENRY W. WARD, that (*here insert the agreement on the part of Evans*).

And the said HENRY W. WARD, in consideration of the covenant of the said party of the first part, doth hereby covenant and agree to and with the said JOHN T. EVANS, that (*here insert the agreement on the part of Ward*).

In Witness whereof, we have hereunto set our hands and seals, the year and day first above written.

Signed, sealed, and delivered
in presence of
EDWARD P. HARTELL.
THOS. J. TURNER.

JOHN T. EVANS. [Seal.]
HENRY W. WARD. [Seal.]

AGREEMENT OF SALE.

Agreement made this day between Thomas J. Raymond, of New York City, of the first part, and Leonard Munroe, of said city, of the other part, as follows:—

Said Thomas J. Raymond, for the consideration hereinafter mentioned, doth hereby agree to deliver to said Leonard Munroe, at his store in said city, as the same may be required from time to time,—the whole to be delivered before the first day of May next ensuing the date hereof,—two thousand pounds Old Government Java Coffee, equal to a sample exhibited.

In consideration whereof, said Leonard Munroe hereby agrees to pay to the said Thomas J. Raymond twenty cents per pound for each and every pound so delivered, in the notes of the said Leonard Munroe, payable three months after date, to be given at the end of each and every month, for the amount of coffee then delivered under this agreement.

Witness the said parties, at New York, this day of A.D. one thousand eight hundred and sixty .

W. P. THORNTON.
K. M. WILSON. } Witnesses present.

THOS. J. RAYMOND.
LEONARD MUNROE.

A BILL OF SALE OF GOODS.

Know all Men by these Presents, that I, Jared K. Long, of Buffalo, for and in consideration of the sum of five hundred dollars to me in hand paid by John Cottrell, of the same place, at and before the sealing and delivery of these presents, the receipt whereof is hereby acknowledged, have bargained, sold, and delivered, and by these presents do bargain, sell, and deliver, unto the said J. Cottrell, *One Thousand* (1000) bbls. Linseed Oil, now in store at Pittsburgh, Pa.

To have and to hold the said goods unto the said J. Cottrell, his executors, administrators, and assigns, to his and their own proper use and benefit forever. And I, the said Jared K. Long, for myself and my heirs, executors, and administrators, will warrant and defend the said bargained premises unto the said J. Cottrell, his executors, administrators, and assigns, from and against all persons whomsoever.

Witness my hand and seal, this tenth day of March, 1868.

Sealed and delivered in
the presence of JARED K. LONG. [L. S.]
JAS. CLARK,
HENRY R. DAMON.

AFFIDAVIT FOR GOODS SOLD AND DELIVERED.

State of , County of , *ss.*

Francis J. Murray, of , in said county, being duly sworn (*or affirmed*), deposes and says that Byron C. Gates, of , county of and State of , is justly and truly indebted unto him, the deponent, in the sum of dollars, for goods sold and delivered by him to the said Byron C. Gates; and that he has given credit to the said Byron C. Gates for all payments and set-offs to which he is entitled; and that the balance claimed, according to the foregoing account, is justly due; and that the said account is correctly stated.

Sworn and subscribed, this day of , A.D. 1868, before me,
HENRY C. BEACH,
Commissioner for the State of

GUARANTEES.

A guarantee is an engagement whereby one man, called the guarantor, binds himself as security for the performance of certain acts by another.

A guarantee, to be binding, should be for a consideration; as in law all promises made without a consideration are valueless.

Though not always necessary, it is preferable that the guarantee be in writing; because the evidence of the fact is then so much easier of proof. In some States, the guarantee must express the consideration for which it was granted.

Guarantees of commission-merchants, binding them to warrant the solvency of the purchasers of the goods they sell on credit, need not be in writing.

The words of a guarantee should be strictly construed, and not taken to mean more or less than the words clearly express. A guarantor is not liable beyond the scope of his engagement: a mere recommendation or overture to guarantee is not sufficient.

A guarantee must be accepted, to make it a contract; and the guarantor must have notice, either direct or implied, of its acceptance within a reasonable time.

In Pennsylvania, by act of April 26, 1855, no action shall be brought upon any special promise to answer for the debt or default of another, unless the agreement, or some memorandum or note thereof, be in writing. This act does not apply to contracts in which the consideration is less than twenty dollars.

Guarantees do not continue to transactions which take place after a change is made in the firm to which they were given, unless such change is expressly provided for.

In some States, unless the creditor can show that it would be useless to proceed against the debtor, he must first institute proceedings against him before he can resort to the guarantor.

A guarantor, after paying the debt, has a right to substitute himself in the place of the creditor, and is entitled to receive from him all the securities held by him for the principal debt.

Guarantee of a Debt not yet incurred.

PITTSBURGH, Dec. 8, 1865.

MESSRS. GEO. H. STUART & BRO.,
13 Bank Street, Philadelphia.

GENTLEMEN:—The bearer, Mr. Henry G. Layton, of this place, intends visiting your city for the purpose of purchasing goods. Should you be disposed to furnish him with such goods as he may call for, we hereby guarantee the payment for any purchases he may make within one month from this date, to any amount not exceeding five thousand dollars. Yours, truly,

S. T. HUMBOLDT & Co.

NOTE.—The consideration in the above guarantee is the selling of goods on credit to H. G. Layton.

Another.

CINCINNATI, Dec. 11, 1865.

GEO. H. WHELAN, ESQ.

DEAR SIR:—I hereby guarantee the payment of any bill or bills of merchandise Mr. J. L. Johnson may purchase from you, the amount of this guarantee not exceeding five hundred dollars ($500), and to expire at the end of three months from date

Respectfully, yours,
BENJAMIN PATTEN.

Guarantee of a Debt already incurred.

LOUISVILLE, KY., Feb. 19, 1868.

MESSRS. M. C. HARRISON & Co.,
New Orleans.

GENTLEMEN:—In consideration of one dollar, paid me by yourselves, the receipt of which I hereby acknowledge, I guarantee that the debt of four hundred dollars, now owing to you by George W. Perkins, shall be paid at maturity. Very respectfully, yours,

LEONARD H. MORTON.

PARTNERSHIP.

A **Partnership** is a voluntary contract between two or more persons to place their property, labor, or credit, or some or all of them, in some lawful business, and to divide the profit, or bear the loss, in certain proportions. (See p. 174.)

A partnership is not constituted merely by an interest, but depends on the joint liability to loss, as well as on the participation in the profits. A stipulated portion of the profits as mere compensation for labor or services does not constitute a partnership.

A **General Partnership** is one formed for trade generally, without limitations, and comprehends whatever business the partners may engage in.

A **Special Partnership** is one which is confined by the terms of the agreement to some particular kind of trade or business, or some particular transaction or speculation.

A **Limited Partnership** is one in which the responsibility of one or more of the partners is limited to the amount invested by him or them in the concern. In a limited partnership the special partner has the advantage of investing where the profits are equal to the gains of actual business, without risking more than the sum contributed. The laws relative to limited partnerships are of a nature to require great care on the part of any one about to become a special partner. The statute law of the State in which such partnership is formed must be complied with literally and accurately. The advice of able counsel should in all cases be taken before entering into such a partnership, in order to avoid assuming the responsibilities and liabilities of a general partner.

A person who lends his name as a partner, though he contribute neither money nor time, nor receive any share of the profits, or who suffers his name to continue in the firm after he has ceased to be an actual partner, is liable to third persons as such.

Each partner has full power to bind the firm by all acts and contracts within the scope of the partnership business.

A partner cannot make the firm responsible for his separate debt, nor enter into engagements binding the firm which are unconnected with, and foreign to, the partnership.

Each partner may buy and sell and make contracts for the firm, and may receive and pay money and become a party to negotiable paper in the name of the firm.

In signing contracts relating to partnership business, partners should always use the proper style of the firm, not merely their own name, nor any other name than the full and exact name of the firm.

In general, however, one partner cannot bind the other by an instrument under seal, unless the other expressly assents, is present when it is executed in the joint name, or subsequently ratifies it; though he may execute a release of a debt due the firm. Nor can one partner bind the firm by a guarantee not in the regular course of business, unless it be afterwards adopted by the firm.

One partner may discharge himself from liability by giving express notice to any customer, or other person, not to trust one or more of his copartners.

A partnership may be dissolved by the expiration of the time limited for its continuance, by the voluntary act of one or all of the parties, by the death, insanity, or bankruptcy of either, and by judicial decree. If no precise period is mentioned for its continuance, a partner may withdraw at any time; and even if formed for a definite time, a partner may, by giving due notice, dissolve the partnership as to all future capacity of the firm to bind him by contract, subjecting himself thereby to a claim for damages for a breach of the covenant.

In cases of a dissolution by death, it is the surviving partner or partners alone to whom belong the right and duty of disposing of the property, collecting the assets, and paying thereout the debts: the representatives of the deceased have no right to do more than to call upon the surviving partner or partners to render an account.

A creditor of a partner may sell only such partner's individual interest in the surplus partnership property, after all claims upon the firm are discharged. The purchaser is not bound to become a partner, nor are the others bound to admit him.

The dissolution of a partnership by consent of the parties should be indorsed on the articles of copartnership, and immediate actual notice communicated to the parties who have had previous dealings with the firm. Notice in a newspaper is sufficient as to persons who have had no previous dealings with the firm; but it is not sufficient for those who have had, as the law requires express notice to the debtors.

Upon dissolution all the members are liable, individually, for the contracts and debts of the firm existing at that time. In general, after dissolution, the power of one partner to bind the firm ceases; but either partner, without agreement as to the mode of liquidation, may sell such property as he may have in possession, and may collect and receipt for debts, being liable to be called to account in a general settlement.

When one partner assigns his interest in the firm, the word "release" must be used, as it alone, it is said, can pass the whole interest.

Guarantees given to a partnership do not continue valid to a new firm.

AGREEMENT BETWEEN PARTNERS.

All partnership agreements should be written, and each partner should hold a copy. Although not essential to their validity that the agreement should be in writing, yet unpleasant feelings and difficulties, as well as serious pecuniary loss, may be prevented by having the terms embodied in clear and distinct language.

Partnership articles should specify the names of the several partners, and the name or firm under which the partnership is to be conducted, the kind of business to be transacted, the time of commencement and intended duration of the partnership, the amount of the capital contributed by each partner, the manner in which the gains and losses are to be shared, whether interest is to be allowed on capital and at what rate, the amount which may be withdrawn yearly by each partner for private use, and the manner of disposing of the partnership effects in the event of a dissolution. Other stipulations may be inserted at the pleasure of the parties.

FORM OF ARTICLES OF COPARTNERSHIP.

Articles of Agreement, made and concluded this *first* day of *January*, in the year A.D. *one thousand eight hundred and sixty-seven*, between ROBERT R. JOHNSON, of the first part, and CHARLES S. BURTON, of the second part, both of Pittsburgh, county of Alleghany, State of Pennsylvania. The said parties have agreed, and by these presents do agree, to associate themselves as copartners for the purpose of carrying on the General Hardware Business on the following terms, to the faithful performance of which they mutually bind and engage themselves, each to the other, his executors and administrators.

FIRST.—The name, style, and title of such partnership shall be R. R. Johnson & Co., and it shall continue for three years from the date hereof, except in case of the death of either of said partners within the said term.

SECOND.—That the said Robert R. Johnson contributes, as his share of the joint stock, merchandise valued at Ten Thousand Dollars ($10,000), a schedule of which is contained in the stock-book of the firm, and the sum of Five Thousand Dollars ($5000) in cash; and that the said Charles S. Burton contributes the sum of Three Thousand Dollars ($3000) in cash.

THIRD.—All profits which may accrue to the said partnership

shall be divided, and all losses happening to the said firm, whether from bad debts, depreciation of goods, or any other cause or accident, and all expenses of the business, shall be borne by the said parties, in the proportion of *three-fourths* by the said Robert R. Johnson, and of *one-fourth* by the said Charles S. Burton.

FOURTH.—The said R. R. Johnson and Charles S. Burton shall devote and give all their time to the business of said firm, and use their utmost endeavors, to the best of their skill and ability, to conduct the business for their mutual advantage, and will not, within the period above-named, engage in any other trade or business to their private emolument or advantage.

FIFTH.—That books of account shall be kept, in which shall be entered a full and exact account of all the purchases, sales, transactions, and accounts of said firm, and which shall always be open to the inspection of both parties, and their legal representatives respectively. An account of stock shall be taken, and an account between the said parties shall be settled, once in every year, and as much oftener as either partner may, in writing, request.

SIXTH.—Neither party shall assume *any* obligation or liability, verbal or written, either in his own name or the name of the firm, for the accommodation of any other person or persons whatsoever, without the consent, in writing, of the other party; nor shall either party lend any of the funds of the copartnership without such consent of the other partner.

SEVENTH.—No large purchase shall be made, nor any transaction out of the usual course of the hardware business be undertaken, by either of the partners, without previous consultation with and the approbation of the other partner.

EIGHTH.—The said Robert R. Johnson shall not withdraw from the funds or joint stock of the firm more than the sum of Eighteen Hundred Dollars per annum, nor more than Three Hundred Dollars in any one month; and the said Charles S. Burton shall not withdraw more than the sum of Eight Hundred Dollars per annum, nor more than One Hundred Dollars in any one month. Each (or neither) party shall be allowed interest on his share of capital invested; and if, at the expiration of the year, a balance of profits be found due to either partner, he shall be at liberty to withdraw said balance, or to leave it in the business, provided the other partner consent thereto.

NINTH.—At the expiration of the aforesaid term, or earlier dissolution of partnership, the stock or its proceeds, after paying the debts of the firm, shall be divided in the proportion of five-sixths to the said Robert R. Johnson, and of one-sixth to the said Charles S. Burton; but, if the said parties or their legal representatives cannot agree in the division of stock then on hand, it is hereby agreed that the matter shall be referred to the arbitration of H. L., C. H., and D. F. (or three competent disinterested persons, selected as may be arranged); and what they shall direct and determine therein shall be binding and conclusive upon all concerned.

TENTH.—And it is further agreed, for the faithful performance of the aforesaid articles of agreement, that either party, in case of any violation of them, or either of them, by the other, shall have the right to dissolve this copartnership immediately upon his becoming informed of such violation.

In Witness whereof, we have hereunto set our hands and seals the day and year above written.

Executed and delivered
in presence of
HENRY C. RODGERS.
JOHN L. DARROW.

ROBERT R. JOHNSON. [Seal.]
CHARLES S. BURTON. [Seal.]

CLAUSES TO BE INSERTED IN PARTNERSHIP AGREEMENTS WHEN DESIRED.

Not to be bound, or indorse bills, for others.—And that neither of the said parties shall, during this copartnership, enter into any deed, covenant, bond, or judgment, or become bound as bail or surety, or give any note or bill of exchange, or accept any bill, with or for any person whatsoever, without the consent of the other first had and obtained.

A majority to control.—That in all matters respecting the transactions of the partnership and the management of the business, the expressed opinion of the majority of the parties to this agreement shall govern and be binding on all of said parties; and in cases of difficulty they shall have power to wind up or sell the concern.

Not to trust any one against the wish of a partner.—And that no merchandise belonging to the firm shall be sold to any person or persons after notice from either of said partners that such persons are not to be credited or trusted.

Neither partner to assign his interest.—And it is agreed between said parties that neither of them shall, without the consent of the others, previously obtained in writing, sell or assign his share or interest in the joint concern, to any person or persons whatsoever.

AGREEMENT TO CONTINUE PARTNERSHIP.

By Indorsement on the Original Articles.

Whereas the within-mentioned partnership has expired by the limitations contained therein (or will expire on, &c.), it is hereby agreed that the same shall continue upon the same terms, with all the provisions and restrictions herein contained, for the further term of five years, from the day of

In Witness whereof, we have hereunto, &c.

Witnesses. ARTHUR B. CLARK. [Seal.]

GEO. C. HARTLEY. MATTHEW H. RALSTON. [Seal.]

M. H. MARTIN.

AGREEMENT TO DISSOLVE A PARTNERSHIP.

By Indorsement.

We, the undersigned, do mutually agree that the within-mentioned partnership be and the same is hereby dissolved; except for the purpose of final liquidation and settlement of the business thereof, and upon such settlement wholly to cease and determine.

Witness our hands and seals, this day of, &c.

Signed, sealed, and delivered

in presence of CHAUNCEY S. DOUGLASS. [Seal.]

HARVEY C. CHESTER. REUBEN H. HOWARD. [Seal.]

PORTER L. FIELDS.

PUBLIC NOTICE OF FORMATION OF PARTNERSHIP.

Notice of Copartnership.—The undersigned have this day formed a copartnership under the name and style of Gregory, Anderson & Co., for the purpose of carrying on the wholesale dry-goods business, at 689 Chestnut Street, Philadelphia.

GEORGE W. GREGORY.
ANDREW L. ANDERSON.
PHILA., Jan. 1, 1868. SAMUEL T. HOLDEN

PUBLIC NOTICE OF DISSOLUTION OF PARTNERSHIP.

Notice of Dissolution.—The copartnership heretofore existing between George W. Gregory, Andrew L. Anderson, and Samuel T. Holden, under the firm of Gregory, Anderson & Co., is this day dissolved by mutual consent (or, has this day expired by limitation, or as the case may be).

George W. Gregory is authorized to settle all claims against, or to receive all amounts due, the above-named firm.

(Or, Either partner will sign in liquidation.)

(Or, The business will be continued by George W. Gregory and Samuel T. Holden, under the name of Gregory & Holden, who are authorized to settle the accounts of the late firm.)

GEORGE W. GREGORY.
ANDREW L. ANDERSON.
Feb. 1, 1868. SAMUEL T. HOLDEN.

PUBLIC NOTICE OF CHANGE OF PARTNERSHIP.

Notice.—Thomas Y. Benton is admitted this day as a member of our firm. The business will hereafter be conducted under the name of Porter, Hudson & Co.

BENSON J. PORTER.
July 1, 1867. JACOB L. HUDSON.

ANOTHER.—ONE PARTNER RETIRING.

Notice.—Mr. Lewis N. Dixon retires from our firm this day. The business will be conducted hereafter under the name of Rudolph & Hunter.

LEWIS N. DIXON.
JARED L. RUDOLPH.
Jan. 1, 1868. PHILIP T. HUNTER.

SHORT FORM OF ASSIGNMENT OF BOND.

For value received, I do hereby assign and set over the within obligation, and all moneys due thereon, unto James M. Walters, his executors, administrators, or assigns, *without recourse.*

Witness my hand and seal, this twentieth day of January, 1868.

Signed, sealed, and delivered
in presence of JOHN L. RAYBURN.
MILTON N. SOMERS
HENRY K PARK.

LANDLORD AND TENANT.

A landlord is one who owns real estate which for a stated period, and at a stipulated rental, is in possession of another, called a tenant. The contract between the two parties is called a lease. It is advisable, in all cases, that leases be in writing, and that each party have a copy. The terms of a lease should be specified clearly; verbal promises are of no effect to add to or vary a written lease: the lease must speak for itself.

A lease from year to year is where no definite time is fixed for its termination; *a lease for years* is every estate which is to expire at a certain specified period.

A tenant for years may underlet, unless forbidden by the lease.

Where a lease for one or more years expires, and by implied consent the tenant remains in possession, he is not a tenant at will, but is considered a tenant from year to year.

If no time is stated for the payment of the rent in a lease for a year, the rent is not due until the end of the year, unless the law of the State is different. In New York, in the absence of special agreement, the rent is due on the usual quarter days.

To terminate a tenancy from year to year, each party is bound to give notice within the time required by the statute law of the particular State. The notice should be in writing, directed to the tenant; if he cannot be found, leaving the notice at the dwelling-house will be sufficient. No notice is necessary to be given to the under-tenants. It is advisable for the landlord to preserve a duplicate of the original notice, with the time and manner of service indorsed on it, and signed by the witness or witnesses.

A tenant from year to year is entitled to *six* months' notice in New York, Vermont, Kentucky, and Tennessee; to three months' notice in Pennsylvania and some of the other States; and to two months in Massachusetts.

A tenant is not responsible for taxes, except when so specified in the lease; and, when paid by him, he can deduct the amount from the rental value.

A landlord is under no legal obligations to repair, unless he has expressly covenanted to do so; nor a tenant, in the absence of a covenant, beyond injuries occasioned by his voluntary negligence.

FORM OF LEASE.

This Agreement Witnesseth, That Henry T. Morton doth hereby let unto Robert H. Walters that certain house and lot situated No. 1801 Green Street, fourteenth ward, city of Philadelphia, for the term of one year from the fifth day of June, 1866, at the rent of six hundred dollars per year, to be paid in quarterly portions in advance; and the said Robert H. Walters doth hereby, for his heirs, executors, and administrators, covenant and promise to pay to the said Henry T. Morton, or his assigns, the said rent in the proportions aforesaid; and the said Robert H. Walters, his executors and administrators, shall and will not, at any time during the said term, let or demise, or in any manner dispose of, the hereby demised premises, or any part thereof, for all or any part of the term hereby granted, to any person or persons whatever, nor occupy or use the same in any other manner than as a private dwelling, without the consent and approbation, in writing, of the said Henry T. Morton or his assigns, first had for that purpose; and at the expiration of the said term yield up and surrender the possession of the said premises, with the appurtenances, unto the said Henry T. Morton or his assigns, in the same good order and condition as the same now are, reasonable wear and tear thereof, and accidents happening by fire or other casualties, excepted.

And the said Robert H. Walters, his executors and administrators, hereby agree that all the personal property on the premises shall be liable to distress; and also all personal property, if removed therefrom, shall, for thirty days after such removal, be liable to distress, and may be distrained and sold for rent in arrear; the said Robert H. Walters, his executors and administrators, hereby waiving all right to the benefit of any laws now made, or hereafter to be made, exempting personal property from levy and sale for arrears of rent.

It is hereby further agreed, that if the above-named Robert H. Walters should continue on the above-described premises after the termination of the above contract, then this contract is to continue in full force for another year, and so on, from year to year, until legal notice is given for a removal.

In Witness whereof, the said Henry T. Morton and Robert H. Walters have hereunto set their hands and seals, the fifth day of June, one thousand eight hundred and sixty-six.

Sealed and delivered in
the presence of
JAMES T. RODGERS.

ROBERT H. WALTERS. [Seal.]
HENRY T. MORTON. [Seal.]

SECURITY FOR RENT.

I, George L. Mason, do hereby agree to be responsible to Henry T. Morton, or his assigns, for the true and faithful performance of the above-named contract on the part of Robert H. Walters.

In Witness whereof, I have hereunto set my hand and seal, the fifth day of June, one thousand eight hundred and sixty-six.

Sealed and delivered in
the presence of
JAMES T. RODGERS.

GEORGE L. MASON. [Seal.]

NOTICE TO QUIT BY THE LANDLORD.

SIR:—Please take notice that you are hereby required to surrender and deliver up possession of the house and lot known as No. 7 Day Street (or as the case may be), which you now hold of me, and to remove therefrom on the first day of   next, or at the expiration of the current year of your tenancy.

Dated this   day of   , 1867.

To MR L. N. SELSER.

J. G. BOND,
Landlord.

NOTICE TO QUIT BY THE TENANT.

Please take notice that on the 1st day of May next I shall quit possession and remove from the premises I now occupy, known as house and lot No. 7 Day Street, in the city of New York.

Dated this first day of Jan. 1867.

Yours, &c.,

To MR J. G. BOND.

L. N. SELSER.

MERCANTILE CORRESPONDENCE.

In all composition, three things require attention:—the thoughts, their arrangement, and the language employed.

On business subjects, as on other matters, he writes best who writes from a full mind. No one is expected to write well on any subject who has but little acquaintance with it. This is the reason why otherwise well-educated persons frequently fail in their efforts to write a good mercantile letter: they are ignorant not only of the technicalities of business phraseology, but of business itself.

The qualifications acquired at school are a good foundation; but they will not dispense with a knowledge of business dealings and of the peculiar styles of expression employed in commercial correspondence. Familiarity with the technicalities of the counting-house is gained only by constant practice; and facility and skill are not obtained until these have been mastered. To a business man, a terse mercantile phrase is as full of meaning as a formula is to a mathematician, and a few words are often all that is necessary to impart what would require from others many circuitous sentences.

A well-written mercantile letter furnishes not only a model for acquiring form and phraseology, but is also a *record* and an *explanation* of the business transacted. Business letters often partake of the nature of contracts, when mistakes, omissions, or uncertainty would involve serious loss. They should be clear and concise; there should be nothing ambiguous, nothing omitted, nothing superfluous. Men in business are too much occupied to waste time either in reading or writing long letters filled with what is irrelevant or useless.

Good writing materials should be selected. It is poor economy to use inferior articles; and the whole appearance of the letter is affected by the quality of the ink and paper used.

The date of a letter should be stated correctly and distinctly, as it is frequently a matter of considerable importance. In England the day is placed before the month; thus, 11th August, instead of August 11th, as in this country. In writing from a city, it is well to mention the street and number.

The form of complimentary address to be adopted depends upon the degree of intimacy and the relative position of the parties. In writing to a gentleman to whom you are an entire stranger, he is addressed as "Sir." "Dear Sir" is used on nearly all occasions, frequently to a stranger, unless a certain formality is required. "My dear Sir" implies a very friendly relationship. A married lady is addressed as "Madam" or "Dear Madam," and an unmarried lady as "Miss" or as "Dear Miss," usually with her last name affixed. "Reverend Sir" is used in addressing a clergyman; "Esteemed Sir" is usual when some degree of formality is required. Judges and Members of Congress should be addressed by the title of "Honorable." In writing to a firm, company, or any number of persons associated in a body, the address is "Gentlemen."

The place where the person resides who is written to, is given, to provide against any accident or attempt at fraud which would destroy the superscription and thus prevent it from being used as evidence.

In answering a letter, after acknowledging its receipt, each point requiring consideration should be taken up in order and discussed in a separate paragraph, before any new subject is mentioned.

Orders should specify exactly what goods are desired, with full directions concerning them. If a communication on other subjects is also sent, the order should be on a separate part of the letter, or, better still, on a separate paper.

In letters containing remittances or enclosures, the amount, or papers enclosed, should be distinctly mentioned, to guard against loss, and that the letter may be used as evidence, if necessary. When drafts are drawn, it is customary to inform the person on whom they are drawn, that he may be prepared to meet them at the proper time.

Some firms have a printed form of receipt, and also a printed form of letter for acknowledging remittances received, which they use in order to save the time and labor required in an extensive correspondence.

Instructions to agents and commission-merchants should be in the plainest terms, with full directions how to act in any contingency, that there may be no misunderstanding or dispute. Agents should keep their principals well advised in reference to the condition and progress of the business with which they are intrusted.

A bill or statement of account is usually sent at stated periods, and should of itself call attention to its settlement. Sometimes the words "Please remit" are written on one end of the bill, for that purpose. Many houses, however, are in the habit of sending out statements which are merely for the purpose of comparing accounts.

When it becomes necessary to request payment, it should be done in gentlemanly terms, even if there has been considerable delay. A man loses more than he gains when he indulges in rash or insulting language. A bitter word, when spoken, may be forgotten; but, when once written, it becomes abiding evidence of the irascibility, if not insult, of the writer. A decided yet respectful manner is productive of the best effects. An air of civility should pervade every letter, yet there should be nothing servile or affected.

In writing to others on business pertaining solely to one's own affairs or for his own benefit, a stamp should be enclosed, with which to prepay the postage. To persons who have a large correspondence, the postage is an item of some importance.

Letters of introduction and recommendation should not be

sealed, that the persons whom they concern may have an opportunity of knowing their contents.

In applications for situations in business houses, the handwriting has much to do with success. It is almost useless for a poor writer to expect employment in a counting-house. Merchants do not wish either the discredit or the inconvenience of bad writing.

When testimonials are required, and it is desired to preserve the original, a copy should be enclosed, and marked "copy" at the top of the page.

All business letters requiring an answer should receive immediate attention. Negligence in this respect is a species of incivility. Every letter, as soon as read and its contents attended to, should be neatly folded, indorsed with the name of the writer and the date of the receipt and answer, and then filed.

E. Speakman & Co.,
Chicago.
Rec'd Jan. 18, /68.
Ans'd " 19, "

It is advisable that copies of all letters, and also all papers of importance, be retained for future reference. A *fac-simile* copy of a letter is admitted as evidence after notice to the other party in the cause to produce the original.

The mere mechanical folding of a letter is not unworthy of attention. A letter carelessly written, clumsily folded, or ill directed, denotes either ignorance of what is proper, or a want of respect to the person addressed.

The superscription should be distinctly written. From neglect of this precaution, thousands of letters are sent every month to the dead-letter office. During the year ending June 30th, 1867, there were received at the Post-Office Department at Washington 4,306,508 letters as unpaid or misdirected. On many the name of the town as well as of the State was omitted from the direction; on some the superscription consisted simply of the name of the town and State, that of the person being omitted, as if totally unimportant; and so careless had been the writers of others that they had not even signed their names.

When sent to a large city, the letter should be directed to the street and number, as well as to the post-office and State. The postage stamp should be placed upon the upper *right-hand* corner. When it is important to know whether the letter has been received or not within a certain time, a request for its return to the writer, if not called for, should be placed upon the *left-hand* end of the envelope.

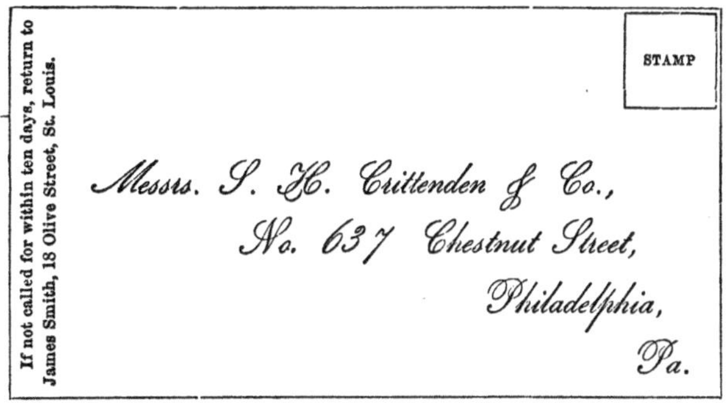

Limited space prevents our offering more than a few forms of letters which relate to transactions of the most frequent occurrence. Nearly all of those here given have been taken from the letter-books of extensive houses, and are presented not as models of superior excellence, but for the purpose of aiding those who wish to become familiar with the language and formula of business correspondence.

MERCANTILE LETTERS.

1. Offering Goods.

New York, Feb. 15, 1867.

Messrs. T. L. Morton & Co.,

Baltimore.

Gentlemen:

We take the liberty of enclosing a few samples of Black Taffetas, just received per Steamer Niagara. They are in patterns of about 14 yards, full 24 inches wide, at $3.15 per yard. Should you need any of them, we shall be happy to receive your order.

Yours, respectfully,

A. W. Colton & Co.,

pr. Jas. T. King.

---

2. Declining Offer to Buy.

Messrs. Gray, Smith & Co. Philadelphia, Aug. 3, 1866.

Gentlemen:—Yours of the 25th ult. is received. We are under the necessity of declining to fill your order upon the terms proposed by you. On receipt of fifteen hundred dollars, we will ship the goods, with the understanding that the balance will be paid within sixty days from the date of shipment. Hoping that these terms will be satisfactory, we remain

Yours, very respectfully,

Henry L. Park & Son.

3. Declining to Purchase.

Messrs. L. H. Alward & Co., Milwaukie, November 1, 1866.
Philadelphia.

Gentlemen:—We are in receipt of your favor of the 30th ult., and have likewise received the samples of Poplins, but, having as many goods of this description as we require for our present sales, we must decline handing you an order from samples forwarded.

Respectfully, yours,
Chandler & Co.

---

4. Order for Goods.

Memphis, Tenn., August 10, 1866.

Messrs. Marshall & Howland,
New York.

Gentlemen:—You will please ship us at your earliest convenience Three (3) Half-chests Imperial Tea (Andreas, ※257), same as in last bill; also, Two (2) Half-chests of *best Imperial* (Queen of the North, ※9, or something better). Ship by Great Western Dispatch, and mark goods as follows:

J. M. Orwig & Bro., *Memphis, Tenn.,*
Care Gould & Linton, *Cincinnati, Ohio.*

Please write across Bill of Lading, "Insured in consignees' open policy in the Globe Insurance Co. of Cincinnati," and send Gould & Linton the amount of Invoice, that they may enter on our policy book. Your early shipment will much oblige

Yours, very truly,
J. M. Orwig & Bro.

---

5. Enclosing Invoice and Bill of Lading.

Per "Wyoming." Philadelphia, March 17, 1867.

Messrs. L. M. Seaton & Co.,
New Orleans.

Dear Sirs:—We confirm our last letter of 12th inst., and hand you herewith enclosed B. of L. and Invoice of Cases E, H, ※632 and 633, ordered by your Mr. Carlton, which we have shipped this day on board Steamer Wyoming. Amt., $1250.\frac{50}{100}$; due June 17th.

Should you need any of our qualities of Cassimeres, we shall be pleased to fill your orders on the best terms possible.

Yours, truly,
Wells, Fisk & Co.

6. Concerning Credit at a Banker's.

"Edinburgh." Liverpool, 12 Feb., 1868.

Messrs. John Simpson & Co.,
Philadelphia.

Gentlemen:—We have your favor of 29th ult., and, as desired, have confirmed a credit for £500 to Messrs. F. & B. Brown & Co.

Your instructions respecting shipment and insurance have our attention. We are, gentlemen,

Your obedient servants,
Green, Richards & Co.

---

7. Advice concerning Shipment.

Messrs. John Simpson & Co., Liverpool, 17 March, 1868.
Philadelphia.

Dear Sirs:—We are advised that the under-mentioned goods are coming to us for shipment on your account, and we purpose forwarding them by the conveyance noted below. Should they not arrive here in time for shipment, a further advice will be sent you.

We state the value as given for entry, and remain

Yours, respectfully,
Green, Richards & Co.

Per S. S. "Delaware," for Philadelphia, sails 22d inst.
J. S. C., 1/3. 3 cases, £224, from F. & B. Brown & Co.

---

8. Enclosing Invoice.

Per the "City of Paris." Manchester, 20 March, /66.

Messrs. John Simpson & Co.,
Philadelphia.

Dear Sirs:—We have the pleasure to hand you herewith invoice of the packages noted below, which we trust will result in all respects to your satisfaction.

To cover present shipment, we apply for funds to Messrs. Green, Richards & Co., as usual.

Great activity prevails in our market, and prices generally are advancing. We are, dear sirs,

Your obedient servants,
F. & B. Brown & Co.

£220. 18. 0. net cash, Mar. 20/66.
J. S. C., 1/3, per steamer "Delaware."

9. Advising Receipt of Invoice.

Mr James L. King, *Boston*. St. Louis, April 5, 1867.

Dear Sir:

Your favor of March 29th, with B. of L. and Invoice, was received in due time. The goods are all that we desired; and for your promptness and care in filling our order, accept our thanks.

Enclosed find in payment Holmes & Bros.' Draft on First National Bank of Boston, at sight, for $\$1875.\frac{50}{100}$. Please acknowledge receipt per return mail, and oblige

Yours, respectfully,

Thos. L. Smith & Co.

---

10. Consigning Goods to be sold on Commission.

Messrs. Samuel G. Porter & Co., Cincinnati, May 11, 1867.

New York.

Dear Sirs:—Your favor of 7th inst. is at hand. We enclose you Invoice and Bill of Lading of 100 bbls. Mess Pork and 50 firkins of Butter, shipped this day per Merchants' Line, to be sold for our account, as per agreement. We request you not to sell for less than Invoice price, and if you succeed in disposing of this lot satisfactorily, you may be almost sure of receiving further consignments from us. We have drawn on you at ten days' sight, through Phœnix Bank, for One Thousand Dollars. Awaiting your advices, and hoping soon to hear from you, we remain,

Very truly, yours,

M. Johnson & Co.

---

11. Enclosing Account Sales.

Messrs. M. Johnson & Co., New York, June 10, 1867.

Cincinnati.

Dear Sirs:—Enclosed we send you Account Sales of Pork and Butter shipped us on May 11th. The Net Proceeds, $1750.62, due per average July 2d, we have placed to the credit of your account; the result, we hope, will be satisfactory.

We shall be pleased to receive further consignments from you, and will endeavor to dispose of them on the most advantageous terms.

Thanking you for past favors, we remain,

Truly, yours,

Samuel G. Porter & Co.

12. Advising of Shipment.

45 Calliope Street,
New Orleans, Nov. 4, 1867.

Messrs. H. R. Stanley & Co.,
Cincinnati.

We herewith enclose Bill of Lading and Invoice of Molasses and Sugars, amounting to $4233.75, which we have this day shipped per steamboat Star of the West, as per your order of 27th ultimo.

We have taken considerable pains to select such lots as we thought would suit you, and hope we have succeeded. Sugars are advancing. We send with this a list of our present quotations. Awaiting your further orders, and grateful for those received, we remain,

Very respectfully,
Your obedient servants,
W. Morrison & Co.

---

13. Advising of Consignment.

Messrs. T. H. Hawkins & Co.,
Boston.

Havana, June 4, 1867.

Gentlemen:—We have this day shipped you, per steamer Juniata, Farington, master, 1200 bbls. P. R. Sugar, T. H. H., and 228 bbls. Cuba S. W. Sugar, L. B. C., to be sold as per our agreement. Please find Invoice and Bill of Lading enclosed.

From the present state of the market, we are induced to hope that this lot will meet with ready sale at good prices. Should you succeed in disposing of this Invoice satisfactorily, we expect to send you another early in next month.

Awaiting your advice, we remain

Yours, respectfully,
Linnard, Bates & Co.,
per S. T. Gerter.

---

14. Enclosing Note for Discount.

Chas. R. Coleman, Esq., *Cashier.*

Baltimore, Feb. 11, 1868.

Dear Sir:—We offer for discount, enclosed, J. Brown's note, Jan. 12th, at ninety days, for $4250.75. By discounting the same you will much oblige

Yours, respectfully,
Thos. H. Whitman & Co.

15. Enclosing Account Current.

Mr. Henry T. Morris, Sandusky, O., Jan. 1, 1867.

Nebraska City.

Dear Sir:

We respectfully call your attention to the enclosed Account Current, with interest calculated to this date, showing a balance in our favor of $\$3275.\frac{50}{100}$. If you find correct, please remit us a Draft at sight for the amount, and oblige

Yours, respectfully,

D. Rundel & Co.

---

16. Enclosing Remittance.

Messrs. J. T. Anthony & Co., Savannah, January 21, 1867.

Manchester, Eng.

Gentlemen:

Your favor of 2d inst., covering statement of account, is at hand, and upon examination we find it correct. Enclosed please find Richardson & Cowden's 1st and 2d of Exchange on Brown, Shipley & Co. for Two Hundred and Sixty Pounds 7/5, in settlement of account to 1st inst.

Please acknowledge receipt, and oblige

Yours, very truly,

B. F. Moore & Co.

per D. B. Martin.

---

17. Another.

Messrs. A. L. Watson & Co., Trenton, April 10, 1867.

Philadelphia.

Dear Sirs:

Enclosed find my Check on First National Bank of this city for Twenty-Two Hundred and Fifty Dollars, in payment of Bills of

July 21	1262.10
" 25	872.00
" 28	115.90
	$2250.00

Please acknowledge receipt, and oblige

Yours, respectfully,

James Anderson.

18. Acknowledging Remittance.

Buffalo, Jan. 12, 1867.

Received from Messrs. George H. Jackson & Co., Five Hundred and Fifty $\frac{25}{100}$ Dollars on account.

$550.$\frac{25}{100}$. H. D. Clinton & Co.

Messrs. George H. Jackson & Co., Buffalo, Jan. 12, 1867.

Utica, N.Y.

Gentlemen:—Above please find receipt for remittance contained in yours of 10th inst., for which we are obliged. We find in your statement a variation in two items, those of December 6th and 19th. Can you favor us with an explanation, as we have no credits reducing the amount of $35 to $25.$\frac{50}{100}$, or $675.$\frac{35}{100}$ to $654.$\frac{75}{100}$?

Waiting your reply, we remain,

Respectfully, yours,

H. D. Clinton & Co.

---

19. Another.

Messrs. Thos. M. Young & Co., Albany, Nov. 13, 1866.

Syracuse.

Gentlemen:—We have the pleasure to acknowledge the receipt of your esteemed favor of 10th inst., containing your Notes dated

Sept. 1, at 3 mos., for 425.66,
" 15, " " 425.66,
Oct. 1, " " 425.67,

Amounting to Twelve Hundred and Seventy-Six $\frac{99}{100}$ Dollars, which we have placed to your credit in settlement of your account.

Please accept our thanks, and, requesting the favor of your future orders, we remain,

Very truly, yours,

Chas. L. Riqua & Co.

---

20. Asking for Settlement.

Mr. Henry G. Sanders, Worcester, May 25, 1867.

Concord.

Dear Sir:—We respectfully call your attention to our statement of account rendered April 3d, a settlement of which at your earliest convenience will much oblige

Yours, very respectfully,

Horace Boyd & Co.

21. Enclosing Draft for Acceptance.

W. B. Perry, Esq., Portland, Dec. 18, 1868.

Castine, Me.

Dear Sir:—We enclose our draft on you for acceptance, which please let us have by return mail, and oblige,

Respectfully, yours,

James Holland & Co.

---

22. Return of Accepted Draft.

Messrs. James Holland & Co. Castine, Dec. 25, 1867.

Gentlemen:—Enclosed please find your draft, dated 18th inst., for $400, with acceptance.

My absence from the city has caused the delay in replying to your favors.

Yours, truly,

W. B. Perry.

---

23. Requesting Payment.

Mr. B. S. Vernon, Rochester, June 19, 18—.

Syracuse.

Dear Sir:—If convenient, please let us have the amount of your bill, March 15th, for $187.50. We desire to close all our accounts by the 30th inst., and have need of all the funds due us. Please remit without delay, and much oblige

Yours, respectfully,

Lansing, Mason & Co.

---

24. Another.

Messrs. Douglass & Heath. Louisville, Nov. 2, 18—.

Dear Sirs:—We are obliged again to ask you for the balance of your account, now four months past due. We are much inconvenienced by your delay, and have waited longer than we think ought to be expected. The account must be speedily settled, and, if we do not hear from you by the 15th inst., will draw on you, at five days' sight. If the draft is not protected at maturity, we shall be compelled to adopt some other mode of settlement.

Very truly, yours,

W. Randolph & Co.

25. ANOTHER.

MR. H. Y. HENDERSON, WILMINGTON, April 5, 1867.
Dover, Del.

Dear Sir:

Enclosed please find our usual monthly statement, amounting to $375.$\frac{25}{100}$, for which, if found correct, we shall be pleased to receive remittance by 30th inst.

Should we receive no remittance by that time, we propose to draw on you at sight for the amount, unless in the mean time we are otherwise advised.

Yours, respectfully,
JAMES S. SMITH & CO.

---

26. ADVISING OF DRAFT.

MR. H. T. HAWKINS, CLEVELAND, June 3, 1867.
Harvard, Ill.

Dear Sir:

As we are in want of funds, we take the liberty of drawing on you at 5 days' sight for bills of

Jan. 10th,	$575.00
Feb. 12th,	300.00
	$875.00

Please protect, and much oblige

Yours, truly,
BROWN & WORTHINGTON.

---

27. ENCLOSING NOTES FOR COLLECTION.

CASHIER FIRST NATIONAL BANK, PHILADELPHIA, July 29, 1866.
Cincinnati.

Dear Sir:—Enclosed find for collection,

Note J. Smith, due Aug. 3/6,	810.20
" J. Jones, " " 8/11,	600.00
Acceptance Morton & Co., due Aug. 10/13,	920.62
	$2320.82

If paid, please remit Draft for proceeds.

Yours, very respectfully,
GEORGE V. MAUS.

28. Letter of Introduction.

Worcester, Mar. 2, 1867.

Dear Sir:—This will introduce to you my friend Mr. Samuel S. Price, of this city. He intends staying a few days in your place, which he visits on business; and I take the liberty of recommending him to your kind attention.

He is a gentleman of excellent acquirements, and we know him to be responsible to the extent of his engagements. Any attention or favor that you may render him shall be considered a personal favor, which I shall be happy to reciprocate.

To Jared L. Morton, Esq. Very sincerely, yours,

Chas. M. Hunter.

---

29. Letter of Recommendation.

To whom it may concern:— Buffalo, Oct. 13, 1868.

The bearer of this, Mr. Edward K. Mitchell, has been in our employ for three years past as salesman and book-keeper, and we have ever found him diligent and faithful in the discharge of his duties, and one who endeavored to make his employers' interest his own. He is correct and reliable in his accounts, and is well qualified to act as book-keeper or correspondent.

We cheerfully recommend him to any who may require the services of a trustworthy and competent person in their counting-house.

Very respectfully,

J. W. Cresson & Co.

---

30. Answer to an Advertisement.

315 Olive Street, St. Louis, April 27, 18—.

Gentlemen:—In answer to your advertisement in the "Democrat" of to-day, for an assistant in your counting-house, I respectfully offer my services to your firm. I am without experience in business, but have a desire to enter mercantile life, am willing to work, and have just graduated from our city High School.

If you will give me a trial, I will devote myself to your interests and endeavor to acquit myself to your entire satisfaction. For reference as to my character or ability, I would offer the names of

Mr. George H. Bowen, 116 Washington Avenue,

Messrs. J. F. Dwight & Co., 20 South Main Street.

Should a personal interview be desired, please address as above.

Very respectfully,

Herman L. Foster.

31. Application for a Situation as Book-keeper.

Messrs. K. K. Langton & Co., Columbus, O., Feb. 19, 1868.
Cincinnati, O.

Gentlemen:—Having learned from Mr. Charles K. Minturn that you desire the services of a book-keeper, I respectfully offer myself as an applicant for the situation. I have been engaged for two years in the wholesale house of L. R. Bullock & Co. as clerk and assistant book-keeper, and have a good knowledge of accounts. My business acquaintance is extensive in the western part of this State and the northern part of Kentucky, and I could therefore influence considerable trade.

I enclose copy of testimonial from my late employers, and would also respectfully refer you, as to my character and ability, to

Messrs.	Albert L. Hancock & Sons,	Wholesale Grocers,	Cincinnati,
"	Stringer, Burt & Co.,	Iron Merchants,	"
	F. L. Williams, Esq.,	City Solicitor,	"

Any communication which you may be pleased to make, addressed as above, will receive prompt attention.

Very respectfully, yours,
Frederick K. Johnson.

---

32. Recommendation enclosed in the above.

(Copy.)

Columbus, June 1, 1867.

The bearer, Frederick K. Johnson, has been in our employ as assistant book-keeper for over two years, and we have always found him to be honest, steady, and correct in his habits and deportment, and well qualified for any position of trust in a counting-house. We cheerfully recommend him as a competent book-keeper, and one who will earnestly apply himself to promote the interests of his employers.

Respectfully,
L. R. Bullock & Co.

---

33. Order for a Book.

Madison, Feb. 26, 1868.

Messrs. S. H. Crittenden & Co., *Philadelphia.*

Enclosed find One Dollar and Fifty Cents ($1.50), for which please send me one copy of the "Crittenden Commercial Arithmetic and Business Manual," and oblige

Yours, truly,
Henry M. Curtis.

INSTALMENT RECEIPT.

No. 13. INSTALMENT RECEIPT.

$2500. **200 Shares.**

WASHINGTON R. R. COMPANY.

Received, Washington, Apr. 11th, 1867, of S. J. Andrews, Two Thousand Five Hundred Dollars, being Twenty-Five Dollars per share, and the Third Instalment on Two Hundred Shares of the Capital Stock of the **WASHINGTON RAILROAD COMPANY;** *for which said shares a full Certificate will be given upon payment of all instalments due thereon, and the surrender of this Certificate.*

Leonard R. Cushing, *Daniel E. Eveland,*
Secretary. *President.*

Copy of an Exchequer Bill issued in the reign of Queen Anne.

£12 10*s*. EXCHEQUER.

A 28/24. Purſuant to an Act of Parliament, Anno 1709, for enlarging the Capital Stock of the Bank of England, &c. This Bill entitles the bearer to twelve pounds, ten ſhillings, with intereſt at a farthing a day. To be received in all aids, taxes, loans, and payments whatſoever to Her Majeſty, and to be paid to the bearer by the Governor and Company of the Bank of England, from time to time, as the ſame shall be paid into the exchequer by any receivers or collectors of Her Majeſty's revenue, aids, taxes or ſupplies; and be thence reiſſued and at all times by ſuch receivers or collectors out of any public money in any of their hands, as directed by the ſaid Act.

BANK DEPOSIT TICKET.

Deposited, April 8th, 1867, at the
MECHANICS' NATIONAL BANK.
By *Brown, Butler & Co.*

	Dollars.	Cts.
BANK NOTES, 5's and upwards	675	00
" " 1's and 2's	25	00
SPECIE	50	00
CHECKS, as follows	325	75
	465	50
	$1541	25

No. 375. 300 Shares.

LEBANON MINING COMPANY

OF LEBANON, MISSOURI.

CAPITAL STOCK
$500,000.

This Certifies that HIRAM MERRELL is entitled to THREE HUNDRED Shares in the Capital Stock of the

LEBANON MINING COMPANY,

Transferable only on the Books of the Company, in person or by Attorney, upon the surrender of this Certificate.

In Witness whereof, the Seal of said Company is hereunto affixed.

Lebanon, April 2d, 1867.

P. Q. RALSTON, Treas'r. W. I. WALLACE, Pres't.

STAMP.

SHARES $50 EACH.

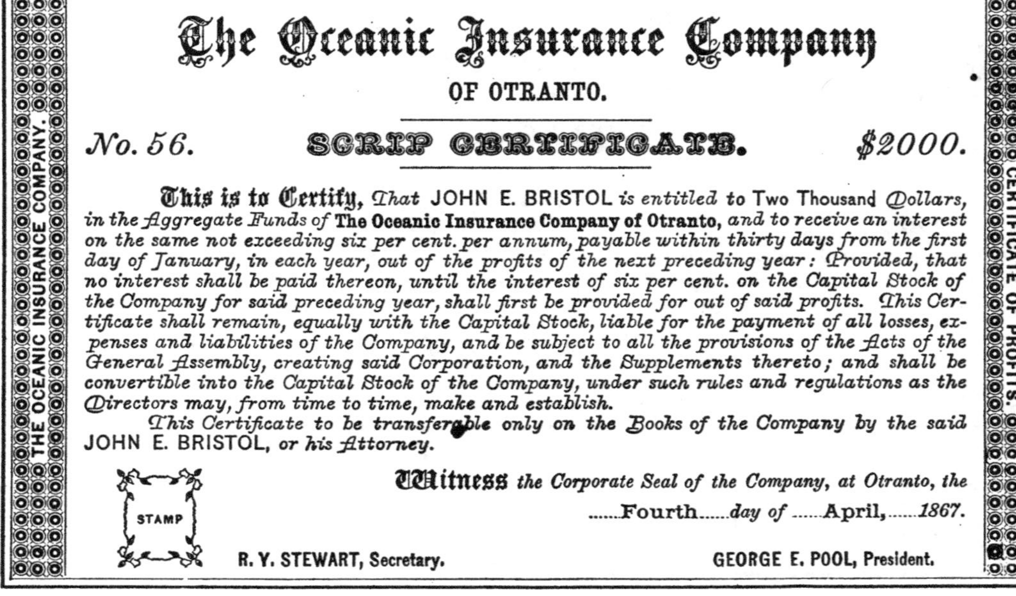

THE OCEANIC INSURANCE COMPANY.

The Oceanic Insurance Company

OF OTRANTO.

No. 56. **SCRIP CERTIFICATE.** *$2000.*

This is to Certify, *That* JOHN E. BRISTOL *is entitled* to Two Thousand *Dollars, in the Aggregate Funds of* **The Oceanic Insurance Company of Otranto,** *and to receive an interest on the same not exceeding six per cent. per annum, payable within thirty days from the first day of January, in each year, out of the profits of the next preceding year: Provided, that no interest shall be paid thereon, until the interest of six per cent. on the Capital Stock of the Company for said preceding year, shall first be provided for out of said profits. This Certificate shall remain, equally with the Capital Stock, liable for the payment of all losses, expenses and liabilities of the Company, and be subject to all the provisions of the Acts of the General Assembly, creating said Corporation, and the Supplements thereto; and shall be convertible into the Capital Stock of the Company, under such rules and regulations as the Directors may, from time to time, make and establish.*

This Certificate to be transferable only on the Books of the Company by the said JOHN E. BRISTOL, *or his Attorney.*

Witness *the Corporate Seal of the Company, at Otranto, the*

*.......*Fourth*......day of ......*April,*......1867.*

STAMP

R. Y. STEWART, Secretary.

GEORGE E. POOL, President.

CERTIFICATE OF PROFITS.

Treasurer's Department. | Register's Office.

1000 No. 60247. | No. 60247. 1000

IT IS HEREBY CERTIFIED THAT

The United States of America

Are indebted unto

S. Hodges Crittenden,

or Bearer, the sum of ONE THOUSAND DOLLARS, *redeemable at the pleasure of the United States after the 30th day of April, 1867, and payable on the 30th day of April, 1882, with interest from the 1st day of May, 1862, inclusive, at Six per cent. per annum, payable on the first day of May and November in each year, on the presentation of the proper coupon, hereunto annexed. This debt authorized by Act of Congress, approved Feb. 25th, 1862.*

Entered .... *E. I. S.*

Recorded .... *M. R.*

Redeemable after Five Years,
and Payable Twenty Years from date.
Loan of Feb. 25, 1862.

Washington, May 1, 1862.
L. E. CHITTENDEN,
Register of the Treasury.

Six Months' interest, due 1st May, 1882, payable with this bond.

30 Act of Feb. 25th, 1862. 30
The United States of America
Will pay the bearer
THIRTY DOLLARS,
for Six Months' interest, due Nov. 1, 1881, upon Bond 60247. L. E. CHITTENDEN,
$1000. *Reg. U. S. Treas.*

30 Act of Feb. 25th, 1862. 30
The United States of America
Will pay the bearer
THIRTY DOLLARS,
for Six Months' interest, due May 1, 1881, upon Bond 60247. L. E. CHITTENDEN,
$1000. *Reg. U. S. Treas.*

30 Act of Feb. 25th, 1862. 30
The United States of America
Will pay the bearer
THIRTY DOLLARS,
for Six Months' interest, due Nov. 1, 1880, upon Bond 60247. L. E. CHITTENDEN,
$1000. *Reg. U. S. Treas.*

www.ingramcontent.com/pod-product-compliance
Lightning Source LLC
LaVergne TN
LVHW010204110826
845151LV00002B/604

* 9 7 8 1 4 2 5 5 3 5 6 1 2 *